VICTIMS OF
PROGRESS

SECOND EDITION

John H. Bodley
Washington State University

 THE BENJAMIN / CUMMINGS PUBLISHING COMPANY, INC.
Menlo Park, California ● Reading, Massachusetts
London ● Amsterdam ● Don Mills, Ontario ● Sydney

Sponsoring Editor: Larry J. Wilson
Production Editor: Gina McMillan Wulff
Book designer: Judith Sager
Cover designer: Robin Gold

Copyright ©1982 by The Benjamin/Cummings Publishing Company, Inc.
Philippines copyright© 1982 by The Benjamin/Cummings Publishing
Company, Inc. All rights reserved. No part of this publication may be reproduced,
stored in a retrieval system, or transmitted, in any form or by any means,
electronic, mechanical, photocopying, recording, or otherwise, without the prior
written permission of the publisher.
Published in the United States of America.
Published simultaneously in Canada.

Library of Congress Cataloging in Publication Data

Bodley, John H.
  Victims of Progress.

  Bibliography: p.
  Includes index.
  1. Social change. 2. Culture conflict. 3. Man,
Primitive. 4. Acculturation. I. Title.
GN358.B63   306   81–8087
 ISBN 0–8053–0950–0   AACR2
  BCDEFGHIJ-AL-898765432

The Benjamin / Cummings Publishing Company, Inc.
2727 Sand Hill Road
Menlo Park, California 94025

PREFACE

The original edition of this book was based largely on conditions existing as of 1970–1972, but since then there has been a dramatic shift toward the political mobilization of indigenous peoples throughout the world. Federations of indigenous peoples have been formed in several regions, and a World Council of Indigenous Peoples now exists. There has also been a recent proliferation of new, nonindigenous organizations designed to support various native efforts to maintain traditional ways of life. These new developments are treated in two new chapters that replace the last chapter of the first edition. I was never fully satisfied with Chapter 9 in that edition because it made the long-term survival of some traditional cultures seem so hopeless. Conditions today are certainly much more dynamic and the outlook for genuine cultural diversity seems more promising than it did in 1970.

In this new edition, I bow to the widespread distaste of my colleagues for the term *primitive* as applied to contemporary cultures, and I employ the less precise terms *tribal, native, traditional,* or *indigenous* in its place. This shift does not represent any retreat from my viewpoint that these cultures represent a unique way of life that offers important contrasts to the cultural patterns of industrial states. The term *primitive* is employed in reference to the Primitivist-Environmentalist perspective on the protection of traditional cultures that is discussed in the final chapter. Hopefully, this specialized usage will not offend anyone, but it may stimulate further discussion of the issues.

This work, like the first edition of *Victims of Progress*, assumes that government policies and attitudes are the basic causal factors determining the fate of tribal cultures, and that governments throughout the world are concerned primarily with the increasingly efficient exploitation of the human and natural resources of the areas under their control. The following chapters examine and document the worldwide regularities characterizing interaction between industrial nations and tribal cultures over the past 150 years. It is an unfortunate record of wholesale cultural imperialism, aggression, and exploitation that has involved every major modern nation regardless of differences in their political, religious, or social philosophies. While blatant extermination policies have become relatively infrequent, basic native policies and the motives underlying them have remained virtually unchanged since the industrial powers began to expand more than 150 years ago.

PREFACE

Victims of Progress will be of special interest in anthropology courses that stress culture change, modernization, and economic development as they relate to tribal cultures. It is also suitable for introductory-level general and cultural anthropology courses in which the instructor wishes to present these topics in greater depth than normally provided by introductory texts. Because this book presents a particular viewpoint on controversial issues, it may be a stimulus for debate. Arguments are stated clearly and abundant case material and documentation are included so that each chapter can be a basis for classroom discussion or supplemental reading.

JOHN H. BODLEY

ACKNOWLEDGEMENTS

This work was supported in part by a summer faculty research stipend awarded me by Washington State University for research during the summer of 1972. I benefited from many stimulating discussions with colleagues and students at Washington State University over the more controversial issues raised in the book. In this regard I would like to specifically thank R. A. Littlewood, Barry Hicks, and John Nelson for their special interest and encouragement. I do not, of course, wish to imply that they necessarily share my views. Peter Aaby of IWGIA (International Work Group for Indigenous Affairs) in Copenhagen also offered early encouragement. I would like to thank those who offered photographs: R. A. and Patricia K. Littlewood, Raleigh Ferrell, Doug Pennoyer, Sam Price, and Dana Keil of Washington State University; Bernard Arcand of McGill University; and Arthur Palmer, Northern Land Council, Darwin, NT, Australia. Robert Kiste of the University of Minnesota gave the manuscript a final reading and offered helpful suggestions. My wife Kathi listened to my ideas as they developed, edited every version of the manuscript, and provided photographs. My son Brett kept me at home writing when I would rather have been in the field.

In 1980 I was on professional leave at the International Work Group for Indigenous Affairs (IWGIA) in Copenhagen, Denmark, to gather and write up new material for the second edition. I am grateful for the many kindnesses extended to me by the IWGIA staff, but I would like to thank especially Helge Kleivan, director of IWGIA documentation and one of IWGIA's original founders, for his enthusiastic support for this research. In London, I also benefited from discussions with Stephen Corry of Survival International.

J.H.B.

INTRODUCTION

Industrial civilization is now completing its destruction of technologically simple tribal cultures. According to the viewpoint of many authorities within industrial civilization, this disappearance or drastic modification of these cultures is considered necessary for the "progress" of civilization and is thought to be inevitable, natural, and, in the long run, beneficial for the peoples involved. However, it is ironic that now that we foresee the imminent possibility of the total disappearance of free tribal peoples, we are just beginning to realize the staggering worldwide costs of industrialization. It is becoming increasingly apparent that civilization's "progress" destroys the environment as well as other peoples and cultures, and that modern civilization may become a victim of its own progress. In view of this we might well question the wisdom of endorsing and encouraging the final disappearance of peoples who reject our "advances" and instead find satisfaction in a technologically simple life in close harmony with its environment.

The impact of modern civilization on tribal peoples has been a dominant research theme in anthropology, but in the past anthropologists often viewed it from the same ethnocentric premises accepted by government officials, developers, missionaries, and the general public. Surprisingly, anthropologists, who discovered ethnocentrism and built their profession by scientifically documenting and analyzing tribal cultures and the process of their "modernization," too often took positions facilitating their destruction. Applied anthropologists attempted to reconcile the natives to the "inevitable" loss of their "maladaptive" cultures and often worked to speed the process while perhaps easing some of the detrimental side effects. Unfortunately many anthropologists disregarded their own humanistic admonitions concerning ethnocentrism, cultural relativism, and the fundamental right of different life-styles to coexist, and developed theoretical concepts and advanced arguments masking the realities of civilization's systematic destruction of tribal cultures.

CONTENTS

ONE

PROGRESS AND TRIBAL PEOPLES

The Industrial Revolution disrupts and transforms all preceding cultures in West and East alike, and at the same time throws their resources into a common pool.

Graham, 1971:193

It is generally recognized that tribal peoples are being drastically affected by civilization and that their cultural patterns and, in many cases, the peoples themselves disappear as civilization advances. For many years anthropologists have made this topic one of their special fields of study, but many seem to have missed its larger significance by failing to stress that the ecological irresponsibility of modern industrial nations and the reckless pursuit of progress are the basic causes of the continuing destruction of tribal peoples. This book is an attempt to dispel some of the widely held ethnocentric misconceptions concerning the disappearance of tribal cultures and to focus attention on the most basic causes, because these causes reveal serious problems within industrial culture itself and must be understood before the world will be safe for cultural diversity.

At the outset the problem must be viewed in long-term perspective as a struggle between two basically incompatible cultural systems—tribes and states. People have led a hunting-and-gathering tribal existence for at least the past half million years, and only for the past 10,000 years or so have any people lived in cities or states. Since the first appearance of urban life and state organization, the earlier tribal cultures were gradually

1

displaced from the world's most productive agricultural lands and were relegated to marginal areas. Tribal peoples persisted for thousands of years in a dynamic equilibrium or symbiotic relationship with civilizations that had reached and remained within their own ecological boundaries. But this situation shifted rather abruptly a mere 500 years ago as Europeans began to expand beyond the long-established frontiers separating tribal peoples from states. However, by 1750, after 250 years of preindustrial European expansion, tribal peoples still seemed secure and successfully adapted to their economically "marginal" refuges—but industrialization quickly swept away all hope for their continued survival.

PROGRESS: THE INDUSTRIAL EXPLOSION

In the mid-eighteenth century the industrial revolution launched the developing Western nations on an explosive growth in population and consumption called "progress," which led to an unprecedented assault on the world's relatively stable tribal peoples and their resources. Within the 200 years since then the world has been totally transformed, self-sufficient tribal cultures have virtually disappeared, and dramatic resource shortages and environmental disasters have suddenly materialized. Now that many researchers are struggling to explain why industrial civilization seems to be floundering in its own success, anthropologists are beginning to realize that the first and most ominous victims of industrial progress were the several million tribal people who still controlled over half the globe in 1820 and who shared a stable, satisfying, and proven cultural adaptation. It is highly significant and somewhat unsettling to realize that the cultural systems of these first victims of progress present a total contrast to the characteristics of industrial civilization (see Bodley, 1976).

The industrial revolution can be called nothing less than an *explosion* because of the totally unparalleled scope and the catastrophic nature of the transformations that it has initiated. Phenomenal increases in both population and per capita consumption rates were the two most critical correlates of industrialization because they quickly led to overwhelming pressure on natural resources.

The acceleration in world population growth rates and their relationship to industrial progress have been well documented. Immediately prior to the industrial revolution, for example, the doubling time of the world's population is estimated to have been approximately

FIGURE 1. *Traditional tribal cultures and industrial civilization are totally contrasting and incompatible systems. This conflict is obvious in the above scene from highland New Guinea where a tribal group is observing the overwhelming presence of modern technology, which has suddenly been thrust upon them.* (Patricia K. Littlewood)

250 years. However, after industrialization was under way, the European population of 1850 doubled in just over eighty years, and the European populations of the United States, Canada, Australia, and Argentina tripled between 1851 and 1900 (Woodruff, 1966). Under the full impact of industrialization, the doubling time of the world's population by 1970 was only thirty-three years. In contrast, clear anthropological evidence shows that tribal populations grow very slowly and tend toward equilibrium with their environments. This relative population balance is due only partly to higher mortality rates; it must also be attributed to a variety of social, economic, and religious controls on fertility, the significance of which is only now beginning to be understood by researchers.

THE CULTURE OF CONSUMPTION

The increased rates of resource consumption accompanying industrialization have been even more critical than mere population increase.

Above all else, industrial civilization is a culture of *consumption*, and in this respect it differs most strikingly from tribal cultures. Industrial economies are founded on the principle that consumption must be ever expanded, and complex systems of mass marketing and advertising have been developed for that specific purpose. Social stratification in industrial societies is based primarily on inequalities in material wealth and is both supported and reflected by differential access to resources. Industrial ideological systems place great stress on belief in continual economic growth and progress, and characteristically measure "standard of living" in terms of levels of material consumption.

Tribal cultures contrast strikingly in all of these aspects. Their economies are geared to the satisfaction of basic subsistence needs, which are assumed to be fixed, while a variety of cultural mechanisms serve to limit material acquisitiveness and to redistribute wealth. Wealth itself is rarely the basis of social stratification, and there is generally free access to natural resources for all. These contrasts are the basis for the total incompatibility between tribal and industrial cultures, and are the traits that are the sources of particular problems during the modernization process.

The most obvious consequences of tribal consumption patterns are that these cultures tend to be highly stable, make but light demands on their environments, and can easily support themselves within their own boundaries. The opposite situation prevails for the culture of consumption. Almost overnight the industrialized nations quite literally ate up their own local resources and outgrew their boundaries. This was dramatically apparent in England, where local resources comfortably supported tribal cultures for thousands of years, but after barely a hundred years of industrial progress the area was suddenly unable to meet its basic needs for grain, wood, fibers, and hides. Between 1851 and 1900 Europe as a whole was forced to export 35 million people because it could no longer support them (Woodruff, 1966). In the United States, where industrial progress has gone the furthest, by 1970 Americans were consuming per capita some fifteen times more energy than neolithic agriculturalists and seven times the world average in nonrenewable resources. They were also busily importing vast tonnages of food, fuels, and other resources from around the world to support themselves.

Indeed few, if any, industrial nations can now supply from within their own boundaries the resources needed to support further growth or even to maintain current consumption levels. In view of these facts it should not be surprising that the "underdeveloped" resources controlled by the world's self-sufficient tribal peoples were quickly appropriated by outsiders to support their own industrial progress.

FIGURE 2. *A Campa Indian of the Peruvian Amazon prepares wild rubber for sale. The ever-increasing need of the industrial nations for resources has been a primary cause of the transformation of tribal cultures.* (author)

RESOURCE APPROPRIATION AND ACCULTURATION

It is indeed obvious that in case after case, government programs for the progress of tribal peoples directly or indirectly force culture change, and that these programs in turn are linked invariably to the extraction of tribal resources to benefit the national economy. From the strength of this relationship between tribal "progress" and the exploitation of tribal resources, we might even infer that tribal peoples would not be asked to modernize if industrial societies learned to control their own culture of consumption. This point must be made explicit, because considerable confusion exists in the enormous culture change literature regarding the basic question of why tribal cultures seem inevitably to be acculturated or modernized by industrial civilization. The consensus, at least among economic development writers (and the view often expressed in introductory textbooks), is the clearly ethnocentric view that mere contact with superior industrial culture causes tribal peoples to voluntarily reject their own cultures in order to obtain a better life. Other writers, however, have seemed curiously mystified by the entire process. A fine example of this latter position can be seen in Julian Steward's summary of a monumental study of change in traditional cultures in eleven countries. Steward (1967:20-21) concluded that while many startling parallels could be identified, the causal factors involved in the modernization process were still "not well conceptualized."

This apparent inability to conceptualize the causes of the transformation process in simple, nonethnocentric terms—or indeed the inability to conceptualize the causes at all—may be due to the fact that the analysts are members of the culture of consumption that today happens to be the dominant world culture type. The most powerful cultures have always assumed a natural right to exploit the world's resources wherever they find them, regardless of the prior claims of indigenous populations. Arguing for efficiency and survival of the fittest, old-fashioned colonialists elevated this "right" to the level of an ethical and legal principle that could be invoked to justify the elimination of any cultures that were not making "effective" use of their resources. These old attitudes of social darwinism are deeply embedded in our ideological system and still occur in the professional literature on culture change. In fact, one development writer recently declared: "Perhaps entire societies will lack survival value and vanish before the onslaught of industrialization" (Goulet 1971:266). This viewpoint has also found its way into modern theories of cultural evolution, where it is expressed as the "Law of Cultural Dominance":

> *That cultural system which more effectively exploits the energy resources of a given environment will tend to spread in that environment at the expense of less effective systems.* (Kaplan, 1960:75)

Quite apart from the obvious ethical implications involved here, upon close inspection all of these theories expounding the greater adaptability, efficiency, and survival value of the dominant industrial culture prove to be quite misleading. Of course, as a culture of consumption, industrial civilization is uniquely capable of consuming resources at tremendous rates, but this certainly does not make it a more *effective* culture than low-energy tribal cultures, if stability or long-run ecological success is taken as the criterion for "effectiveness." Likewise, the assumption that a given environment is not being exploited effectively by a traditional culture may merely represent a failure to apply the familiar biological concept of carrying capacity that would reveal the wisdom of tribal systems. We should expect, almost by definition, that members of the culture of consumption would probably consider another culture's resources to be underexploited and to use this as a justification for appropriating them.

"Optimum" Land Use for Hill Tribes

The recent experience of the Chittagong Hill peoples of East Pakistan (now Bangladesh) provides an excellent example of the process by which industrialization leads to a shortage of resources at the national level and ultimately results in acculturation for tribal peoples who have preserved their resources more effectively. Along with other parts of the world—thanks to the intervention of the industrial nations—East Pakistan experienced a major population explosion that became so severe that by 1965 population densities reached an overall average of 470 people per square kilometer and the soil resources of the country were being pushed to the limits. As the crunch on resources worsened, the government made dramatic efforts to emulate the industrialization-economic development route of the developed nations, and soon directed special attention to the still largely self-sufficient Chittagong Hills tribal areas, which had so far managed to remain outside of the cash economy and had avoided major disruptions due to industrial influences. The tribal areas were beginning to show population growth and subsequent pressure on their own resources due to shortening swidden cycles. But with only 35 people per square kilometer, they remained an island of low population density and "underdeveloped" resources in what had suddenly become an impoverished and overpopulated country.

External exploitation of tribal resources in the interests of the national economy initially focused on the forests of the Chittagong Hills. Twenty-two percent of the district was declared a forest "reserve," a "Forest Industries Development Corporation" was organized by the provincial government, and in 1953 lumber and paper mills were in operation to facilitate the modern commercial utilization of the region's bamboo and tropical hardwoods. In 1962 the largest river in the tribal area was dammed to supply hydroelectric power to help feed the rising energy demands of East Pakistan's urban affluent. In the process, however, 673 square kilometers of the best tribal agricultural land were converted into a lake, thus further aggravating the land scarcity that was already developing because of earlier disruptions of the population-resources balance and requiring the resettlement and "rehabilitation" of many hill people.

Still dissatisfied with the level of resource exploitation in the Chittagong Hills, in 1964 the Pakistani government enlisted an eleven-member international team of geologists, soil scientists, biologists, foresters, economists, and agricultural engineers to devise a master plan for the integrated development of the area based on what they considered to be optimum land-use possibilities. The team worked for two years with helicopters, aerial photographs, and computers. They concluded that regardless of how well the traditional economic system of shifting cultivation and subsistence production may have been attuned to its environment in the past, today it "can no longer be tolerated" (Webb, 1966:3232). The research team decided that the hill tribes should allow their land to be used primarily for the production of forest products for the benefit of the national economy because it was not well suited for large-scale cash cropping. The report left no alternative to the tribal peoples.

> More of the Hill tribesmen will have to become wage earners in the forest or other developing industries, and purchase their food from farmers practicing permanent agriculture on an intensive basis on the limited better land classes. It is realized that a whole system of culture and an age-old way of life cannot be changed overnight, but change it must, and quickly. The time is opportune. The maps and the basic data have been collected for an integrated development toward optimum land use. (Webb,1966:3232)

THE ROLE OF ETHNOCENTRISM

While resource exploitation is clearly the basic *cause* of the destruction of tribal peoples and cultures, it is important to identify the underlying ethnocentric attitudes that are often used to justify what are actually exploitative policies. *Ethnocentrism*, the belief in the superiority of one's own culture, is vital to the integrity of any culture, but it can be a threat to the well-being of other peoples when it becomes the basis for forcing irrelevant standards upon tribal cultures. Anthropologists may justifiably take credit for exposing the ethnocentrism of nineteenth-century writers who described tribal peoples as badly in need of improvement, but they often overlook the ethnocentrism that occurs in the modern professional literature on economic development. This is ironic because ethnocentrism threatens tribal peoples even today by its support of culturally insensitive government policies.

Crude Customs and Traditions

The ethnocentrism of culture change professionals can furnish government policies with the kind of support that is clearly demonstrated in the following example from India. A group of Indian scholars and administrators presented an extremely unsympathetic view of tribal culture in a series of papers and speeches at a seminar on new policy directions for the hill tribes of North East India, which was held at Calcutta in 1966 (Mittra and Das Gupta, 1967). At the outset, some participants in the seminar complained that prior British administrators had committed the fundamental error of placing tribal culture above the "basic need for human progress" (Moasosang, 1967:51), because for a time they had attempted to prevent the economic exploitation of the region by nontribal peoples. Throughout the seminar the entire range of tradtional culture was attacked on clearly ethnocentric grounds. The tribal economic system was called backward, wasteful, and obviously in need of "scientific permanent farming" (Nag, 1967:90); an Indian professor complained of "crude customs and tradtions" and characterized the tribal Garo peoples as being steeped in "primitive ignorance," "tradition-bound," and "static." More thorough research was called for to determine whether or not Garo society could be lifted out of its "morass of backwardness, traditionalism and pseudo-modernism" (Kar, 1967:80–90).

In one paper curiously entitled "An Outlook for a Better Understanding of Tribal People" (Thiek, 1967:103–109), an enlightened tribal member characterized his tribal kin as backward, quite lacking in culture, and living in darkness. Not only were these people described as cultureless, but according to an educated official they also lacked language.

> *You see, unfortunately here they do not have a language,*
> *what they speak is an illiterate dialect, lacking grammar and*
> *orthography.* (Chatterjee, 1967:20)

Somewhat earlier, an Indian sociologist supported the conclusion that tribal languages were "merely corruptions of good speech and unworthy of survival." He wanted to see these people adopt the "more highly evolved" Indo-Aryan languages, because he considered the tribal peoples to be nothing more than backward hindus (Ghurye, 1963:187–190).

Technological Ethnocentrism

Development writers with tractors and chemicals to sell have expressed more ethnocentrism in their treatment of traditional economic systems than for any other aspect of tribal culture. These writers automatically assume that tribal economies must be unproductive and technologically inadequate and therefore consistently disregard the abundant evidence to the contrary. It has long been fashionable to attack the supposed inefficiency of shifting cultivation and pastoral nomadism, and the precariousness of subsistence economies in general. But it could easily be argued that it is really industrial subsistence techniques that are inefficient and precarious. There is no doubt that mono-crop agriculture, with its hybrid grains and great dependence on chemical fertilizers, pesticides, and costly machinery, is extremely expensive in terms of energy demands and is highly unstable because of its susceptibility to disease, insects, and the depletion of critical minerals and fuels. The complexity of the food distribution system in industrial society also makes it highly vulnerable to total collapse because of the breakdowns in the long chain from producer to consumer. In contrast, tribal systems are highly productive in terms of energy flow and are ecologically much stabler, while they enjoy efficient and reliable distribution systems.

It is a virtual article of faith among cultural reformers that all people share our desire for what we define as material wealth, prosperity, and progress and that others have different cultures only because they have not yet been exposed to the superior technological alternatives offered by industrial civilization. Supporters of this view seem to minimize the difficulties of creating new wants in a culture and at the same time make the following highly questionable and clearly ethnocentric assumptions:

1. The materialistic values of industrial civilization are cultural universals;
2. Tribal cultures are unable to satisfy the material needs of their peoples;
3. Industrial goods are, in fact, always superior to their handcrafted counterparts.

Unquestionably, tribal cultures represent a clear rejection of the materialistic values of industrial civilization, yet tribal individuals can indeed be made to reject their traditional values if outside interests create the necessary conditions for this rejection. The point is that far more is involved here than a mere demonstration of the superiority of industrial civilization.

The ethnocentrism of the second assumption is obvious. Clearly, tribal cultures could not have survived for half a million years if they did not do a reasonable job of satisfying basic human needs.

The third assumption—the obvious superiority of industrial goods and techniques—deserves special comment because there is abundant evidence that many of the material accouterments of industrial civilization may well not be worth their real costs regardless of how appealing they may seem in the short run. To examine briefly a specific example, it could be argued that the bow is superior to a gun in certain cultural and environmental contexts, because it is far more versatile and more efficient to manufacture and maintain. A single bow can be used for both fishing and hunting a variety of game animals. Furthermore, bow users are not dependent on an unpredictable external economy, because bows can be constructed of local materials and do not require expensive ammunition. At the same time, use of the bow places some limits on game harvesting and demands a closer relationship between man and animal, which may have great adaptive significance. Hames (1979) has shown that Amazon Indians who have adopted shotguns have dramatically increased their hunting yields, but that these gains do not entirely offset the extra labor that must go into raising the money to support the new technology. Furthermore, the increased hunting efficiency also means that certain vulnerable species are more likely to be depleted.

Many of the ethnocentric interpretations of tribal cultures are understandable when it is realized that development writers often mistakenly attribute to them the conditions of starvation, ill-health, and poverty, which are actually related to civilization and industrialization. Self-sufficient tribal peoples do not belong in the underdeveloped category. It must be clarified that "poverty" is a totally irrelevant concept in tribal societies and that poverty conditions do not result from subsistence economies *per se*.

Tribal Wards of the State

Writers on international law and colonial experts often called on the *wardship principle* in an effort to justify harsh governmental programs of culture change directed against tribal peoples. This so-called legal principle reflects the grossest ethnocentrism in that it considers tribal people's to be incompetent or even retarded children. It defines the relationship between tribal peoples and the state to be that of a benevolent parent-guardian to a ward who must be protected from his or her own degrading culture and gradually reformed or corrected. According to the wardship principle, the state is under a strong moral obligation to make all tribal peoples share in the benefits of civilization—that is, in health, happiness, and prosperity as defined primarily in terms of consumption.

This legal inferiority of tribal peoples has indeed contributed significantly to the speed with which their acculturation or "reform" can occur and has worked marvelously to satisfy both the conscience and the economic needs of modern states.

Placing tribal peoples in the legal category of incompetent children seems to reflect a significant tendency to view tribal culture as abnormal, sick, and mentally retarded. This obviously ethnocentric theme runs throughout the colonial literature, in which the civilization process is often described as *mental* correction, but this same theme continued to appear in the modern literature. Recent economic development writers, as we noted, lumped tribal peoples indiscriminately with under-developed peoples, referred explicitly to economic underdevelopment as a "sickness," spoke of the "medicine of social change," and compared change agents to brain surgeons (Arensberg and Niehoff, 1964:4-6). It would appear that the basic attitudes of some modern cultural reformers were quite unaffected by the discovery of ethnocentrism.

A Sacred Trust of Civilization

As we have seen, the modern civilizing mission undertaken by states against tribal peoples was supported by a variety of ethnocentric assumptions, some of which were recognized as principles of international law. It should not be surprising, therefore, that prestigious international organizations such as the United Nations also threw their support behind official attempts to bring civilization to all peoples—whether or not they might have desired it.

During the second half of the nineteenth century the colonizing industrial nations began to justify their scramble for foreign territories as a fulfillment of a sacred duty to spread their form of civilization to the world. When the major imperialist powers met in 1884-1885 at Berlin to set guidelines for the partitioning of Africa, they pledged support for the civilizing crusade and promised to favor and assist missionaries and all institutions "calculated to educate the natives and to teach them to understand and appreciate the benefits of civilization" (General Act of the 1884-1885 Berlin Africa Conference). This position was reiterated and took on an even more militant tone in Article Two of the Brussels Act of

1892, which called on the colonial powers to raise African tribal peoples to civilization and to "bring about the extinction of barbarous customs." This constituted a clear, internationally approved mandate for ethnocide in the interests of progress.

While such attitudes are perhaps to be expected from colonial nations at the height of their power, they seem somewhat out of place when expressed by world organizations dedicated to peace and self-determination of peoples. Nevertheless, the 1919 League of Nations Covenant in Article 22 gave "advanced nations" responsibility for "peoples not yet able to stand by themselves under the strenuous conditions of the modern world," thereby placing many tribal peoples officially under tutelage as "a sacred trust of civilization." In fact, this sacred trust proved to be a profitable colonial booty for the trust powers because it gave them the internationally recognized right to exploit the resources of thousands of square kilometers of formerly nonstate territory while making no allowance for the wishes of the peoples involved. Under the 1945 United Nations Charter many of these same tribal peoples were identified as "peoples who have not yet attained a full measure of self-government," and their continued advancement was to be promoted by their guardians "by constructive measures of development" (Articles 73 and 76, UN Charter). Here again, reponsibility for deciding what constitutes a tribal people's welfare is effectively taken from them and is legally placed in the hands of outside interests. The carefully worded and seemingly nonderogatory phrases "peoples not yet able to stand by themselves" and "nonself-governing" are glaringly ethnocentric and derogatory because these peoples have governed themselves for thousands of years without the support of civilization. Of course, they were unable to defend themselves against the incursions of militant, resource-hungry states. But many modern nations only exist at the discretion of more powerful nations, and the UN Charter would not advocate making all militarily weak nations surrender their political autonomy to their stronger neighbors.

CIVILIZATION'S UNWILLING CONSCRIPTS

It now seems appropriate to ask the obvious question—how do autonomous tribal peoples themselves feel about becoming participants in the progress of industrial civilization? Because of the obvious power at their disposal, members of industrial civilization have become so aggressively ethnocentric that they have difficulty even imagining that another life-style—particularly one based on fundamentally different premises—could possibly have value and personal satisfaction for the peoples following it. Happily arrogant in their own supposed cultural superiority, industrial peoples assume that those in other cultures must realize their obsolescence and inferiority and eagerly desire progress toward the better life. This belief persists in the face of abundant evidence that independent tribal peoples are not anxious to scrap their cultures and would rather pursue their own form of the good life unmolested. Peoples who have already chosen their major cultural patterns and who have spent generations tailoring them to local conditions are probably not even concerned that another culture might be superior to theirs. Indeed, as a general principle it can perhaps be assumed that people in any autonomous, self-reliant culture would prefer to be left alone. Tribal peoples, if left undisturbed, are very unlikely to volunteer for civilization or acculturation. Instead:

> . . .acculturation has always been a matter of conquest . . . refugees from the foundering groups may adopt the standards of the more potent society in order to survive as individuals. But these are conscripts of civilization, not volunteers. (Diamond, 1960:vi)

Free and Informed Choice

The question of choice is a critical point because many development authorities continue to stress that tribal peoples should be allowed to choose progress. This view was obvious at a 1936 conference of administrators, educators, and social scientists concerning education in Pacific colonial dependencies, where it was stated that choices regarding cultural directions "must lie with the indigenous peoples themselves" (cited Keesing, 1941:84). Anthropologists at a more recent international conference in Tokyo took the same position when they called for "just and scientifically enlightened programs of acculturation which allow the peoples concerned a free and informed basis for choice" (Eighth International Congress of Anthropological and Ethnological Sciences, Resolution on Forced Acculturation, 1968, cited Sturtevant, 1970:160). Apparently no one noticed the obvious contradiction between a scientific culture change program and free choice, or even the possible conflict between free and informed. The official position of the Australian government on free choice for the Aborigine in 1970 indicates the absurdities to which such thinking can lead.

PROGRESS AND
TRIBAL PEOPLES

The Commonwealth and State governments have adopted
a common policy of assimilation which seeks that all persons of
Aboriginal descent will choose to attain a similar manner and standard
of living to that of other Australians and live as members of a single
Australian community . . . . (Australia, Commonwealth Bureau
of Census and Statistics, 1970:967)

It must be stressed that those who so glibly demand choice for tribal
peoples do not seem to realize the problems of directly operationalizing
such a choice, and at the same time refuse to acknowledge the numerous
indicators that tribal peoples have already chosen their own cultures
instead of the progress of civilization. In fact, the question of choice itself
is probably quite ethnocentric and irrelevant to the peoples concerned.
"Do we choose civilization?" is not a question that tribal peoples would
even ask, because they in effect have already answered it. They might
well consider the concept of choosing a way of life to be as irrelevant in
their own cultural context as asking a person if he or she would choose to
be a tree.

It is also difficult to ask whether or not tribal peoples really desire
civilization or economic development because affirmative responses will
undoubtedly be from individuals already alienated from their own
cultures by culture modification programs, and their views may not be
representative of their still autonomous tribal kin.

Other problems are inherent in the concept of free and informed
choice. Even when free to choose, tribal peoples would not generally be in
a position to really know what they were choosing and would certainly
not be given a clear picture of the possible outcomes of their choice,
because the present members of industrial cultures do not know what
their own futures will be . Even if tribal peoples could be given a full and
unbiased picture of what they were choosing, obtaining that information
could destroy their freedom to choose, because the degree of contact
involved in such an "educational " program might destroy their self-
reliance and effectively deny them their right to choose their own tribal
culture. An obvious contradiction exists in calling for culture change in
order to allow people to choose or not to choose culture change. The
authorities at the 1936 conference referred to above were caught in just
such Alice-in-Wonderland double-talk when they recommended the
promotion of formal education programs (which would clearly disrupt
native culture) so that the people could freely decide whether or not they
wanted their cultures disrupted:

CHAPTER
ONE

> . . .*it is the responsibility of the governing people, through
> schools and other means, to make available to the native an adequate
> understanding of non-native systems of life so that these can be ranged
> alongside his own in order that his choices may be made.* (cited
> Keesing, 1941:84)

Such a program of education might sound like a sort of "cultural smorgasbord," but in fact there is really only one correct choice allowed— tribal peoples must choose progress.

One further problem overlooked in the "free choice" approach is that of the appropriateness of industrial progress or of any foreign cultural system in a given cultural and environmental context—even if freely chosen. Should Eskimos be encouraged to become nomadic camel herders or to develop a taste for bananas? Does the American "car complex" belong on a Micronesian coral atoll of four square kilometers? What will be the long-term effects of a shift from a self-reliant subsistence economy to a cash economy based on the sale of a single product on the uncertain world market? There are certain inescapable limits to what can constitute a successful human adaptation in a given cultural and environmental setting.

We Ask to Be Left Alone

At this point we will again ask the question posed earlier regarding whether or not tribal people freely choose progress. This question has actually been answered many times by independent tribal peoples who, in confrontations with industrial civilization, have (1) totally ignored it; (2) deliberately avoided it; or (3) responded with defiant arrogance. Any one of these responses clearly could be interpreted as an open rejection of further involvement with progress.

Many of the Australian Aborigines reportedly chose the first response in their early contacts with members of Western civilization. According to Captain Cook's account of his first landing on the Australian mainland, Aborigines on the beach totally ignored both his ship and his men until they became obnoxious. Elkin (1951) confirms that this complete lack of interest in white people's habits, material possessions, and beliefs was characteristic of Aborigines in a variety of contact settings. In many cases tribal peoples have shown little concern or interest in early contacts with civilized visitors because they simply assumed that the visitors would soon leave and they would again be free to pursue their normal lives undisturbed.

Among contemporary tribal peoples that have had only minimal contact and who still retain their cultural autonomy, rejection of outside interference is a general phenomenon that cannot be ignored. The Pygmies of the Congo represent a classic case of determined resistance to the incursions of civilization. Turnbull (1963), who studied the Pygmies intensively in their forest environment, was impressed with the fact that in spite of long contact with outsiders they had successfully rejected foreign cultural elements for hundreds of years. Attempts of Belgian colonial authorities to settle them on plantations ended in complete failure, basically because the Pygmies were unwilling to sacrifice their way of life for one patterned for them by outsiders whose values were irrelevant to their environment and culture. According to Turnbull, the Pygmies deliberated over the changes proposed by the government and opted to remain within their traditional territory and pursue their own way of life. Their decision was very clear.

> *So for the Pygmies, in a sense, there is no problem. They have seen enough of the outside world to feel able to make their choice, and their choice is to preserve the sanctity of their own world up to the very end. Being what they are, they will doubtless play a masterful game of hide-and-seek, but they will not easily sacrifice their integrity.* (Turnbull, 1963)

Avoiding Progress: Those Who Run Away

Direct avoidance of progress actually represents what must be a very widespread, long-established pattern of cultural survival whose implications should not be ignored by those who so eagerly promote culture change.

Throughout South America and many other parts of the world, many basically nonhostile tribal peoples have made their attitudes toward progress abundantly clear by choosing to follow the Pygmies' game of hide-and-seek and actively avoiding all contact with outsiders. In the Philippines, a special term meaning "those who run away" has been applied to tribal peoples who have deliberately chosen to flee in order to preserve their cultures from government influence (Keesing, 1934:87).

Many little known tribal peoples scattered in isolated areas around the world have, in fact, managed to retain their cultural integrity and autonomy until quite recently by quietly retreating farther and farther into more isolated refuge areas. As the exploitative frontier has gradually engulfed these stubborn tribes, the outside world periodically has been surprised by the unexpected discovery of small pockets of unknown

FIGURE 3. *A Batangan man from the interior of Mindoro, Philippines. This tribe is only one of the many that prefer to flee and hide as civilization advances.* (Pennoyer)

"stone-age" peoples who have clung tenaciously to their cultures up to the last possible moment. The extent and full significance of this phenomenon have seldom been recognized by the public at large and certainly not by professional agents of culture change. Most recently the Tasaday of the Philippines have captured worldwide attention as unique survivors of the stone age, but the phenomenon is clearly much more common than this one famous case would indicate. In South America many different groups have been discovered recently who were using stone tools and were deliberately avoiding contact with outsiders. These determined people are generally peaceful, except when harassed too severely. To avoid contact they prefer to desert their homes and gardens and thrust arrows point-up in their paths, rather than resort to violence. All that even the most persistent civilized visitors usually find—if they do manage to locate their well-hidden villages—will be empty houses and perhaps smoldering cooking fires. If a village is disturbed too often, the people simply abandon the site and relocate in a more isolated place. When, after continuous encroachment, their resource base shrinks to the point that it will no longer support their population and there is no place to retreat to, or when violent attacks by civilized raiders and introduced illnesses reduce their numbers to the point that they are no longer a viable society, then they must surrender to progress.

How successfully some of these groups have managed to avoid contact can be seen in the case of the Akuriyo Indians of Surinam. These hunting-and-gathering people were first seen by outsiders in 1937, when a Dutch expedition discovered them while surveying the Surinam-Brazil border. After this brief encounter they remained completely out of sight for nearly thirty years until American missionaries began to find traces of their camps. The missionaries were determined to make contact with them in order to win them for Christianity, but it was three years before they finally succeeded with the assistance of ten missionized Indians, shortwave radios, and airplanes. They tracked the Akuriyo along their concealed trails through a succession of hastily abandoned camps until they caught up with a few women and children and an old man who, with obvious displeasure, asked the first man to greet them, "Are you a tiger that you smelled me out?" This small group had been left behind by others who had gone in search of arrow canes to defend themselves against the unwanted intruders. The Indians allowed the missionary party to remain with them only one night. Refusing to reveal either their tribal or their personal identities, they fed and traded with the intruders, and then insisted that they leave. The mission Indians sang hymns and tried to tell them about God, but the Akuriyo were unimpressed. According to the missionaries:

> *The old chief commented that God must really be good. He said he knew nothing about Him, and that he had to leave now to get arrow cane.* (Schoen, 1969)

Obviously these people were expressing their desire to be left alone in the most dignified and elegant terms. But the missionaries proceeded to make plans for placing Christianized Indian workers among them and requested "for the sake of this tribe" that the Surinam government grant their mission exclusive permission to supervise further initial contacts with the Akuriyo. Within a short time contact was reestablished and the mission was able to encourage about fifty Akuriyo to settle in mission villages. Tragically, in barely two years 25 percent of the group had died and only about a dozen people still remained in the forest (Kloss, 1977).

While the Akuriyo are an example of a group avoiding contact in a remote area, many other examples can be cited of small tribes that have survived successfully on the very fringes of civilized areas. One of the most outstanding of such cases was the surprising discovery in 1970 that unknown bands of Indians were secretly living within the very boundaries of the famous Iguazú falls national park in Argentina (Bartolomé, 1972).

Some will no doubt argue that these cases do not represent real rejections of civilization and progress because these people were given no real choice by their hostile neighbors. They actually could not have shared the benefits of civilization and so were forced to pretend that they really didn't desire them. It is also pointed out that such people often eagerly steal or trade for steel tools. This argument misses the real point and represents a misunderstanding of the nature of culture change. It must not be forgotten that stability and ethnocentrism are fundamental characteristics of all cultures that have established a satisfactory relationship with their environment. Some degree of change, such as adopting steel tools, may well occur to enhance an ongoing adaptation and to prevent *greater* change from occurring.

CULTURAL PRIDE VERSUS PROGRESS

The pride and defiance of numerous tribal peoples in the face of forced culture change is unmistakable and has often been commented upon by outsiders. The ability of these cultures to withstand external intrusion is certainly related to their degree of ethnocentrism or to the extent to which tribal individuals feel self-reliant and confident that their own culture is best for them. The hallmark of such ethnocentrism is the stubborn unwillingness to feel inferior even in the presence of overwhelming enemy force.

A fine case of calm but defiant self-assurance of this sort is offered by a warrior-chief of the undefeated Xavante of central Brazil, who had personally participated in the 1941 slaying of seven men of a "pacification" mission sent to end the Xavante's bitter fifty-year resistance to civilization. As further evidence of their disdain for intruders, the Xavante shot arrows into an air force plane and burned the gifts it dropped (*Life*, 1945, vol. 18:70-72). After one Xavante community finally accepted the government's peace offers in 1953, the air force flew the chief to Rio de Janeiro in order to impress him with the overwhelming superiority of the Brazilian state and the futility of further resistance. To everyone's amazement, he observed Rio, even from the air, with absolute calm. He was then led into the center of a soccer field to be surrounded by thousands of applauding fans, and it was pointed out to him how powerful the Brazilian state was and how unwise it was for the Xavante to be at war with it. The chief remained quite unmoved and responded simply: "This is the white man's land, mine is Xavante land" (Fabre, 1963:34-35). According to news accounts, in 1972 the Xavante were again fighting to defend their land against developers. It was reported that they "are possessed with extraordinary racial pride" and "firmly believe that they should preserve their culture" (cited Akwesasne Notes, Summer 1972).

THE PRINCIPLE OF STABILIZATION

According to theories of cultural evolution, adaptation, and integration, resistance to change is quite understandable as a natural cultural process. If the technological, social, and ideological systems of a culture gradually specialize to fit the requirements of successful adaptation to a specific environment, other cultural arrangements become increasingly difficult, if not impossible, to accommodate without setting in motion major disruptive changes which have consequences that cannot be foreseen. Resistance to change—whether in the form of direct avoidance of new cultural patterns, overt ethnocentrism, or open hostility to foreigners—may thus be seen to be a significant means of adaptation because it operates as a "cultural isolating mechanism" (Meggers, 1971:166) to protect successfully established cultures from the disruptive effects of foreign cultural elements. It should be stressed that the resulting "stability" refers to a relative lack of change in the major cultural patterns and does not imply complete changelessness in all the nuances of culture because minor changes probably occur constantly in all cultures. Stability is such a fundamental characteristic of cultures that it has been formulated as a general principle, "that a culture at rest tends to remain at rest" (Harding, 1960:54). A corollary of this so-called principle of stabilization states:

> When acted upon by external forces a culture will, if necessary, undergo specific changes only to the extent of and with the effect of preserving unchanged its fundamental structure and character. (Harding, 1960:54)

It is also significant, as change agents are well aware, that resistance

CHAPTER
ONE

to change is based not only on the natural resistance or inertia of already established cultural patterns, but also on the realization by the people concerned of the risks of experimenting with unproven cultural patterns. Either the probable rewards of new ways must appear to be obviously worth the risks, or some form of coercion must be applied. However, change agents who are convinced of their own cultural superiority tend to overlook the fact that native fears over the possible dangers of untested innovations may be quite justified. Peoples that reject such unproven cultural complexes as miracle grains, pesticides, and chemical fertilizers may prove in the long run to be wiser and better adapted to their natural environments.

For peoples in relatively stable, self-reliant cultures, resistance to change is a positive value. It is only in our own culture that such emphasis is placed on change for its own sake, and among those who make a profession of promoting change, that cultural stability is given a negative connotation and is identified as backwardness and stagnation.

TWO

THE UNCONTROLLED FRONTIER

The history of the European settlements in America, Africa, and Australia,
presents everywhere the same general features—a wide and sweeping
destruction of native races by the uncontrolled violence of individuals, if not of
colonial authorities, followed by tardy attempts on the part of governments to
repair the acknowledged crime. . . . Desolation goes before us, and
civilization lags slowly and lamely behind.

Herman Merivale, 1861

If, as has been argued in Chapter 1, tribal peoples are not eager to exchange their basically satisfying cultures for the dubious benefits of civilization, we are faced with the basic problem of explaining how their unwillingness has been overcome. It can be assumed that little "progress" can be made as long as tribal peoples remain basically autonomous, sovereign societies that are both politically and economically self-sufficient. Therefore, the problem is to explain how this autonomy has been broken. In general it appears that three processes have been at work to weaken tribal resistance and to prepare the way for further transformations:

1. The uncontrolled frontier;
2. Military force;
3. The peaceful extension of administrative control;

For analytic purposes these processes will be distinguished arbitrarily and treated in separate chapters, even though frequently they may overlap in a given area.

THE FRONTIER PROCESS

The initial breakdown of tribal autonomy was accomplished in many areas of the world by the direct action of the countless individual traders, settlers, missionaries, and labor recruiters who, in seeking their own self-interest, dealt directly with native peoples in frontier areas beyond government control.

Many definitions have been proposed for the term *frontier,* but for our purposes those concerned with resource exploitation and the role of the state will be most useful. Billington, for example, defines the frontier as:

> ... *the geographic area adjacent to the unsettled portions of the continent in which a low man-land ratio and abundant natural resources provide an unusual opportunity for the individual to better himself economically and socially without external aid.* (Billington, 1963:7)

In this definition, the significant point is that frontier resources are considered to be freely available for exploitation by outsiders. Webb (1952:2) speaks of the frontier as "an area inviting entrance" with its free gifts of land and minerals, and , along with many other historians, he explicitly disregards the aboriginal population. Indeed, a common aspect of the frontier process is the fact that the prior ownership rights and interests of aboriginal inhabitants are totally ignored as irrelevant by both the state and the invading individuals. Another significant aspect of the above definition is that in frontier areas individuals are given the opportunity to better themselves without external aid, that is, without any effective legal restraint by the state. This combination of free resources and free enterprise serves to distinguish the frontier process from the use of military force and from formal native administration, both of which involve direct and effective government control.

Without the restraints of law, individuals used force or deception to ruthlessly and profitably obtain the land, labor, minerals, and other resources they sought. In the process, tribal societies were disrupted, weakened and embittered, or simply exterminated. There is certainly no mystery to be explained here. It has long been recognized that frontier violence, the dispossession of tribal peoples from their homelands, the destruction of their subsistence bases, the introduction of exotic diseases, the ready availability of guns and alcohol, and numerous forms of economic exploitation have all directly led to depopulation, apathy, dependence, and detribalization. What *is* remarkable is the extent of the destruction and the fact that this familiar and significantly uniform pattern has been repeated over the years throughout the world, and still continues in some areas today with the implicit approval of the governments involved.

The broad outlines of the frontier process have been fully understood at least since the 1836-1837 publication of the thousand-page "Official Report and Minutes of Evidence of the British House of Commons Select Committee on Aborigines." The fifteen-member committee was ordered to consider measures for the protection of native right in frontier areas and spent ten months interviewing more than forty settlers, soldiers, politicians, missionaries, and natives from South Africa, Canada, Australia, New Zealand, the South Seas, and British Guiana. Their cautious general conclusion was that frontier contacts had been "a source of many calamities to uncivilized nations."

> *Too often, their territory has been usurped; their property seized; their numbers diminished; their character debased; . . . European vices and diseases have been introduced amongst them, and they have been familiarized with the use of our most potent instruments for the subtle or the violent destruction of human life, viz. brandy and gunpowder.* (British Parliamentary Papers, 1837:5)

Furthermore:

> *From very large tracts we have, it appears, succeeded in eradicating them; and though from some parts their ejection has not been so apparently violent as from others, it has been equally complete, through our taking possession of their hunting-grounds, whereby we have despoiled them of the means of existence.* (British Parliamentary Papers, 1837:6)

This committee called on Britain in the strongest terms to end this admittedly unnecessary oppression of natives, and suggested several specific measures to bring order to the frontiers. Apparently, however, their evidence and recommendations were not widely accepted, because since that time similar official investigations have been independently repeated in several countries, the same list of problems has been drawn up, and more suggestions made, but frontier abuses have not stopped. Considering this fact, it seems appropriate to risk "overemphasis" and review here some of the more outstanding regularities characteristic of the uncontrolled frontier since about 1820.

I Didn't Know It Was Wrong to Kill Indians

The 1836-1837 Select Committee on Aborigines noted in its report that in frontier areas indigenous peoples were being classed as "savages," and it warned ominously that this could result in their being treated as something less than human. It is clear from the committee's own published findings that in frontier areas around the world in the 1830s, tribal peoples were indeed being considered less than human and were being treated accordingly. For example, it was reported that in Canada it was long considered a "meritorious" act to kill an Indian. Significantly, the Dutch Boers in South Africa felt the same way toward natives, according to a letter received by the committee stating: "A farmer thinks he cannot proclaim a more meritorious action than the murder of one of these people." Reportedly, in South Africa it was customary to speak of killing natives with the same indifference applied to shooting partridge, and in fact one settler boasted proudly of personally killing 300 natives. At the same time the tattooed heads of New Zealand Maori were being offered for sale as curiosities in Australia (British Parliamentary Papers, 1837:3-15).

The committee reported that "many deeds of murder and violence" undoubtedly had been committed by the settlers in Australia, and, in fact, the same violence had continued on the Australian frontier for at least a hundred years, sometimes taking remarkably treacherous forms. In Victoria, Aborigines were known to have been poisoned by arsenic mixed with flour (Corris, 1968:153-157), while strichnine was reportedly used to eliminate Aborigines in western Australia in 1861. In the Northern Territory in 1901, "It was notorious, that the blackfellows were shot down like crows and that no notice was taken" (Price, 1950:107-108). As recently as 1928, thirty-two Aborigines were killed in that area in reprisal for the death of a Dingo hunter (Price, 1950:106-114). Violent anti-Aborigine slogans were again heard in Australia's Northern Territory in the late 1970s as the Aborigines pressed for legal recognition of their land rights (see Figure 4).

The frequent attitude of settlers on the American frontier can be summarized by Sheridan's famous statement, "The only good Indian is a dead Indian," and hardly need be elaborated upon here. However, it is not always remembered that in South American frontier areas the same approach is still being taken. In southern Brazil professional Indian

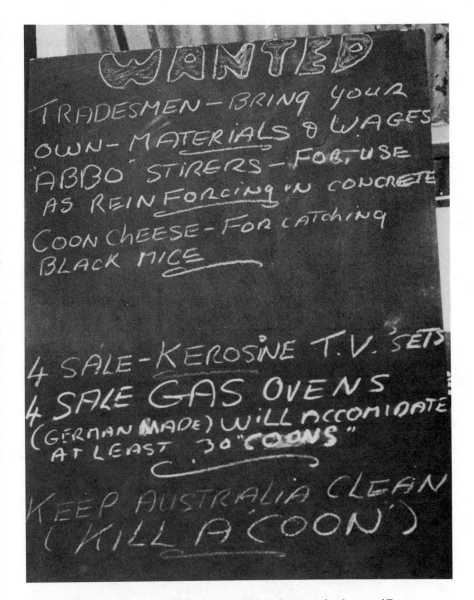

FIGURE 4. *A sign in the Daly Waters Pub indicating the degree of European backlash to the granting of Aboriginal land rights in the Northern Territory. 1978.* (Arthur B. Palmer Northern Land Council Darwin Australia)

hunters were killing the Xokleng Indians until their final pacification in 1914 (Henry, 1941). In São Paulo, one man claimed to have killed 2,000 Kaingang Indians in 1888 by poisoning their drinking wells with strichnine (Moreira Neto, 1972:312). In the northeast, the famous Brazilian ethnologist Curt Nimuendaju reports that an entire village of 150 Timbira Indians was treacherously wiped out by a band of settlers in 1913. In this case the murderers were brought to trial, but all were acquitted (Nimuendaju, 1946:30). In nearby Paraguay in 1903, settlers were killing Guayaki Indians and using their bodies to bait jaguar traps (Münzel, 1973). In 1941 it was reported that local settlers still felt that killing Guayaki was not a crime, but rather "a praiseworthy action, like killing a jaguar." The simple rationalization for such violence was that since the Guayaki were not baptized Catholics, they were not human beings (Chase-Sardi, 1972:195).

By 1962, after decades of continual harassment, a Guayaki band of fifty people finally surrendered. It was discovered that every man in the Guayaki group carried bullet wounds received in clashes with the local German colonists, many of whom proudly displayed Guayaki "trophies" in their homes (Chase-Sardi, 1972:197-199). As recently as 1971 there were clear indications that the indiscriminate killings of the Guayaki were continuing (Münzel, 1973).

FIGURE 5.   *A Cuiva Indian of the llanos of Colombia relaxes in a hammock. The Cuiva are among the tribal groups that have been repeatedly attacked by settlers invading their traditional territories.* (Bernard Arcand)

The Guayaki situation has close parallels in other South American countries. In 1968 shocking news reports came from Brazil of the massacre of several Indian groups, including the Cinta-Larga, and others in Rondonia and Mato Grosso. In these cases hired killers used arsenic, and dynamite and machine guns from light planes. In Colombia, anthropologist Bernard Arcand (1972) has reported that the Cuiva Indians in the llanos are constantly subject to attacks from neighboring cattlemen. He found many Indians bearing bullet scars and was himself fired upon while accompanying them. In 1967, in the same area of Colombia, settlers treacherously massacred fifteen Indians and were acquitted in a jury trial because it was considered customary to kill Indians. In his own defense one of the admitted killers stated, "I didn't believe it was wrong since they were Indians." Even more significantly, another stated:

> *I killed those Indians because I knew that the government*
> *would not reprimand us nor make us pay for the crime that was*
> *committed.* (Akwesasne Notes, summer 1972:26)

This statement raises an interesting question about the role of the government in the uncontrolled frontier process. It is frequently claimed that atrocities committed by settlers are beyond the control of any government to prevent, but a closer look at the facts casts doubt upon such claims. Even in 1837, the Select Committee refused to accept this explanation, and condemned the indifference and slackness of local authorities, which the committee felt had allowed entire tribes to be exterminated. The committee specifically pointed out that white settlers were seldom punished for their crimes against natives, but that courts were very thorough in meting out punishment to natives for their abuses against settlers. In frontier Australia at that time, a simple legal mechanism was used to protect whites who openly killed Aborigines: the testimony of surviving aboriginal witnesses was not admitted because they were "ignorant of the existence of a God or a future state" (Corris, 1968:105). When the authorities finally took action against known offenders and ordered the hanging of seven whites for massacring twenty-eight aboriginal men, women, and children in New South Wales in 1838, the murderers protested with a familiar excuse that demonstrated official connivance at such crimes.

> *We were not aware that in killing blacks we were violating*
> *the law or that it could take any notice of our doing so, as it has*
> *(according to our belief) been so frequently done before.* (cited Price, 1950:108)

There can be little doubt that many of these open crimes against tribal peoples would not have been committed, and certainly not as openly, if local officials had not cooperated in them. In Brazil in 1968, the evidence for large-scale involvement in Indian massacres by many public officials of the Indian Protectorate Service was so overwhelming that the organization was abolished. In 1971 in Paraguay, officials of the Native Affairs Department refused to take any action against known Indian hunters or even to conduct investigations into the well-known crimes being committed against the Guayaki (Münzel, 1973). Such official ignorance of frontier crimes, and the general failure of legal processes to protect tribal peoples, would certainly suggest that lack of control has been a deliberate policy on many frontiers.

Dispossession

Generally the primary purpose of the killing of tribal peoples has been to remove them from the land. In many cases less violent, but equally effective, methods have been used to accomplish this purpose.

In South Africa in the 1830s, the Select Committee reported that the Boers were in the habit of extending their territory by simply herding their cattle into native territory, destroying native gardens, and taking over their houses. Protesting natives were informed that complaining would not help them because the government would be unconcerned (British Parliamentary Papers, 1837:29). One hundred years later natives were still being actively dispossessed as squatters by white farmers in the frontier areas of South Africa. The justification for this action was the familiar argument that the natives were merely subsistence farmers and deserved to be treated as squatters since they were not engaged in any systematic forms of agriculture. The twentieth-century version of the dispossession process has been described in simple detail by a South African education professor.

> *When the new owner of the land enters into possession he generally summons a meeting of the squatters, informs them that he is the new owner of the land, announces how many native families he proposes to retain on his property, selects those he desires, and gives the remainder notice to quit at a certain date after they have reaped their crops. The dispossessed natives have the alternative of seeking a new landlord who will receive them as "labor tenants" or of attempting to find a place in a near-by Native Reserve or of gravitating towards an urban area.* (Loram, 1932:170)

In South America remarkably similar processes have also been applied in the twentieth century. Nimuendaju (1946:60) reported that in the Brazilian northeast in the 1930s it was common practice for ranchers to deliberately break down fences and drive their cattle through Timbira gardens in order to force the Indians to abandon their village sites. Dispossessed Indians appealed to the Indian Protectorate Service and petitioned state and federal government officials for help, but their pleas were ignored. As recently as 1963 cattlemen were still driving out the Timbira and even burning their villages with impunity (Moreira Neto, 1972:321).

Other modern examples could be cited from throughout South America, colonial Africa, and the American frontier, but the important point is that all of these cases illustrate that the unwillingness of governments to protect the rights of tribal peoples against the interests of intruding settlers has resulted in their dispossession. The problem of land policies is examined in more detail in a later chapter, but at this point it must be emphasized that one primary impact of frontier dispossession has been the disturbance of traditional subsistence patterns, forcing tribal people into participation in the market economy. Dispossessed Aborigines on the Australian frontier and Indians in the American West were unable to feed themselves by hunting and were forced either to beg food from the missions and government welfare posts or to work for settlers at menial tasks in order to stay alive. African farmers and herders also experienced severe subsistence hardships when they were pushed off their lands, and, as Loram indicated above, few alternatives were open to them but to labor for whites.

While certainly direct physical violence has been a prominent frontier process, it must also be emphasized that the *economic* exploitation of tribal peoples in an uncontrolled frontier situation has been just as destructive of traditional culture. In the following sections brief case studies are presented that demonstrate the impact of the rubber trade in the Amazon and the Congo, and the labor trade in the Pacific. Finally, the patron system of debt slavery is examined, and an assessment is made of the demographic impact of the frontier on tribal populations.

Atrocities of the Putumayo

World demand for rubber began to rise in the 1870s after the development of vulcanization, and particularly after 1900, when the automotive industry began to become important. As a result, the price of rubber soared, and the Amazon regions of Brazil and Peru, which were the

primary sources of natural rubber, became major new frontier areas as
thousands of outsiders arrived to share in the wealth. This initiated a
period of frantic economic activitiy called the rubber boom, which
continued until about 1915, when East Indian plantation rubber captured
the world market. Regular labor was scarce in the Amazon, but because
tribal Indians were numerous in many of the rubber zones, they quickly
became the backbone of the new extractive industry. The Indians were
especially useful because they could be made to work for cheap trade
goods, required little to maintain, and knew the rubber forests perfectly.
Best of all, however, the prevailing attitudes of the local government and
military officials were highly favorable toward allowing relatively
uncontrolled economic exploitation of the Indians, who were considered
to be savages in need of civilization.

Given this setting, serious abuses were almost certain to occur. In
fact, what followed was the ruthless exploitation and incredibly violent
destruction of thousands of people, which must have fully equaled the
cruelest periods of the Spanish conquest. The need for Indian laborers in
the rubber zones became so great that merely luring them to work with
trade goods was not enough, and undisguised slaving activities became
institutionalized. Slave raids, popularly known as *correriás*, were
commonly reported occurrences even outside the rubber zones and
involved armed gangs assaulting isolated Indian settlements, killing the
resisting men, and capturing the women and children to be sold as slaves.
Not surprisingly, these activities were widely approved as economically
advantageous and necessary civilizing measures, as the following
commentary by a contemporary Peruvian writer indicates.

> *It is not strange, then, that, there exists the cruel
> procedure known with the name of* correriás, *which consists of
> surpising the habitations of some tribe and taking the members of it
> prisoner. These prisoners are taken to far territories and are dedicated
> to work. . . . This catechization has the advantage that the indiviudal
> soon obtains precise concepts of the importance that his personal work
> has in the commerce of civilized people. . . . In our century, the
> procedure is cruel and wounds all the fibers of our sensibility;* but one
> must recognize the powerful and rapid help that it lends to
> civilization. (Palacios i Mendiburu, 1892:289–290, my
> translation, emphasis supplied).

Under the direction of large corporations such as the British-owned
Peruvian Amazon Company, Ltd., a highly profitable system of rubber

production was formulated in which a number of regional company officials controlled managers who organized the scattered tribal populations into local sections and directed the actual rubber-gathering activities. Section managers kept careful records of their Indian laborers and assigned them specific rubber quotas, which had to be carried to the regional administrators at regular intervals. Many of these lower-level company officials, or rubber barons, wielded enormous power and lived lavishly in great houses surrounded by Indian servants and concubines, and armed bodyguards. In the Putumayo district of Peru, where some 12,000 Indians were reported to be working in 1905 (Fuentes, 1908), it was common knowledge that direct physical violence was used regularly to increase production. Indians who failed to meet their assigned quotas or who attempted to escape were flogged and tortured or simply shot. Even though these actions occurred quite openly and were widely reported, the government refused to take any action against known offenders.

Finally, in 1907 an outraged Peruvian as a private citizen presented the local court and newpapers with a carefully documented formal denunciation of unspeakable atrocities committed against the Putumayo Indians. The denunciation, which named twenty prominent individuals as responsible, detailed specific crimes of rape, slavery, torture by flogging and mutilation, and mass murder by shooting, poisoning, starvation, and burning—all of which reportedly resulted in the deaths of thousands of Indians. These reports shocked the nation, and the president of Peru called on local officials to make investigations. Because of the involvement of a British company, the matter was even debated in the British parliament and Sir Roger Casement was sent to investigate. A local Peruvian judge, Carlos Valcarcel, also conducted his own investigation; soon the overwhelming testimony of eyewitnesses and the discovery of mass burials and other physical evidence left no doubt that crimes of immense proportion had occurred (Valcarcel, 1915). Some indication of the scale of the atrocities may be obtained by comparing the estimated 50,000 pre-1886 Indian population of the Putumayo district with the estimated population of only 10,000 by about 1910 (Steward, 1948; Casement in Hardenburg, 1912:336-337). The precise figure will never be known, but it is certain that thousands of Indians died.

The attitude of the local government officials toward these crimes was continued denial and inaction. The judge who had pursued the case was suspended, and the most prominent of the accused company officials was praised for his talent and capital with which he had brought economic progress to the department (Fuentes, 1908:113). In this case the frontier was being left deliberately uncontrolled.

CHAPTER
TWO

Heart of Darkness

We have now to record the operations of a System which Conan Doyle has described as the "greatest crime in all history." . . . *And it is undeniable that all the misdeeds of Europeans in Africa since the abolition of the over-sea slave trade, pale into insignificance when compared with the tragedy of the Congo. Indeed, no comparison is possible as regards scale, motive, and duration of time alike.* (Morel, 1972:105)

Events in the Congo closely paralleled and occurred at the same time as the situation in the Amazon. But in the Congo, government involvement was more direct and the scale of the atrocities committed even greater. The Congo Free State, under King Leopold of Belgium from 1885 to 1908, and the adjacent French Congo were based on a system of economic exploitation under which local company officials and government servants were urged to obtain maximum production of rubber and ivory by using whatever means they found most profitable. This exploitation was carried out by government officials under the guise of taxation, and by concessionaire companies that were given complete freedom of operation. Officially, of course, murder and slavery were illegal, but in fact they were employed on a massive scale by individuals eager to increase their profits, and here as in the Amazon, the courts seemed quite unwilling to punish known offenders. Local officials employed government troops to terrorize villagers into greater production, and the concessionaire companies hired undisciplined private armies for the same purpose. Women and children were held captive in special hostage houses to force the men to greater exertions, or were themselves forced to labor in the rubber forests. Villages were burned and looted and entire districts were devastated because, if production declined, the population was said to be in a state of rebellion. As a result of such oppression, disastrous rebellions did occur, subsistence pursuits came to a halt, and disease and starvation became widespread. While there is no certain estimate of the depopulation occurring as a consequence of all these conditions, there is no doubt that it was enormous. Morel, who founded the Congo Reform Movement in England to fight the abusive system, estimated that an incredible 8 million people died in the nearly twenty-five years of Free State exploitation alone (Morel in Louis and Stengers, 1968:7). He cites an estimate that in one district 6,000 natives were killed and mutilated every six months (Morel, 1920:123). Whatever the actual figures, the Congo must have been the scene of some of the worst frontier violence in modern times.

The atrocities set off an outcry in Europe after they were publicized by the Congo Reform Movement and in such books as Morel's *Red Rubber* (1906) and Conrad's novel *Heart of Darkness*. Eventually a number of official inquiries were conducted, resulting in the annexation of the Congo Free State by Belgium in 1908, which brought the establishment of more normal forms of colonial administration.

"Blackbirding" in the South Seas

> *It would be difficult to exaggerate the evil influence of the process by which the natives of Melanesia were taken to Australia and elsewhere to labour for the white man. It forms one of the blackest of civilization's crimes.* (Rivers, 1922)

From approximately 1860 to 1910 the South Pacific became the scene of frontier violence and exploitation similar to that occurring in the Amazon and Congo. Certainly frontierlike disturbances had arisen earlier in connection with the sandalwood trade, but widespread threats to tribal autonomy did not occur until the American Civil War brought British cotton imports to a halt and stimulated the development of plantations in Queensland, Australia, and Fiji. Unfortunately for the planters, labor was scarce in these areas because white Australians were considered unsuitable for tropical labor, and the native Fijians refused plantation work. Consequently, in 1863 the Queensland planters began sending ships into Melanesia to recruit cheap tribal labor, and the profitable but outrageously exploitative operation known as "blackbirding" became firmly established.

It is generally acknowledged that the completely uncontrolled recruiting during the early years relied heavily on deception and often amounted to little more than kidnapping. It was often impossible, for lack of interpreters, to explain the real purpose of recruitment to the islanders. Frequently the islanders were led to believe that they would be away for three months of fun, when actually they were being induced to sign a three-year indentured labor contract. Shrewd captains devised a variety of ingenious means to fill the holds of their ships with recruits. In order to lure wary natives close enough to be pulled into their boats, they employed the famous "missionary trick," in which they masqueraded as missionaries and even passed out Bible tracts that were actually pages from old almanacs. The most direct methods involved ramming canoes to spill their occupants into the sea, or the "eye drop" trick, which consisted of luring native canoes to the stern of the ship for trade and then dropping heavy pieces of metal to sink them (Docker, 1970:47). It is true that islanders sometimes deliberately boarded the recruiting ships in order to obtain trade goods or because they were simply runaways, but force and deception were the prime means of recruitment.

Unwilling natives were often killed accidentally before they could be dragged aboard ship, and it was not uncommon for them to jump overboard and drown while attempting to escape. Further deaths resulted from fighting between recruits when enemies from different islands were thrown together, or when mutinous recruits were shot and thrown overboard by the crews. In one famous case, seventy recruits were killed in this manner (Docker, 1970:82-84). Disease on board ship also took many lives because of overcrowding, poor food, and inadequate medical attention, and, in some cases, up to half of the cargo died before reaching the plantations (Scarr, 1968:16). Once on the plantations, the recruits might be sold—rather, their "passage" would be paid by the highest bidder—and they could then look forward to three years of labor, ten to twelve hours a day, six days a week, at an annual wage that was only 5 percent of what low-paid government officials earned at that time. Health conditions were little better on the plantations than aboard ship, and annual mortality rates for new recruits sometimes ran as high as 18 percent (Docker, 1970:205). In spite of all these outrages, the recruiting continued for more than forty years, during which over 60,000 natives were legally imported to Queensland alone, and the process was stoutly defended against critics who called it slavery.

However, the open abuses finally became too obvious for the government to ignore completely, and various Select Committees and Royal Commissions met in 1869, 1876, 1885, 1889, and 1906 to suggest means of regulating the process. Strict measures were enacted requiring the licensing of recruiters for specific shipments, assigning government inspectors to accompany each ship, and specifying how passengers were to be treated and informed what their contracts really meant. In practice, of course, the regulations were often openly defied, and the government inspectors were often incompetent and underpaid political appointees who retired to their cabins when irregularities occurred. The utter failure of the many regulations to achieve their purpose was well illustrated by the 1885 Royal Commission, which interviewed 480 natives in Queensland and found that virtually none had been legally recruited (Docker, 1970:223-224).

As usual in frontier situations, the courts tended to move very gently to punish known offenders. This was certainly true with the famous case of the *Daphne,* a recruiting ship arrested on suspicion of slavery in 1869 off Fiji by Captain Palmer of the British Navy. The ship's bare hold was jammed with a hundred totally naked, underfed natives who were about to be sold to Fijian planters. It was peculiar that no interpreter was available to question the natives and that the ship's captain was authorized only to carry fifty natives to Queensland and not a hundred to Fiji. The circumstances looked suspicious to Captain Palmer, who was familiar with the African slave trade and under orders to investigate illegal recruiting activities in the islands. But the Australian courts felt differently: the natives themselves were not allowed to testify, because, as non-Christians, they would not be able to take the oath. It was ruled that as long as *contracts* were involved, whatever occurred could not be considered slavery, and the case had to be thrown out (Palmer, 1871).

Whatever the effects of the unrestricted recruiting may have been for the individual tribesmen involved, the impact on the home villages was devastating. As in the Congo and the Amazon, normal village economic, ritual, and social life was thoroughly disrupted with a significant proportion of the active male population absent, and serious depopulation resulted from the new diseases introduced and from the increased violence aggravated by the guns and alcohol received from the labor recruiters.

The Patron System of Debt Peonage

In many of the world's frontier areas, unregulated contacts between isolated tribal peoples and civilized traders have been conducted on the basis of an exploitative system of debt peonage, which has certainly been less violent than the types of contact previously described, but which has also resulted in profound tribal disorganization. In many parts of North and South America, Siberia, and India, traders concerned primarily with their own advancement have been quick to take advantage of tribal peoples in their unfamiliarity with money and their desire for certain kinds of trade goods. Following a remarkably uniform pattern everywhere, traders advance goods to the natives on credit in exchange for furs, rubber, lumber, fish, nuts, labor, or crops, to be delivered in the future. The trick is that by continually advancing more goods, the trader or patron manages the transactions so that the debt is never fully paid, and an extravagant profit is reaped by the simple expedient of overcharging for the goods he advances and grossly undercrediting for the articles he takes in exchange. The tribal individual is gradually drawn into a relationship of total dependence on the trader and is forced to work harder as he finds himself further in debt and more attracted by increasingly more expensive goods. His difficulties are often complicated by other rules of the system by which debts are inherited, and that discourage the use of cash, or prohibit a debtor from transferring to other traders. All of these

CHAPTER
TWO

features of the system open it to flagrant exploitation, and in many cases the result is a situation resembling slavery.

Comparative research has shown that the long-term effects of this system have followed an extremely regular pattern even in widely separated areas of the world, and generally involve the gradual abandonment of traditional subsistence activities and the weakening of tribal sociopolitical organization, until the basic autonomy of tribal culture is destroyed. These regularities were demonstrated clearly by Murphy and Steward (1956:353) in their comparison of the impact of the Amazon rubber trade and the North American fur trade on native peoples.

In other contexts and with minor modifications, debt peonage can destroy tribal autonomy by dispossession. This has happened widely in India, where the system known as agrestic serfdom has been used—in spite of government attempts at legislative control—as a means of robbing tribal peoples of their land.

In the Amazon, the modern *patron* himself is often completely dependent on his Indian debtors for their labor and the forest products they supply. However, he still pushes his profits to the absolute limit, because laws limiting the amount of indebtedness for which an Indian can be held responsible are simply not enforced. In recent years in the

FIGURE 6. *Campa Indians from the Peruvian Amazon. Like many forest Indians in South America, the Campa have been exploited unmercifully by outsiders* (K. M. Bodley)

Peruvian Amazon it was common practice for patrons to charge Indians double for trade goods and credit them with half of the value of their products. Greedier patrons have been known to shift decimal points in their account books and charge up to twenty times the fair market value for certain articles. In one case a Campa Indian spent two years cutting valuable mahogany logs for his patron to pay for a twenty-five dollar shotgun (Bodley, 1970:108). It is not surprising that such practices undermine both traditional social systems and economic patterns.

DEMOGRAPHIC IMPACT OF THE FRONTIER

*Wherever the European has trod, death seems to pursue
the aboriginal.* (Charles Darwin, cited Merivale, 1861:541)

Severe depopulation of tribal peoples is a characteristic feature of the frontier process and has been reported by observers from all parts of the world over the past 150 years. As early as 1837 the members of the Select Committee found tribal populations to be declining at alarming rates in areas influenced by British colonists. They noted that the Indians of Newfoundland had been completely exterminated by 1823 and that the Canadian Cree had declined from 10,000 to 200 since 1800. They also found "fearful" depopulation in the Pacific where reportedly the Tasmanians would soon be extinct, and that the Australian Aborigines were simply vanishing from the earth.

In retrospect, it is now clear that what the Select Committee was seeing at that time was only the beginning of a truly catastrophic decline in tribal populations that continued in most areas of the world for another hundred years. Table 1 represents an attempt to indicate the scale of at least some of this depopulation. According to these figures, tribal populations in lowland South America (east of the Andes and exclusive of the Caribbean) and North America (north of Mexico) were reduced by almost 95 percent or by nearly 18 million by 1930. It is noteworthy that in these areas much of this reduction occurred *since* 1800 and can be only partly attributed to the Spanish and Portuguese conquests, which, of course, decimated large populations in the Orinoco, the lower Amazon, and eastern Brazil and Bolivia prior to 1800. Certainly in North America, with the exception of some portions of the southwest and California, and the eastern seaboard, most of the depopulation was again after 1800. In

Table 1.
World Survey of Tribal Depopulation

	Precontact Population	Population Lowpoint	Depopulation
North America (U.S. and Canada)[a]	9,800,000	490,000	9,310,000
Lowland South America[b]	9,000,000	450,000	8,550,000
Oceania			
Polynesia[c]	1,100,000	180,000	920,000
Micronesia[d]	200,000	83,000	117,000
Melanesia			
Fiji[d, e]	300,000	85,000	215,000
New Caledonia[f]	100,000	27,000	73,000
Australia[g]	300,000	60,500	239,500
Africa			
Congo[h]			8,000,000
		Estimated Total Depopulation	27,860,000

[a,b]Dobyns, 1966:415.
[c,d]Keesing, 1941.
[e,fe,f]Roberts, 1927.
[g] Rowley, 1970:384.
[h] Morel in Louis and Stengers, 1968:123. (Suret-Canale, 1971:36-37, gives a much more liberal estimate of some 12 million for the depopulation of the French Congo alone between 1900 and 1921).

Polynesia, Micronesia, and Australia, where fairly complete, although conservative, estimates have been made, the population was reduced by approximately 80 percent, or more than 1.25 million since 1800. If moderate allowances are made for further depopulation in areas not included in Table 1, such as Siberia, southern Asia, island southeast Asia, southern Africa, and Melanesia, and if Morel's modest estimate for the Congo is accepted, it might be conservatively estimated that during the 150 years between 1780 and 1930 world tribal populations were reduced by at least 30 million as a direct result of the spread of industrial civilization. A less conservative and probably more realistic estimate would place the figure at perhaps 50 million. Such an incredible loss has no parallel in modern times and must certainly have been a major factor in the "acculturation" of tribal peoples.

These population losses have perhaps greater meaning when their impact on specific tribal groups is examined, because it is clear that countless groups were never able to recover from such massive depopulation and simply became extinct while those that did survive were seriously weakened. The speed with which many groups were engulfed by the frontier was certainly a critical factor in the ultimate outcome. The Tasmanians, for example, were reduced by almost 98 percent from a population of 5,000 to 111 within thirty years. In western Victoria the aboriginal population of perhaps 4,000 was reduced to 213 full bloods after less than forty years of settlement, and within fifty years anthropologists could find no one who could reliably describe their traditional culture (Corris, 1968). In California, 75 percent of an estimated 85,000 Yokut and Wintun Indians were swept away by epidemic diseases in 1830-1833 (Cook, 1955). In recent times there have been reports of extremely rapid rates of decline for many South American tribal groups. In Tierra del Fuego, for example, the nomadic Indians such as the Ona and Yahgan, who may have numbered more than 8,000 as recently as 1870, were effectively extinct by 1950. It is estimated that in Brazil alone eighty-seven of 230 groups known to be in existence in 1900 were extinct by 1957 (Ribeiro, 1957), while many other surviving groups experienced drastic declines following white contacts. Some of the most dramatic cases recorded for Brazil are the Caraja, estimated to number 100,000 in 1845, 10,000 in 1908, and 1,510 in 1939 (Lipkind, 1948:180). The Araguaia Kayapo, who numbered 8,000 in 1903, were reduced to twenty-seven by 1929 (Dobyns, 1966). More recently, the Kreen-Akarore were reduced from 300 to thirty-five in 1979, just six years after agreeing to establish permanent contact with the national society (Davis, 1977:69-73, Latin America Political Report 1979, Vol. 13(3):19). Depopulation of this magnitude would clearly constitute a major source of stress for any culture, and particularly when it occurs in the context of conquest and economic exploitation.

The causes of tribal depopulation have generally been well understood, at least since the Select Committee's 1837 Report clearly designated frontier violence, disease, alcohol, firearms, and demoralization as the principal causes. Since that time, however, there have been some ethnocentric attempts to attribute depopulation to inherent tribal decadence and racial inferiority, and to suggest that civilization merely accelerated a decline that was already occurring. This view has been supported by some missionaries and government inquiries, and by not a few scholars, such as the historian Roberts, who spoke vaguely of "a general racial decline, an indefinable *malaise* of the stock itself" (Roberts, 1927:59). This explanation is no longer regarded seriously by anthropologists and was vigorously rejected years ago by the British anthropologists Rivers (1922) and Pitt-Rivers (1927), who examined the depopulation of the Pacific and showed how culture contact was responsible.

The only real problem remaining for more recent writers to debate has been the difficulty of assessing *which* contact factors are the most critical. Some would place special emphasis on the role of disease; others stress the importance of direct physical violence. Certainly both of these factors were important, but they should not distract attention from other indirect factors, because there seem to be very complex interrelationships and feedback mechanisms operating among all the variables leading to depopulation. For example, dispossession often forced enemy groups into severe competition for greatly reduced resources, and the availability of firearms made the resulting conflicts far more destructive than previous conflicts. These increased conflicts, combined with other new disturbances in economic and social patterns (such as those related to debt peonage), often placed new stresses on tribal societies and weakened them to the point that they willingly accepted outside control and welfare. Even depopulation itself is a form of stress that can lead to further depopulation by threatening the subsistence base. Rivers (1922) speculated that the sudden total transformation experienced by many tribes caused a form of shock that made people stop producing or desiring children, and in some cases they simply died because life was no longer worth living. While this explanation is now in disrepute, it would seem difficult to disprove.

It appears that increased mortality alone does not account for the complete disappearance of so many tribal peoples: other cultural variables must be involved. Ironically, the special adaptive mechanisms of primitive cultures designed to prevent *overpopulation*, such as abortion, infanticide, and the not infrequent ideal of a small family, may have actually contributed to *depopulation* and even extinction when frontier conditions drastically elevated mortality rates. There is little reliable data on this point because the importance of these population-regulating devices has only recently been recognized, but anthropologists have specifically cited these factors to explain the depopulation of the Tapirape in Brazil (Wagley, 1951), and for Yap in Micronesia (Schneider, 1955).

THREE
WE FOUGHT
WITH SPEARS

Nothing much is said about the sufferings on our side. Yet we fought with spears, clubs, bows and arrows. The foreigners fought with cannons, guns and bullets.

F. Bugotu, 1968, Solomon Islands

The early anthropologists who have studied the culture change process did not generally place sufficient emphasis on the role of military force in bringing about the initial breakdown of tribal autonomy. According to the standard definition presented in the famous "Memorandum for the Study of Acculturation" (Redfield, et al., 1936), *acculturation* is the result of groups with different cultures entering into "continuous firsthand contact, with subsequent changes in the original cultural patterns of either or both groups." The memorandum indicated that the contact situation could be friendly or hostile, but certainly it gave no hint that force might be a major cause of acculturation. Even some modern anthropology textbooks continue to stress that acculturation often results from demands for change coming from tribal peoples themselves, due to their exposure to higher standards of living or the idea of progress— almost as if such "demonstration effects" were the basic cause of culture change (Starr, 1971:514, 516). Considered in a different light, giving full weight to the historical record, acculturation can in many cases be seen as the direct outcome of the defeat of individual tribes in separate

43

engagements in a very long war fought between all tribal peoples and industrial civilization throughout the world.

While it is not appropriate here to attempt a major history of military actions against tribal peoples, this chapter does emphasize the extent and nature of this military pressure, and shows how it has frequently initiated culture change by destroying tribal autonomy.

In many parts of the world, tribal peoples fought back fiercely when they saw their traditional cultures threatened by outsiders and when they realized that those outsiders had come to stay and intended to impose their will on them. Often they were forced into one-sided battles to defend their lives against militarily superior enemies, and in most cases the outcome was never long in doubt when natives were engaged with regular troops armed with modern weapons. Defeat on the battlefield was invariably followed by the surrender of cultural autonomy and the imposition of government administrative control leading ultimately to further culture change.

In general, two major varieties of military action against tribal peoples can be distinguished: punitive raids and wars. The difference between these categories is that punitive raids tend to be short punishments for specific offenses committed by the natives and the intent is merely to establish administrative control. Wars, however, may involve protracted campaigns, often for the purpose of extermination or the forced removal of native populations that are not in themselves of direct economic value. Both approaches have been widely applied and have had profound impacts on tribal culture, as is discussed in the following sections.

THE PUNITIVE RAID

The basic purpose of a punitive raid is to impress a tribal population with the overwhelming force at the government's disposal, and to thereby gain their "cooperation." It is simply a form of intimidation, always with the threat of greater force in the background, and it normally does not intend the total annihilation of a people.

The punitive raid has been used widely in New Guinea and throughout the Pacific, where the native population was too valuable as a source of labor to risk its extermination. The Germans conducted frequent raids in their New Guinea colony and frequently carried them to excessive lengths. When two white men and eight native laborers were killed by unpacified natives, the government responded by sending an expedition that killed eighty-one people, destroyed houses and canoes, and carried off women and children as prisoners (Reed, 1943:136-137). Such overreaction was a common feature of punitive raids. In 1928, when two native policemen in Australian New Guinea were killed by the Kwoma in a dispute over the rape of a village woman, the government massacred seventeen villagers in return (Reed, 1943:154-155). By coincidence, in the same year Australian police killed seventeen Aborigines near Alice Springs (Rowley, 1967:73). Even if these raids were considered a necessary form of retribution for specific "crimes" committed by the natives, there was seldom any effort to determine who the guilty parties were or to balance the punishment to fit the crime.

Naval battleships and cruisers were often used in the Pacific by the French, Germans, British, and Americans to impress recalcitrant natives. This occurred as late as 1920, when the Americans stopped a revolt in Samoa with naval guns (Keesing, 1941:173). The Germans made regular use of their warships in New Guinea but did not always gain the intended result. The natives may have been impressed with the noise, but often merely returned to their villages when the barrage was over and planted taro in the shell holes (Reed, 1943:136).

Punitive raids were also institutionalized in colonial Africa. In South Africa they were known as *commandos,* and were often conducted by detachments of armed settlers whose leaders were officially acknowledged by both the government and the military. The usual excuse for a raid was to regain "stolen" cattle, but they often resulted in the indiscriminant destruction of tribal life and property.

Perhaps the most raided tribal group in Africa were the Nuer of the Sudan, who Evans-Pritchard found to be arrogant and suspicious in 1930. The British usually sent expeditions or patrols against tribes in the Sudan that refused to submit to government administration or that were fighting among themselves. The Nuer proved to be one of the most difficult of such groups to subdue because they simply refused to be humbled and had abundant empty land in which to hide. According to the count of a recent historian, armed force was used against the Nuer and related tribes sixteen times between 1902 and 1932 (Beshir, 1968:19).

Such raids probably accomplished several things: they caused loss of life, which was a significant disruption of tribal society in itself, and they seriously disturbed the subsistence economy when stored food or gardens were destroyed. The psychological impact of such displays of overwhelming force would also do much to undermine native morale and the self-confidence necessary for tribal autonomy. When these disturbances were combined with the other difficulties characteristic of the uncontrolled frontier, the surrender of tribal peoples to the government becomes quite understandable.

It should be emphasized that punitive raids are not a thing of the past and were never restricted to colonial governments. It is well known that such raids were a common tactic of the U.S. Army in the Indian Wars and were widely applied in Latin America. In Brazil, organized irregular troops, known as *bandeiras*, often punished Indian tribes in the nineteenth century. Thanks to modern technology, punitive raids can now be conducted more easily and much more effectively. In 1965 newspapers reported that Brazilian air, naval, and ground forces were used against the Marubo, a small Indian tribe in Amazonas that attacked settlers who had invaded their territory (Bowman, 1965). At about the same time in the Peruvian Amazon, the Peruvian air force used napalm to punish Campa Indians who were thought to be in support of leftist rebels. Bombing raids and armed patrols were also used by the Indonesian government in 1965-1966 to control 4,000 "disaffected" Arfak people in West Irian (Indonesian New Guinea); they reportedly left 1,200 dead (Hastings, 1968:17).

WARS OF EXTERMINATION

Major campaigns and wars of extermination waged against tribal peoples have usually been for the purpose of removing the population so that their territory could be utilized by outsiders to benefit the national economy. The immediate justification for such action, as with punitive raids, has often been the need to protect settlers or colonists from "marauding savages," or to quell tribal rebellions, or it has simply been viewed as a quick means of spreading civilization and progress. It is generally acknowledged that in most cases rebellions and raids by tribal peoples were the direct result of pressures exerted against them by outsiders and could have been prevented if they had been left alone—but that policy was not often economically advantageous.

Wars against tribal peoples became extremely frequent throughout the world as European expansion began, and probably reached a high point in the period between 1850 and 1910. It is well known that the Indian Wars in the United States continued almost without respite from 1820 to 1890, but it is not often realized that similar wars were occurring in South America at the same time, and sometimes on just as large a scale as in North America. Africa, particularly the southern and eastern regions, was also the scene of almost continual military action during the same period. In Asia, campaigns were conducted against tribal peoples in Formosa by the Japanese; in the Philippines by the Spanish and then by the Americans; in Indochina by the French; and in Burma and Assam by the British. In the Pacific, the Maori Wars of 1860-1872 and the New

Caledonia revolt of 1878-1879 were the most significant major military actions. These tribal wars have received relatively little attention in history texts because they were overshadowed by other political and economic events occurring in Europe and America at the same time, but they were nevertheless extremely dramatic and critical struggles for the peoples most directly involved.

GUNS AGAINST SPEARS

Half measures do not answer with natives. They must be thoroughly crushed to make them believe in our superiority. . . . I shall strive to be in a position to show them how hopelessly inferior they are to us in fighting power although numerically stronger. (Lord Chelmsford, British Commander in the Zulu Campaign, cited Furneaux, 1963:32)

It is generally true, of course, that modern weapons gave government forces a distinct advantage in conflicts with tribal peoples, particularly in large-scale battles between troops and natives still unfamiliar with the effects of firearms. Conventional forms of resistance were usually futile and often ended tragically, like the Matabele rebellion in Rhodesia in 1896, which was decisively ended when machine gun fire mowed down spear-carrying warriors by the hundreds with "bullets that came like hail in a storm" (Wellington, 1967:245). In many areas, magical as well as thoroughly empirical defenses were developed by tribal peoples to counteract such weapons. In New Guinea a special salve was invented that was supposed to deflect bullets (Reed, 1943:134), while on the American plains, the "ghost dance" shirt was intended to turn bullets to water, and in the Amazon Campa shamans attempted to blow at the bullets as protection. Guerrilla tactics generally proved more effective, however, and better still was the acquisition of firearms.

While these campaigns were often short, one-sided affairs, tribal peoples were not infrequently capable of incredibly stubborn resistance and sometimes struck back major blows against their enemies. In Burma, the British spent more than ten years suppressing rebellious tribesmen (La Raw, 1967:131), and the Naga were even more troublesome, as will be shown. The odyssey of Chief Joseph and the Nez Perce in 1877 is well known, as well as the massacre of General Custer and 264 men of the Seventh Cavalry in 1876. Perhaps even more dramatic, though less familiar, was the destruction of more than 800 of the British forces sent against the Zulu in 1879 at Isandhlwana and Rorke's Drift. The soldiers were attempting to teach the Zulu that they were "hopelessly inferior," but in this case spears prevailed against guns. That same year in nearby Basutoland, 300 rebellious Pluthi warriors, armed with a few guns, managed to withstand a siege of their fortified hilltop refuge for eight months against 1,800 soldiers with artillery. The most stubborn cases of resistance often occurred when tribal people were able to obtain firearms from traders and learned to use them before major conflicts broke out. This availability of firearms certainly prolonged the Maori Wars and was an important factor in many other areas as well.

In order to illustrate more fully the varied nature of the military conflicts between modern states and tribal peoples, the following specific examples are examined in greater detail: the defeat of the Indians in southern South America between 1870 and 1885; the Maori Wars of 1860-1872; the resistance of the Naga in Assam; the German extermination campaign against the Herero of Southwest Africa in 1904; and the Japanese method of controlling the Formosan Aborigines from 1902 to 1909.

The distinction between these wars and the wars that Europeans waged among themselves was not merely the usual one-sidedness of the fighting, but rather that their purpose was often the total destruction of a way of life and the subjugation if not destruction of entire populations. Military defeat of tribal peoples by industrial states involves far more than a mere change in political structure. When the Pluthi were defeated, their cattle and land were immediately taken from them, and their women and children became involuntary laborers for white farmers. In effect, the Pluthi ceased to exist as a distinct tribal entity.

The Conquest of 15,000 Leagues

> *We have six thousand soldiers armed with the latest*
> *modern inventions of war to oppose two thousand Indians that have no*
> *other defense but dispersion, nor other arms than the primitive lance.*
> (Avellandeda-Roca, 1878, cited Portas 1967:7, my translation)

In 1820 most of central Chile and the Argentine pampas were occupied by thousands of autonomous Araucanian and Tehuelche Indians who had successfully held back the frontiers of European settlement during nearly 300 years of continuous fighting. The Indians fell back, however, when the effects of the industrial revolution began being felt in southern South America, and European immigrants began to arrive in greater numbers bringing new patterns of warfare. By 1883, after a series of major military operations, they were finally defeated and vast areas of rich agricultural land were opened for the benefit of white settlers. On the pampas most tribes were virtually annihilated by the military campaigns, while in Chile, after the successful conclusion of the War of the Pacific, seasoned troops turned on the Araucanians and they were reduced to disorganized and isolated pockets. These Indian wars in southern South America were strikingly similar to those occurring in North America at exactly the same time, yet their scope, and the kind of military force that was required to defeat the Indians, is not widely appreciated.

In Argentina by the early 1870s, a semi-static defense system had evolved to protect the expanding agricultural settlements from the attacks of dispossessed Indians. The system consisted of a continuous line of ten major forts and nearly seventy smaller forts stretching 1,600 kilometers from the Andes to the Atlantic. The large forts were bastions, each garrisoned by hundreds of soldiers, while the smaller were fortifications of walls, moats, and watchtowers, armed with cannon and perhaps ten to twenty troopers. Included in the line were 370 kilometers of walls, and trenches 3 meters wide and 2 meters deep, which were intended to impede the passage of Indian horsemen. Daily patrols were sent from each fort to the right and left along the line to check for incursions by the Indians. When Indians were detected in the vicinity, cavalry troops were quickly dispatched to intercept them, and if they could be caught, bloody one-sided battles ensued. In one such action in 1872, the battle of San Carlos, 1,665 cavalrymen clashed with 3,500 Indians. Four soldiers and 200 Indians died. Lances and bolas proved completely ineffective against repeating rifles and artillery, and the Indians' only real defense was surprise attacks and rapid flight. This inability to match their enemies' armament was dramatically apparent in an 1878 incident, when a lone trooper with a rifle killed six Indians and captured nine. Earlier the Indians had successfully held their territory against the advances of soldiers and settlers, but modern firearms rapidly changed the situation. As one Argentine military official described it:

> *The remington came, and with the remington, the*
> *offensive, the Indians were finished and the desert was conquered.*
> (General Ignacio Fotheringham, cited Portas, 1967:19, my
> translation)

The defense network described above was really neither static nor defensive, because it was constantly being moved forward and new land was declared free of Indians. As the Indians surrendered, they were required to sign treaties acknowledging the sovereignty of Argentina and pledging themselves to fight against rebel Indians. Many national leaders were dissatisfied with the relatively slow pace of the advance and openly called for an aggressive war against the Indians. Finally in 1878 the government approved the "final solution"—a lightning "conquest of fifteen thousand leagues" in which five columns of 6,000 soldiers advanced into Indian territory to carry out what President Nicolás Avellaneda called "a great work of civilization" and a "conquest for humanity" (Garra, 1969:433). Within six months the frontier had been advanced some 640 kilometers until it stood on the south bank of the Rio Negro. More than 5,000 Indians were either killed or captured, and the nation's agricultural territory almost doubled at a cost of thirteen soldiers killed (Portas, 1967:7, 76). The campaign continued beyond the officially authorized frontier until 1885, when the general in charge of the forces south of the Rio Negro proudly reported the complete end of the humiliating frontier with the "savages":

> . . . today not any tribe remains in the field that is not voluntarily or forcibly reduced; and if any number of Indians still exist, they are isolated wanderers, without forming groups worthy of consideration. (General Lorenzo Wintter, cited Garra, 1969:522, my translation)

Indian settlements were indiscriminately destroyed and looted in the campaign, and it appears that many who were not killed were taken captive and removed to uncertain fates, while their women "voluntarily" became wives for the soldiers and settlers. This kind of culture contact had decisive effects. By 1913-1914 little more than a hundred Tehuelche still survived, and by 1925 the Puelche were nearly exterminated (Cooper, 1946:131,138). The Argentine Araucanians apparently survived in greater numbers, but their total military defeat left them thoroughly demoralized and willing to accept the authority of the government.

Forcing the Maori into Civilization

> And the word of the Maori is, we'll fight for ever, for ever and ever. (Maori answer to the call for their surrender at Oarakau, 1863, cited Harrop, 1937:190)

In 1840 perhaps a thousand settlers, traders, and missionaries shared New Zealand with at least 100,000 Maori who were willing to tolerate the foreigners and even aid them in order to receive new manufactured goods such as muskets. By 1858, due to the usual frontier disturbances, the Maori population had dwindled to about 56,000, and thanks to rapidly increasing immigration the white population had risen to nearly 40,000. As the balance swung in its favor, the government felt strong enough to pursue a vigorous policy of Maori land alienation for sale to settlers and land speculators in spite of widespread Maori resistance. As usual in such situations, the colonists demanded the best land for farming and grazing; they rationalized their greed by pointing out that Maori possession of the land was an interference with the industrial and commercial progress of the colony. After all, the land was "the greatest curse the natives have" and taking it from them was " the greatest boon you could confer on them" (cited Sinclair, 1961:4-5). As early as 1854 the 12,000 colonists in Auckland Province in the North Island had already acquired some 324,000 hectares from the Maori, of which only 3.5 percent were actually being cultivated; and in Wellington Province, 6,000 colonists "purchased" 3.6 million hectares from the Maori and were cultivating less than one-tenth of a percent.

These proceedings caused considerable resentment among the Maori, who realized they were being rapidly dispossessed. Calling upon their traditions of warfare and chiefdom-level political organization, and borrowing from the British model, they began uniting to resist further land alienation. In 1858 they elected their own "king," designed flags, and began organizing troops. Declining Maori customs, such as tattooing, were revived, and there were moves to sever economic ties with the colonists and to demand that they be completely expelled from New Zealand. Soon a general feeling arose on both sides that war was inevitable. In 1860, when the Taranaki Maori passively resisted the work of a survey team preparing to subdivide a large block of their land, the governor declared martial law and called on the military to enforce the government's will. The colonists were eager to teach the Maori a lesson and were confident that the fighting would be short, decisive, and profitable.

In fact, the Maori proved to be formidable opponents, even though their total fighting force could hardly have numbered over 8,000 men. They managed to fight for twelve years against a force that in 1864 amounted to some 22,000 soldiers, including nearly 10,000 British regulars. The war cost the colony 1,500 casualties, including 500 killed, and a bill of approximately 1.3 million pounds from the crown to pay for the military operations. The Maori suffered an estimated 4,000 casualties in killed and wounded, and in the end were forced to bow to the government and surrender their autonomy (Cowan, 1922:553; Harrop, 1937:196, 312).

While Maori resistance did not succeed, it was certainly far stronger than the colonists expected, in part because the Maori were well armed and knew how to use their muskets. They were also extremely skillful at fortifying positions and built numerous redoubts, complete with trenches, rifle pits, walls with loopholes, parapets, and towers, that rivaled those designed by the best-trained military engineers. Maori courage and fighting ability won frequent praise and admiration from their enemies. In the first major campaign in Taranaki in 1860-1861 a force of 1,500 Maori besieged the town of New Plymouth and prevented 3,000 troops from gaining any significant victories. The common British stereotype of colonial wars, involving a handful of redcoated infantry coolly fighting off hoards of natives, was often curiously reversed in the Maori Wars. In 1864 at Oarakau, 300 Maori with women and children entrenched themselves on a hilltop, where they were surrounded by 1,800 soldiers. The Maori, outnumbered six to one, were short of food, water, and ammunition, and were poorly armed, but they refused all demands for their surrender. For three days they withstood shellfire and grenades and repulsed four bayonet assaults before thirst forced them to retreat. In the final hours they were so short of ammunition that they were forced to improvise wooden bullets and fearlessly defused grenades thrown at them in order to use the powder. They withdrew in good order, advancing silently and deliberately into the fire of the troops surrounding them, but only a few managed to escape. In all, over half of their number were killed, and half of the survivors were wounded (Cowan, 1922:365-407). General Cameron, who led the British troops, spoke in tribute of their courage, and soldiers of the Sixty-fifth Regiment erected a tablet in a local church as a memorial to the Maori who fell at Oarakau (Harrop 1937:192).

Naga Resistance in Assam

The Naga hill tribesmen in Assam frustrated British attempts to extend administrative control over them and to end their headhunting and raiding for more than fifty years. In the nearly twenty years between 1832 and 1851 ten military expeditions were sent against them, inflicting incredible losses, but many of the Naga still refused to surrender their political autonomy.

The first British expedition to enter Naga territory in 1832 consisted of 700 well-armed soldiers, but the Naga resisted their advance with every weapon at their disposal and seemed to ignore the devastating effects of gunfire. They yelled and threw spears at the soldiers, rolled rocks on them from the ridgetops, burned grass in their paths, planted punji sticks, poisoned their wells, built stockades, and attacked continuously. In the face of such opposition the British managed only to temporarily occupy and destroy one village before withdrawing (Elwin, 1969:114). In 1850 another military expedition of 500 men and four artillery pieces besieged a Naga fortification for sixteen hours before capturing it. The 1851 expedition burned a village that refused to give it provisions and was thrown a fierce challenge by the Naga, who had nothing but scorn for its guns and muskets:

> . . . *we will fight with spear and shield and see who are the* best men. (Elwin, 1969:142)

The British commander eagerly accepted the challenge and promptly attacked the Naga village of 2,000 warriors with 150 soldiers armed with muskets, two 3-pounder artillery pieces, a mortar, and 800 native allies. The Naga were panic-striken by the musketry and artillery, and lost 100 killed and another 200 wounded, while the soldiers escaped without a single casualty and proceeded to burn the village.

The fighting was not all one-sided, however, because the Naga continued to raid and constantly harassed the soldiers. In 1879 they killed an administrator and 35 troops, and 6,000 warriors besieged the administrative center for twelve days. In 1879-1880 expeditions sent to punish them suffered over 100 soldiers killed (Elwin, 1969).

It gradually became apparent that regardless of how many villages were burned and how many Naga were killed, they remained unhumbled, and it became ridiculously costly to continue punishing them when their territory offered relatively little of economic value. Numerous suggestions began to be made that the Naga be left entirely alone and that all attempts to extend British sovereignty and civilization over them be suspended. In 1854 all British troops were actually withdrawn, but by 1886 attempts at administrative control were renewed, and efforts were under way to build roads and establish economic contacts between the tribesmen and the lowlanders. These less militant efforts were moderately successful, but the Naga continued to resist penetration of their areas by lowlanders and still strongly resented any undue interference in their affairs. After India gained independence in 1947, the Naga openly rebelled again; this time they demanded to be recognized as an independent state. By 1956 they had organized a guerrilla force of 15,000 men armed with Japanese weapons hidden during World War II. The Indian Army attempted to end the rebellion, but the government was finally forced to make Nagaland a state within the Indian Union in 1963. However, the Naga have continued to fight for total independence (Elwin, 1961; Burling, 1967).

Extermination of the Herero

> *We tried to exterminate a native race, whom our lack of wisdom had goaded into rebellion.* (German Professor Boon, in

FIGURE 7. *An Herero woman of Botswana wearing traditional headpiece. The Germans attempted to exterminate this tribe in 1904 and drove them into the Kalahari desert.* (R. Lee, Anthro-Photo)

lecture to the Royal Colonial Institute of London, 1914, cited Wellington, 1967:204)

The Germans founded their protectorate of Southwest Africa in 1884 on the familiar principle that native peoples must simply step aside and allow Europeans to use both their persons and their land as the Europeans desired. However, in this case they did not bother with the slightest pretense of humanitarian concern for the advancement of what one governor had labeled "the most useless of natives" (cited Cornevin, 1969:387). The 300,000 tribal inhabitants of this arid desert region consisted primarily of nomadic cattle herders such as the Hottentots and the Bantu Herero, who numbered perhaps 100,000 (Murdock, 1959:370; Cornevin, 1969:386). Unfortunately, their interests in the land were totally incompatible with German plans. The German administration prepared to use military force against the tribes as soon as settlers began to arrive in 1892, seeking the few areas of valuable grazing and farmland that, of course, were already occupied by the tribal people. In 1893 an official policy of forced dispossession was initiated when 250 German soldiers and two artillery batteries surrounded a sleeping Hottentot village and massacred 60 men and 90 women and children. In turn the Herero were attacked in 1896 and threatened with a "war of extermination" if they refused to surrender their best lands to the settlers and withdraw to the waterless reserves designated for them (Wellington, 1967:180-188).

The moral justification for this policy was a simple argument in favor of social darwinism and economic efficiency, which was forthrightly explained in 1907 by Paul Rohrbach, leader of the territory's Settlement Commission:

> . . .*the native tribes must withdraw from the lands on which they have pastured their cattle and so let the* White man *pasture his cattle on these self-same lands. If the moral right of this standpoint is questioned, the answer is that for people of the culture standard of the South African Natives, the loss of their free national barbarism and the development of a class of workers in the service of and dependent on the Whites is primarily a law of existence in the highest degree. For a people, as for an individual, an existence appears to be justified in the degree that it is useful in the progress of general development. By no argument in the world can it be shown that the preservation of any degree of national independence, national prosperity and political organization by the races of South West Africa would be of greater or even of equal advantage for the development of mankind in general or the German people in particular than that these races should be made serviceable in the enjoyment of their former territories by the White races.* (cited Wellington, 1967:196)

The Herero soon found themselves without grazing land and virtually cattle-less because an epidemic in 1897 carried off two-thirds of their cattle. By 1903 more than half of the remaining cattle had been appropriated by unscrupulous traders. They could tolerate their situation no longer. In 1904 some 8,000 Herero warriors rose against the colonists, and within a few days 150 Germans were killed. Two months after the outbreak of fighting, a Herero chief explained the causes of the war in a letter to the military governor. Speaking bitterly of German abuses, he stated that the war had really been started by the whites, and he vowed to fight to the death.

The Germans were well prepared to make good on their earlier threats of a war of extermination. General Von Trotha was quickly dispatched from Germany, and in 1904 surrounded 5,000 Herero with an army of 1,500 riflemen, thirty field guns, and twelve machine guns. Many Herero escaped in the fighting and were driven into the Kalahari desert to die of thirst. Von Trotha refused to negotiate and proclaimed that anyone who remained in the country would be shot.

> *The Herero people must now leave the country, if they do not I will compel them with the big tube [artillery]. Within the German frontier every Herero, with or without a rifle, will be shot. I will not take any more women and children [prisoners], but I will drive them back to their people or have them fired on.* (cited Wellington, 1967:208)

These orders were ruthlessly carried out by the soldiers for months (even to the extent of deliberately poisoning waterholes), and thousands of Herero died. By 1906 their population had been reduced to a mere 20,000 landless fugitives. The Hottentots also joined in the fighting, but by 1907 the war was officially declared over. It had been a disastrous campaign for the Germans as well. They lost over 1,600 men and had fielded a force of up to 19,000 men at an estimated cost of some 23 million pounds. The total native loss in life was estimated at some 100,000 or approximately two-thirds of the labor force as the Germans viewed it. In the end, even Rohrbach, whose policies of land confiscation had directly contributed to the fighting, was willing to admit his "blunder," because "the actual extermination of a race could be politically and economically disastrous" (Wellington, 1967:213; Cornevin, 1969; Cana, 1946).

Advancing the Guard-Line in Formosa

When the Japanese took over Formosa in 1895 some 3 million "civilized" people occupied less than half the island while the remainder was occupied by 120,000 tribal people. Pressure on the tribal areas was understandable in view of their relatively light population and because of the resources in timber, camphor, gold, and agricultural land contained within them. As soon as the Japanese administration had succeeded in putting down the Formosan rebels in 1902, they turned their attention toward controlling the Aborigines and helping them progress toward civilization. The Aborigines were particularly bothersome because they frequently attacked and took the heads of outsiders who approached their frontiers too closely. This made it very difficult to extract timber and camphor from aboriginal territory, and virtually excluded the utilization of their agricultural land in the interests of the total economy. According to an official report published by the Formosan Bureau of Aboriginal Affairs (1911), the Japanese developed two methods for dealing with the

FIGURE 8. *A Taiwan hill tribesman, defeated by the overwhelming force of the Japanese Army, 1902-1910.* (Courtesy of Government of Formosa, Bureau of Aboriginal Affairs)

problem. The first method was called "gradual development" and involved winning aboriginal cooperation through slow, peaceful penetration, but this did not always work quickly enough; the second, and more direct, "suppression" method was often resorted to.

Suppression of "savages" Japanese-style was very similar to the Argentine approach, except that the Japanese were able to make use of much more sophisticated weaponry. The approach was simply to encircle virtually the entire aboriginal area with a military cordon and then gradually advance toward the center. The cordon itself, called a guard-line, consisted of a line of small guardhouse redoubts situated on ridgetops and paralleled by a road and a wide swath of cleared forest serving as a fire zone. Important innovations included the use of telephone communication, barbed-wire entanglements, electric fences, and land mines, which "have great effect in giving alarm of the invading savages" (Government of Formosa, 1911:16). Grenades were used regularly in fighting, and field guns were placed in strategic locations where, according to the official report, "one gun is sufficient to withstand the attack of several tribes" (1911:16). In 1909 the guard-line was 493 kilometers long and throughout its length, approximately every 500 meters, guardhouses garrisoned with two to four armed guards were located, while every kilometer and a half there was a special superintendent station.

Like the Argentine line of forts, the Formosan guard-line was never intended to be a permanent frontier between state and tribal areas, but it was to be constantly advanced. The guards regularly conducted patrols and ambushes inside the line, and moved the line forward at every opportunity, with or without the consent of the Aborigines. Between 1903 and 1909, seventy-five advances were made, eighteen under "hostile" conditions. Certainly the report was accurate in describing the advance as both "an aggression and progression into the savage territory" (1911:20).

"Punitive expeditions" were frequently sent across the guard-line to punish the Aborigines for their attacks on outsiders. In 1897 one particularly "savage" tribe killed a policeman and a year later killed two more officers at a pacification station. In response, according to the report:

> . . .a punitive expedition, consisting of about 5 companies of infantry, was dispatched against this tribe. The Troops destroyed all the dwellings of the tribe. As a result, they surrendered to the Government. (1911:35)

A more elaborate punishment was arranged for another tribe that had managed to kill thirty camphor workers and a policeman within their territory in 1906. A special 11 kilometer guard-line was placed around the area, and the tribe's villages were assaulted from the line while two cruisers bombarded them from off the coast. In this action, six villages and their gardens were destroyed and forty tribal people were killed.

In a typical advancement of the guard-line under hostile conditions—a campaign of 107 days, using 886 fighting men, and 1,000 support forces for labor and transport—a tribal area of 222 square kilometers, "containing many camphor and other valuable trees" as well as tribal hunting grounds, was captured. The Aborigines constructed defenses and fought tenaciously, but were finally overcome by rifles and grenades at close quarters. Territory captured in such a manner was immediately made available for outside exploitation, as the report carefully explained.

> The territory thus included within the guard-line becomes a peaceful district, where various settlers may engage in the

agricultural, timber and camphor industries with greater
safety. . . . This act necessarily excites a dislike among the savages, but
it intends, by no means, the plundering and destruction of the district
occupied by them. It is simply intended to utilize the vast undeveloped
territory now held by the Aborigines in the island. (1911:20)

Some measure of the intensity of the resistance in Formosa can be obtained by comparing the figure of 4,341 Japanese and Formosans killed by the Aborigines between 1896 and 1909, with the 500 Europeans killed by the Maori in New Zealand between 1860 and 1872.

FOUR

THE EXTENSION OF GOVERNMENT CONTROL

*The government of any race consists rather in implanting in them ideas of
right, of law and order, and making them obey such ideas.*
Bronislaw Malinowski, 1929

Military force brought government control, which ended the lawless
frontier process and initiated the formal and orderly process of native
administration. Such administration was designed to continue native
exploitation through legal means. It was a simple matter to assume
political control over already decimated and defeated native populations
that faced no alternative but submission. But while governments did not
hesitate to use armed force to crush native resistance, in some areas
humanitarian concerns prompted the use of peaceful pacification
techniques to subdue still hostile or potentially uncooperative native
groups.

By whatever means necessary, agreements were made and treaties
signed with the natives that surrendered full and final authority for their
lives to the government and made them submissive wards of the state—
whether or not they understood what this meant. When large native
populations survived and when it was in the interest of the state to
maintain them with minimal disturbance, various systems of indirect
rule were devised to ease the impact of government control. Successful
rule ultimately depended on census data, elaborate records, and
administrative bureaucracy, but it also required the accurate data on

native customs that were provided by anthropologists working under direct government supervision or with the support of national and international research institutions.

AIMS AND PHILOSOPHY OF ADMINISTRATION

Official statements frequently justify the extension of government control over tribal populations as an effort to bring them peace, health, happiness, and other benefits of civilization and minimize economic factors. But there can be little doubt that the extension of government control was directly related to protecting the economic interests of nonindigenous peoples moving into formerly exclusive tribal areas. Considering the basic incompatibilities between the economic and social systems of tribal and industrial cultures, it is clear that tribal cultures would have to give way and be transformed if the resources of their territories were to be efficiently exploited for the benefit of the world market economy.

FIGURE 9. *A Tswana tribal assembly in Botswana is addressed by government officials. Throughout the world, tribal populations have been forced to surrender their full political autonomy.* (Irven DeVore, Anthro-Photo)

Governments could not allow the frontier process to continue indefinitely, even though it may have been extremely profitable for some individuals, because it was often very destructive of native labor and other resources, and, as we have seen, it often led to expensive military campaigns. The maintenance of law and order became a critical concern. If settlers were to successfully acquire land and utilize native labor, the government had to provide *security*, because native unrest and uprisings could quickly sweep away their economic gains. Economic development of the tribal population itself also became important in many areas, but this will be treated in a separate chapter.

TRIBAL PEOPLES AND NATIONAL UNITY

Many newly independent nations have followed an active policy of exerting control over tribal areas in the professed interests of national unity. Economic considerations aside, government authorities see the existence of fully autonomous tribal populations within the boundaries of the state as a challenge to their authority and a possible invitation to aggression by foreign powers. This has been particularly true where, as is often the case in South Asia, tribal populations occupy remote border areas. Perhaps one of the principal reasons for the recent efforts of the Indian government to extend its control over the North East Frontier Agency (NEFA) was its proximity to her potential foe, the People's Republic of China, and the rising nationalism of the Naga. Prime Minister Nehru warned India of the dangers of leaving a political vacuum along the frontier and strongly emphasized the need for full integration of India's tribal populations.

It has become fashionable to describe tribal peoples as national minorities, and as such even to speak of them as obstacles to national unity and sources of instability. Newly independent nations have been eager to politically incorporate zones that former colonial governments had left relatively undisturbed, on the theory that such zones had been deliberately perpetuated in order to create division within the country.

Cunnision (1967) has noted the irritation of governments over the presence of tribal nomads in Asia and Africa, where they are regarded as a stigma, an affront to national pride. The main complaint is that the life style of the nomad seems to be completely incompatible with the aims of the state. Nomads, after all, do not go to school, cannot easily be reached by state medical services, and are "lawless," but worst of all they may regard tribal loyalties above national loyalties.

CHAPTER
FOUR

THE TRANSFER OF SOVEREIGNTY

Most nations throughout the modern period, and, indeed, many authorities on international law since the beginning of colonial expansion in the sixteenth century, have acknowleged tribal societies to be small independent sovereignties, and have recognized that in order to legally govern them, tribal sovereignty would need to be transferred to the state either by conquest or by treaty. Many early Spanish publicists and theologians, such as Franciscus Victoria, Dominic Soto, Las Casas, and Alaya, stressed that non-Christian peoples constituted sovereign "nations." These writers challenged both the *validity* of European claims to sovereignty based solely on "discovery" and the *justice* of rights based on conquest. It was generally agreed that non-Christian lands were not empty, *territorium nullius*, and, therefore, that they were not freely open to acquisition by Europeans.

Even after the industrial revolution had begun and the modern period of colonial expansion was under way, the prevalent opinion among legal authorities continued to recognize the sovereign rights of all peoples living in organized societies, regardless of their level of "civilization." In the nineteenth century, this opinion was supported by the French publicists Pradier-Fodéré, Salomon, Bonfils, and Jèze; the Italian Pasquale Fiore; and the German Hefter.

As colonial expansion began to reach a peak in the late nineteenth century, however, important modifications of this position were begun. By an act of Congress in 1871 the United States declared, contrary to some 350 years of international legal opinion, that it would no longer make treaties with Indian tribes as if they constituted sovereign nations. The French annulled by decree any and all sovereign rights of traditional rulers in French Equatorial and French West Africa in 1899 and 1904, respectively. Legal authorities quickly fell in line. In 1876 the American lawyer Dudley Field (who helped found the International Law Association in 1873), argued that tribal lands could be acquired by direct occupation. In 1914 the British lawyer John Westlake opinioned that territorial claims could only be recognized in states that were organized strongly enough to protect the interests of white settlers. In the 1920s other authorities on international law, such as Oppenheim and Lawrence, asserted that tribal societies were not developed sufficiently to be considered sovereign entities and that these territories were therefore outside the family of nations where they could be legally claimed by any foreign power. In 1889 an Australian legal decision actually declared Australia to have been *territorium nullius*—unoccupied, waste territory, legally free for the taking—when it was annexed by Britain in 1788. This approach certainly eliminates the costly inconvenience of paying land claims to dispossessed Aborigines and has also been the implicit policy of many Latin American nations expanding into Indian territory.

While the Institute of International Law, meeting in Lausanne, France, in 1888, rejected the notion that the rights of independent tribes could legally be ignored, and while it condemned wars of extermination against tribal peoples, useless severities, and tortures, it declared that the legal transfer of sovereignty could be carried out by the mere extension of government control over a region (Snow, 1921:173-201).

There is certainly no question here of the morality of the procedure as a whole, aside from the details of how it is conducted, and this declaration suited perfectly the needs of colonial administrators.

TREATY-MAKING

> *Treaties with aboriginal tribes . . . are made for the*
> *purpose of arranging the terms of the guardianship to be exercised over*
> *the tribe.* (Snow, 1921:207-208)

Treaty-making as the first step in extending government control was carried out widely in North America and Africa as the frontiers of settlement were extended. Representatives of the governments involved merely located individuals who were assumed to be tribal leaders and obtained their marks on official documents transferring tribal sovereignty to the state and at times extinguishing their claims to the land. An example of the sweeping powers that governments assumed over tribal populations on the basis of such agreements is represented by the following treaty of 1884 between various Bechuanaland chiefs and the British.

> *I give the queen to rule my country over white men and*
> *black men; I give her to publish laws and to change them . . . to appoint*
> *judges . . . and police . . . to arrest criminals . . . to hold them as*
> *prisoners . . . to collect money (taxes) . . . to impose fines. . . .* (cited
> Lindley, 1926:36)

In the terms of the treaty of Waitangi in New Zealand in 1840, an assembly of chiefs ceded "absolutely, and without reservation, all the rights and powers of sovereignty . . . over their respective territories" to the British crown. German treaties were, if anything, more inclusive: they could

CHAPTER
FOUR

involve the transfer of a tribal people's rights to "have their own laws and administration, the right to levy customs and taxes, the right to maintain an armed force," and "all the rights" that Europeans recognize in a sovereign prince (Lindley, 1926:38-39). In several areas, the right to make such treaties was delegated by the government to special chartered companies. In Rhodesia, the British South Africa Company, under Cecil Rhodes, obtained an open-ended Royal Charter from Britain in 1888 that, like sixteenth-century Spanish charters, allowed the company

> *. . . to acquire by any concession agreement grants or treaty all of any rights interests authorities jurisdictions and powers of any kind or nature whatever, including powers necessary for the purposes of Government and the preservation of public order.* (cited Wellington, 1967:241-242)

Treaty-making often concluded military campaigns as part of a formal surrender ceremony, but even under peaceful conditions, the threat of force was always in the background. It was also not unusual for lavish gifts to be presented to the signing dignitaries, often accompanied by promises of new authority and special privileges to be accorded by the government. It appears that in signing these agreements many tribal leaders either acted largely in their own immediate self-interest, or else did not really understand the terms and full implications of the treaty and felt themselves under duress. Sometimes tribal leaders clearly recognized the threat to their political independence that such treaties constituted, but were unable to resist them. When the Germans approached a Hottentot chief in Southwest Africa in the 1880s, with a request that he accept German protection, the chief demanded to know what protection was and from what they were to be protected. He was promised continued jurisdiction over his people if he accepted protection, but he quickly recognized the inconsistency and pointed out that "everyone under protection is a subject of the one who protects him" (Wellington, 1967:177).

BRINGING GOVERNMENT TO THE TRIBES

As indicated above, treaty-signing was merely a first step in establishing government authority, often intended merely to legitimatize sovereign claims to much larger areas. However, regardless of the dominion established over them on paper, tribal peoples remained autonomous until the government physically established contact with them and initiated their political integration into the national polity by

1. Appointing political authorities over them.
2. Imposing the state's legal-judicial system, including police and imprisonment.
3. Levying and collecting taxes.
4. Instituting military recruitment.
5. Collecting census data.
6. Extending the national educational system and health services.

The methods followed by states to initially break down tribal resistance in order to bring these national institutions to the tribes varied considerably in detail in different parts of the world. But, in general, they were often well-organized, large-scale programs based on the assumption that loyalties were to be developed and hostilities were to be overcome by peaceful means. These efforts thus differed sharply from earlier attempts to overcome resistance by the use of overwhelming military force in raids and wars, and could be correctly characterized as peaceful pacification. The emphasis was on the material benefits to be derived from cooperation with the government, and gift-giving was often a prominent part of the procedure. Perhaps this pacification process can best be visualized by examining several specific examples from various parts of the world.

The Base-Camp System in New Guinea

> Soon all villages in Australian New Guinea will have been formally brought under control of the Administration; most of them, in their turn, unwillingly, and resisting what must be, no matter how it is glossed over, an act of conquest. (Rowley, 1966:63)

When the civil administration was established in Australia's Mandated Territory of New Guinea in 1921, a vigorous program for exploration and the peaceful extension of government control was immediately initiated. Material inducements were especially prominent in this procedure, and an important factor in the urgency of the program was the need for supplying the growing demand for laborers on the European copra plantations on the coast. At this time the territory was divided into areas according to the degree of government influence to help determine which areas had received least attention and to map progress as it was achieved. These categories are summarized in the following manner by Townsend

(1933:424). They reflect the various degrees of influence and illustrate effectively how control was measured.

1. *Complete Government Control.* An area in which an unarmed native policeman could make an arrest and count on the assistance of local villagers.
2. *Partial Government Control.* Where arrests could be made, but where the local villagers would not necessarily assist.
3. *Government Influence.* Where arrests would not be actively resisted, and where European lives and property would be safe.
4. *Area Penetrated by Patrols.* Without opposition, but where "proper contact" still had not been established.
5. *Unknown Area.*

At the discretion of the government, various areas were declared "uncontrolled areas," and the entry of unauthorized individuals was strictly forbidden in order to prevent the usual frontier difficulties from disturbing the orderly process of peaceful penetration.

To extend control into the latter two categories, the government developed what was called the base-camp system. In this system an armed patrol, well stocked with trade goods and headed by a European patrol officer with perhaps a dozen native police, established a base camp in an area already under government influence. The camp site was carefully selected in order not to indicate any special alliance with any particular village, which might have been interpreted as an indication of hostility by neighboring villagers. While the patrol remained in this base camp, various highly prized trade goods such as steel tools, salt, and cloth were offered in exchange for food, thus establishing contact with many of the villagers in the surrounding area. At this point the patrol moved out to actually visit these villages for the first time and the villagers were requested to build a rest house to make a longer visit possible. Townsend indicates that the villagers were not always eager to fulfill this request because they "loathe interference in domestic affairs," but they were usually convinced through the services of an interpreter. When the rest house was completed, the patrol might have visited for several days and planted fruit trees for the use of future patrols.

The presence of a government camp distributing valuables in the partially controlled area would eventually attract visitors from the "unknown" areas, who might have arrived fully armed to receive their gifts and then quickly depart. They would return again, however, and would finally invite the patrol officer to visit their own village to distribute gifts to them directly. The officer would agree to do so on condition that they build a road for him. When the new village was visited, gifts were indeed distributed and the government's objectives were explained through interpreters, while the material rewards of "belonging to the government" were stressed. A few months later a major feast would be conducted for all the tribes in the area at government expense as further proof of goodwill. Peace agreements were negotiated between hostile groups, and carefully selected native police were brought in to live at strategic points throughout the new area to help enforce the peace and to act as unobtrusive teachers. As soon as possible *luluais* or village chiefs were appointed to serve as intermediaries between the government and the village. Each chief was presented with a red-banded, blue-peaked cap as a badge of honor, and a village book that eventually would be filled with census data. Often the chief was assisted by an interpreter-assistant known as a *tultul*, who would be taken to the coast and given several months of training and who might also have served as a medical orderly in the village.

An average base-camp patrol operation lasted about three months and was normally a peaceful and successful procedure. Patrols were under orders not to use firearms except in self-defense, but occasionally trouble broke out and sometimes officers were killed while attempting to arrest participants in intertribal fighting. After friendly contact was established and luluais and tultuls were installed, a patrol officer made annual inspection tours. However, the real measure of successful penetration occurred when the labor recruiters were allowed to operate freely. As Townsend (1933:428) explains:

> It is not long before European recruiters of labour work through, and in the next few years each village has members who have worked for white men, and are strong advocates of the white man's Government.

Considerable difficulties were experienced in New Guinea pacifying the headhunting Sepik River district during the 1920s. In 1924 four European officers, a detachment of thirty police, and a twelve-ton patrol boat established themselves near the halfway point along the 800 kilometer river and began sending out heavily armed patrols. The first patrol to be attacked responded with rifle fire, and thereafter the tribal population resorted to passive resistance. Villagers simply informed the officers that they had no intentions of following their orders and often

CHAPTER
FOUR

FIGURE 10. *A New Guinea* luluai, *government-appointed chief, in official hat and clothes supplied by the government. His cheek bulges with betel nut.* (Littlewood)

simply deserted their villages when the patrol boat was sighted. To cope with this problem the officers kidnapped the old men left behind in the deserted villages and housed them in pacified enemy villages near headquarters until they agreed to arrange for communication with the resisters. Within eighteen months, 400 kilometers of river inhabited by some 10,000 people was declared safe to travel, but "ingrained hostility" still existed. Two years after the establishment of district headquarters the district officer called a meeting of 200 men to gain their approval for the government's acquisition of a plot of tribal land to be leased to a mission station. The brief meeting ended when one man made the following statement and everyone filed out:

> *Several days' journey up the river there is a white man, the District Officer. Several days' journey downstream there is a white man, the missionary. That makes two. Two too many.* (Townsend, 1933:431)

The last reported headhunting raid on the river occurred in 1927, but the government arrested those involved, hung seven, and imprisoned the rest.

The Mokolkol people in New Britain were probably the most difficult case of resistance to pacification efforts anywhere in New Guinea. According to Fenbury's (1968) account, the Mokolkol were a small group of forest nomads who refused trade or any form of peaceful contact with outsiders and occasionally raided their neighbors to obtain steel tools. They occupied a small tract of mountain forest within just 80 air kilometers of Rabaul, the district capital, and were a constant source of embarrassment to the administration. In 1931 a patrol officer approached a Mokolkol village with his police, distributed his "gifts," and sat down to wait for the villagers to receive them. The Mokolkol ran out, grabbed the gifts, and disappeared—only to return four days later to attack the patiently waiting patrol. With this reception, the defeated patrol returned to the coast with two dead and four wounded. Two years later another officer was sent in, but this time with rolls of barbed wire and orders to construct a compound and lock up any "wild men" that he could capture. The Mokolkol played hide-and-seek with the patrol, and they were able to capture only four children and three elderly men and women. These captives were taken to Rabaul, but the adults failed to adjust to their new surrounding and soon died. Finally, in 1950 a patrol of fifty-four men stealthily surrounded a village of twenty-seven people that had been located by aerial reconnaissance and rushed in handcuffing captives. This time two men, one woman, and four children were arrested and taken to Rabaul, where they were successfully indoctrinated in the advantages of cooperation with the government.

Throughout Australian New Guinea the basic process of peaceful penetration continued relentlessly from the 1920s into the 1970s, except for an unavoidable pause during World War II. By 1950 some 168,350 square kilometers of territory was not yet fully controlled, but by 1970 only 1,735 square kilometers remained in that category (Grosart, 1972:266-269).

Peaceful Pacification in Brazil

The techniques of government penetration used so effectively in New Guinea were first developed in Brazil by Rondon, founder of the Indian Protection Service. Officials of the Indian Service worked under the strict motto "Die if necessary but never kill," and during given pacification efforts, perhaps lasting months or even years, they were not allowed to shoot Indians even in self-defense. The usual procedure called for a small team to enter hostile Indian territory and build a house and compound at a strategic location, placing gifts in conspicuous places in hopes of establishing a silent barter system. In many cases the Indians promptly attacked the team's base, but the house was well shielded with sheet metal, and the Indians' arrows usually had little effect. If they approached too closely, the team was permitted to shoot over their heads to scare them away. Eventually the Indians would decide that the team really intended no harm, and direct contact would take place. Pacification was usually followed by resettlement, schooling, and perhaps other forms of supervision by Indian Service officials at Indian "posts." In 1967 the service was reorganized as the National Foundation for the Indian (FUNAI) after disclosure that many of its officials had been involved with wealthy investors in efforts to liquidate tribes hindering their interests. The new Indian Foundation has been very active recently in efforts to remove Indians from the path of the Trans-Amazon highway.

Unfortunately, in spite of the obvious humanitarian concerns of many of the former Indian Service officials and the present FUNAI workers, pacification has often had a disastrous impact on tribes who proved unable to adjust to their suddenly changed cultural environments.

In other areas of South America, such as in Peru and Ecuador, the Summer Institute of Linguistics, a well-organized and equipped group of missionary-linguists, has established initial contacts with many isolated and potentially hostile groups in basically the same manner, except that they have been able to make widespread use of airplanes.

Soviet Reconstruction: Red Tents and Red Boats

The tribal peoples of Russia's Far East in Siberia were left virtually undisturbed by the government, and many groups, such as the Chukchi, had no idea that they were part of Russia until rivalry with Americans in nearby Alaska began developing around 1900 and focused special attention on the area. However, an effective policy toward the political incorporation of these peoples did not really begin until after the revolution, when the new government discovered that the tribal peoples were living outside the Soviet Constitution and were in need of "extreme measures for their salvation" and of "rapid inclusion within the sphere of Soviet authority" (Levin and Potapov, 1964:490). In 1924 a special agency called the Committee for Assistance to the Peoples of the Northern Regions (the "Committee of the North") was assigned the task of bringing the tribal peoples into the Soviet system.

The scattered nature of the population and their nomadic habits constantly frustrated efforts at political reorganization. Mobile red tents carried by reindeer or by boats ("red boats") attempted to follow the nomads and offer them political indoctrination, cultural programs, medicine, and education. By special decrees, the tribal populations were exempted from particularly bothersome duties of citizenship, such as payment of taxes, military recruitment, and work levies. "Capitalist" traders were thrown out and the government became the sole supplier of desirable trade goods. An offensive was launched against traditional leaders who resisted the new program, and they were ousted to be replaced by clan assemblies. The ultimate aim was the elimination of nomadism and the concentration of the population in settlements for easier administration. Resettlement programs were finally developed to expedite this end and thousands of nonnative immigrants were brought in concurrently. Stationary "cultural bases" equipped with hospital and veterinary facilities, boarding schools, radios and movie projectors, and model workshops were established in the most remote areas as inducements to facilitate the resettlement plan.

Tribal "Action Programs" in Southeast Asia

For thousands of years tribal peoples have occupied the interior hilly uplands of Southeast Asia, where they apparently maintained a relative balance with their natural environment and a successful symbiosis with the various civilizations on the lowland plains. Trade and cultural diffusion certainly occurred between the tribal populations and the civilizations surrounding them, but the tribes retained their basic autonomy. This tribal independence was possible because the lowland civilizations were ecologically adapted to their own environment and were interested in maintaining the hill tribes as effective buffer zones separating them from neighboring states. World political considerations, beginning in the 1960s, have suddenly made the "loyalty" of the hill peoples a matter of major concern for the governments claiming ultimate sovereignty over them, and a variety of programs have been devised to win their support peacefully. An example of the recency of these efforts is the fact that Thailand's hill tribes, who may number some 200,000 people, were not even counted in the nation's 1960 census, and then there was no clear government policy on whether they were even to be considered citizens (Kunstadter, 1967:20, 375).

With the rise of communist-inspired guerrilla activities, however, Thailand became very interested in the tribal peoples, and by 1967 numerous government agencies were showing a sudden new interest and often developing special programs for them. These organizations included the Provincial Police, the Border Patrol Police, the Ministry of Education, the Ministry of Health, the Ministry of Defense, the

Department of Forestry, and the Hill Tribes Division of the Department of Public Health with its Hill Tribes Research Center and other programs. Considerable *international* involvement also suddenly began in direct support of these national efforts. This included the United States Information Service, the United States Operations Mission, the United States Department of Defense, the Southeast Asia Treaty Organization, UNESCO, the World Health Organization, the Asia Foundation, and at least eleven Protestant missionary organizations and several Roman Catholic orders.

The general intent and organization of these various programs parallels closely Soviet policy toward Siberian peoples described above, where the emphasis was on political indoctrination supported by the rapid provision of bountiful material rewards. Specifically, Thailand's Border Patrol Police Program and the Defense Ministry's Mobile Development Program offer striking parallels to Soviet Red Tent and Culture Base programs. The usual procedure for the Border Patrol Police in carrying out their mission of befriending the hill tribes was to send patrols into the hills in order to persuade the tribal people to build airstrips in exchange for gifts of food, tools, and medical aid. The airstrips were then used to fly in other medical aid and technical assistance. During these visits the people were told "informally" about the national government, and photographs of the king and queen and the "emerald buddha," a symbol of the national religion, were distributed. In 1964 the border patrol police removed approximately a hundred young tribal leaders from some forty villages to a district town for technical training and political indoctrination. They were then sent back to their villages as instructors.

The Mobile Development Program also distributed thousands of photographs of the king and queen and the emerald buddha, but went a major step further with the establishment of model villages in the remote areas.

Model villages were equipped with schools, TV sets, playgrounds, street lights, running water, toilets, and medical facilities, and were perhaps even more elaborate than the Soviet culture bases. Critics who would suggest that such a life-style was quite inappropriate within the hill tribe context, and that promoting such standards of material consumption might in the long run have a disastrous impact on the people, their culture, and their environments, are answered by Huff as follows.

> *We must also be careful not to underestimate the villager's capacity to change his way of life. Arguments that he does not need, does not want, and cannot get TV, electric power, machinery, and other luxuries may turn out to be shortsighted, in which case the*

*MDUs' [mobile development units] instinct in establishing and
supporting the model village concept will look somewhat better in
retrospect.* (Huff, 1967:463)

THE POLITICAL INTEGRATION
PROCESS

The extension of government control marks a highly significant event in
the history of any tribal society, for it means that at this point they cease
being politically autonomous "little sovereignties"; they cease being
"tribes" as the term is being used here. Upon their official incorporation
into the state, tribal peoples must conform to and become integrated with
the social and political institutions characteristic of state organization.
The tribe is no longer fully responsible for settling disputes and
maintaining internal order, and certainly has limitations placed upon its
political decision-making processes. At the same time a new set of
problems is created by the need to formally define the relationship
between the tribal population and the state government, and with
nontribal individuals who now have special interests in the tribal area
and its resources.

There has been wide variation in different independent countries
and colonial administrations in the extent to which political and legal
powers have been delegated to or withheld from tribal peoples. At one
extreme is the so-called direct rule system, in which *all* authority is held
by outsiders, while at the other extreme is the creation of a political
bureaucracy incorporating tribal individuals and extending down to the
village level. Many variations on the theme of indirect rule lie between
these two extremes, but it must be stressed that regardless of which
political integration strategy is followed, the result is always profound
transformation of traditional tribal organization.

French Direct Rule

According to French colonial theory, control was to be imposed as
rapidly as possible over native populations, with virtually no allowances
made for incompatibilities between native sociopolitical organization
and the French model. Native officials or canton chiefs were, of course,
utilized, because it would have been impossible in many areas to have
actually placed French administrators in every local village (in Africa

12,500 Europeans controlled over 15 million natives), but these native officials were considered to be *government employees* and not representatives of traditional cultures.

Maunier, a member of the French Academy of Colonial Sciences, argued that in the interests of utility, convenience, prosperity, and justice, it was necessary for the French to abolish the rights of traditional leaders and tribal councils, and to replace them eventually with French administrators and French courts, presided over by Frenchmen. In many cases French authorities totally denied the legal existence of any tribal social unit above the family. It was felt that in this way the tribe could be remade, "to accommodate it to new needs" (Maunier, 1949:568-569). Direct rule seems to have been a deliberate and well-planned policy, reflecting a fundamental belief in French superiority.

Chiefs appointed by the French in tropical Africa were responsible for the collection of taxes, the requisition of forced corvée labor, forced crop cultivation, military recruitment, the provision of support for visiting dignitaries, and the maintenance of an armed police force. They themselves were subject to imprisonment and corporal punishment for failure to carry out these duties, and to complicate their situation, often their authority was not recognized by the villagers. Needless to say, this placed these puppet chiefs in extremely uncomfortable positions and led to many abuses.

Under direct rule in French tropical Africa, two legal systems operated side by side. French law and the French court applied to all cases involving natives and Europeans. The *indigénat* system, or indigenous justice, applied to all cases involving only natives. In this system at the village level, the canton chief was for a time allowed to judge minor cases and impose fines of up to five days in prison. But in 1912 the chief could no longer impose any fines and could only *mediate* disputes, and by 1924 full authority was entrusted to Europeans. French administrators operated with full discretionary powers to investigate, arrest, judge, and execute the sentence, and there was no practical appeal from their decisions. Infractions were defined by the administrator's interpretation of customary law and by decree, and included such crimes as: "Any disrespectful act or offensive proposal *vis-à-vis* a representative or agent of authority" or songs, rumors, or speeches "intended to weaken respect for French authority" (Suret-Canale, 1971:331-336).

French-style direct rule was widely condemned by other colonial authorities, who claimed that it was too harsh on native custom, involved too much government, was too inconsistent and unstable, and, more specifically, that it deliberately refused to work through native political organization (Roberts, 1927:149-151).

Indirect Rule

By the 1920s and 1930s *indirect rule* came to be widely accepted as the only valid approach to native administration, although as an administrative structure it was often difficult to distinguish from *direct rule* on more than theoretical grounds. The method was pioneered and developed as both a practical working system and a philosophy by Lord Lugard during his service as high commissioner among the Islamic rulers of northern Nigeria between 1900 and 1907, and was propagated through his book *The Dual Mandate in British Tropical Africa,* first published in 1922. Indirect rule involved maintaining and strengthening traditional native leaders and creating them where they did not exist. Tribes, tribal councils, clans, and villages were generally recognized as legal entities; native courts presided over by natives were encouraged, but with specific limits on their authority. In Lugard's view (1965:214-218), one of the primary purposes of indirect rule was the necessity to prevent the total breakdown of native society and the collapse of all social order, which was being initiated by the arrival of Europeans and would certainly be accelerated by the abuses unavoidably associated with arbitrary direct rule. The demands for recognition of native rights being made by anti-imperialists and humanitarian organizations, such as the Aboriginal Protection Society and the Congo Reform Movement, combined with the obvious failures of French direct rule, were all probably influential in fostering the acceptance of indirect rule, but practical considerations were undoubtedly paramount.

"Growth from within" was one of the key philosophical concepts behind indirect rule. It was assumed that tribal peoples would thereby be allowed to develop along their own lines. However, more cynical observers have called indirect rule, "direct rule by indirect means," and Pitt-Rivers (1927:276-277) argued that the only difference between the two forms of rule was that direct rule achieved the goal more rapidly and that in the long run detribalization and deculturation occurred either way. Indeed, there is considerable evidence to suggest that indirect rule was designed to preserve native political institutions only to the extent necessary to maintain order and to assure the availability of native labor. It is significant that in areas where tribal populations were numerically insignificant indirect rule was usually dispensed with in favor of more efficient or rapid methods. Indirect rule was clearly intended to involve the adaptation of the traditional political system to the political and economic requirements of the state, but this transformation was to be carefully directed.

The system of native administration in preindependence Kenya, as described by Dilley (1966:26-30), may be briefly examined as a typical example of indirect rule in operation.

In Kenya Colony, according to the guidelines of the Native Authority Ordinance of 1912, authority over the native population at the local level was vested in *headmen,* or *councils of elders* who were selected by the local people subject to the recommendations of the white district commissioner and the final approval of the governor. Headmen were salaried and were given wide powers to maintain order and see that governmental regulations were carried out in the local area. In addition to the headmen, native councils existed in each district (sometimes paralleling European-run district councils), comprised of natives appointed and presided over by the district commissioner, but with considerable authority to pass resolutions and levy taxes. In addition, native tribunals or courts existed, which in 1932 under the supervision of the administration handled some twenty-five thousand civil cases and 7,000 criminal cases. There were also tribal police at the province level.

Systems similar to this were applied by the British throughout Africa. In India the tribal peoples of NEFA were allowed to form tribal councils that also served as courts with broad powers. Australian New Guinea operated with the headmen or *luluais* until 1950 when local government councils were established.

In many areas indirect rule was eventually ended by "independence" in which a native elite, educated by the former colonial rulers, took over the state bureaucratic structure and local appointed headmen were abolished or became elected positions, and dual (native-white) forms of local government were abolished in favor of a single administrative hierarchy.

The Protective Legislation Approach

In the case of tribal peoples who were greatly outnumbered by invading populations and were not themselves useful as sources of labor (such as in lowland South America, North America, and Australia), native administration tended to take the form of a welfare operation. After their traditional cultural autonomy had been destroyed by conquest, or in some cases by treaty, these peoples were treated merely as incompetent and impoverished citizens to be sheltered in special institutions and by special legislation. Canada, for example, provided for the gradual development of some degree of self-government for reservation Indians in its Indian Act of 1869, but the United States did not allow any significant political activity among its Indian population until the Indian Reorganization Act of 1934, which permitted tribal councils. In lowland South America, isolated Indian populations are sometimes technically subject to special protective legislation, and there may be official state organizations, such as Colombia's commissions for Indian protection and welfare, Brazil's National Foundation for the Indian, and Venezuela's National Indigenist Commission—all in principle designed to look after Indian welfare—but there is little deliberate effort to preserve any semblance of traditional sociopolitical structure. In spite of all these organizations for their protection and regardless of special laws, Amazonian Indians continue to be openly exploited by outsiders taking advantage of their lack of sophistication because little real effort is made to implement protectionist policies.

In British India there was a long tradition of protective legislation for tribal peoples in combination with a form of indirect rule. As early as 1855 the Santal Parganas District was declared a *nonregulation area,* making the general laws of the country inapplicable to it, and it was administered directly by special commissioners with full judicial authority. This approach was extended to other Indian tribal areas by the Scheduled Districts Act of 1874 and the *backward tract* provisions of the Government of India Act of 1919. *Scheduled tribes* and *tribal areas* were designated in the 1950 constitution of independent India, and tribal advisory councils were established under the supervision of the local governors who could suspend any state laws at their discretion (Ghurye, 1963; Elwin, 1969).

Suspension of normal state laws or the creation of extraordinary political arrangements are everywhere viewed as only temporary measures to allow tribal peoples time to gain familiarity and competence with the normal political-legal structures of the state. In many countries few, if any, boundaries are maintained between the dominant society and the tribal population. In these cases tribal populations may participate in normal state political processes at least theoretically on an equal footing with any other citizen, and there is relatively little in the way of special protective legislation or distinctive administrative structures. This seems to be the approach of many independent African and Asian nations and partially independent areas such as Papua New Guinea and Micronesia, where little effort has been made even to maintain former ethnic identities.

An exception to this general pattern is represented by the Soviet Union, which in 1926 began forming national *rayons* or territorial political units ostensibly representing national minorities. At the lower levels the rayons were composed of clan assemblies and councils patterned after rural soviets, and including clan federations and rayon native executive councils and congresses. This policy of recognizing nationalities or ethnic groups was merely an efficient way of following the larger national policy of helping tribal peoples "develop and consolidate Soviet state structure among themselves in the forms corresponding to the national ways of life

of the peoples" and was to be "a gradual transition to the normal
territorial system of soviets" (Levin and Potapov, 1964:492). In the
People's Republic of China there has been a similar effort to recognize the
existence of national minorities by designating *autonomous regions* that
were to be integral parts of the nation but could enjoy considerable
self-government subject to the approval of the National People's
Congress (Diao, 1967:171-173).

ANTHROPOLOGY AND NATIVE ADMINISTRATION

Representatives of government have seldom questioned the
value of ethnological data for purposes of administration. In modern
times practically every nation with expanding frontiers has supported
inquiries into the customs of native peoples in areas of projected or
accomplished occupation. . . . Colonization programs, if they have not
been dedicated to the destruction of indigenous populations, have
necessitated a knowledge of local customs. (H. G. Barnett, 1956:2)

Throughout most of the nineteenth century and before indirect rule and
other administrative refinements became widely institutionalized,
governments felt little need to acquire specialized knowledge of the
cultures that were being transformed and eradicated. Gradually,
however, it became apparent that such knowledge could make the task of
administration and transformation much more efficient and effective,
and that it might even prevent tribal uprisings. Missionaries and
administrators lacked the necessary training, were too busy with other
duties, and were too biased by their roles to obtain reliable scientific data
on tribal culture. What was needed was the assistance of anthropologists.

The United States led the way in 1879 by organizing the Bureau of
American Ethnology, which, as its first director, J. W. Powell (1881:xiv)
explained in his first annual report, endeavored to produce results of
"practical value in the administration of Indian affairs." From about 1890
on, British colonial administrators became increasingly interested in
anthropological research. Many gained some anthropological training at
the Universities of Oxford and Cambridge and went on to publish
significant monographs. In 1926 the International African Institute was
founded with the primary purpose of relating scientific research to the
"practical tasks" that were facing Europeans who were working for the
"good" of Africa (Lugard, 1928). Support for this institute came from
virtually all the major colonial powers, including Great Britain, France,

Belgium, Italy, South Africa, Germany, and the United States, but a great deal of the research effort of the institute was conducted by British social anthropologists in British colonies. Since the 1920s numerous national and international institutes have arisen in support of anthropological research in relation to native administration. Examples of the latter include the South Pacific Commission founded in 1948 and the Inter-American Indian Institute founded in 1940, while innumerable national research institutes have been founded. Most independent former colonies have also actively supported administration-related anthropological research (Barnett, 1956; Forde, 1953; Brokensha, 1966).

In general, government administrators have received the most support from anthropologists in such areas as sociopolitical organization, law and judicial processes, land tenure, and the general problem of economic development. British anthropologists were ardent supporters of indirect rule which, according to Malinowski, was considered by all competent anthropologists to be "infinitely preferable" to direct rule (Malinowski, 1929:23). They also stressed the functional interrelatedness of culture in their research so that administrators could best evaluate the impact of their policies (Manners, 1956). Prominent British functionalists such as Malinowski and Radcliffe-Brown traveled widely and helped establish anthropology departments and special training programs for colonial administrators in South Africa and Australia. During their association with colonial governments, anthropologists generally assumed a neutral position in their work and limited themselves to providing data while they avoided direct involvement in policy-making.

FIVE
LAND POLICIES

The land, of course, must be transferred from the hands of the Natives to those of the Whites. . . . So the Natives must give way and either become servants of the Whites or withdraw to the reserves allotted to them.

Newspaper Article,
German Southwest Africa,
1901, cited Wellington, 1967

Perhaps the most critical government policies to affect tribal peoples were those relating to their possession of the land: any modification of the traditional man-land relationship would undoubtedly have a major impact on all aspects of tribal culture. As soon as government control was firmly established and the administrative structures were in operation, attention was turned to the problem of defining tribal land rights in order to maximize economic productivity. While considerable variation existed in different countries, the general effect of the land policies imposed by governments was reduction of the territory available to tribal populations and modification of their traditional systems of tenure in favor of state-controlled systems. In turn, these results made traditional economic systems and related social and ideological patterns extremely difficult, if not impossible, to maintain. It should be emphasized that none of these changes were due to mere "contact" and simple diffusion, but rather to deliberate state policy. These policies will be examined in the following pages, but to better appreciate their effects it is necessary to first understand traditional tribal systems of land tenure and how they contrast with state systems.

THE TRIBAL MAN—LAND RELATIONSHIP

In traditional tribal cultures, access to land was generally controlled by a complex network of kinship relationships, the principles of which were often totally foreign and incomprehensible to outsiders. It is common to encounter examples of complete misunderstanding of tribal land-tenure systems in the writings of government administrators and colonial experts who felt that native land rights were always obscure and confused. Tribal land rights *were* often complex to be sure, but certain facts do stand out. In the first place, group boundaries were well defined and defended against encroachment from neighboring groups. Ownership was vested in the kin group or community, or figuratively in the chief, and it was inconceivable that anyone would have the right to permanently alienate land from the group. The concept of *ownership* at other than the group or tribal level was quite irrelevant, because land was to be *used* by individuals and not owned in the usual sense. Access to and use of land was virtually guaranteed to all tribal members. Even though specific rights were often overlapping and subject to numerous conditions, land allocation remained both well regulated and flexible. It was highly adaptive to have a variety of cultural mechanisms of land allocation to ensure an equitable balance between land resources and population. Aside from its obvious economic significance, the land itself often held important symbolic and emotional meaning for the people as the repository for ancestral remains, clan origin points, and other sacred features important in tribal mythology.

It is important to note that tribal land-use patterns made the concept of waste or unoccupied land as irrelevant as the concept of private ownership. Pastoralists, shifting agriculturalists, and hunter-gatherers often exploited their territory in long-term cycles and left large areas undisturbed to recuperate before returning to them. Furthermore, not all portions of tribal land are necessarily exploited in exactly the same manner, because some zones might be reserved for certain specialized uses. These details are, of course, unlikely to be of much consequence to policy-makers concerned primarily with increasing the cash value of the land. Governments have usually been quick to claim what they interpreted to be wasteland, and in the process have often destroyed the larger man-land equilibrium systems evolved by tribal cultures.

LAND POLICY VARIABLES

It is generally recognized in international law that the aboriginal inhabitants of a region possess rights in their lands that cannot legally be ignored (Buffalo Law Review, 1978, Vol. 27(4), Bennett, 1978). This is acknowledged explicitly in Article Eleven of the International Labour Office's Convention 107, which provides that:

> *The right of ownership, collective or individual, of the members of the populations concerned over the lands which these populations traditionally occupy shall be recognized.*

In fact, these rights have not always been recognized, or they have been legally circumvented through a variety of means, as will be shown.

Land laws are often complex, and in any discussion of land policies concerning tribal peoples several variables must be kept in mind. There may be virtually no recognition of any native rights in the land, as was the case in Australia until recently, but more often *some* rights are recognized in *some* categories of tribal land. These rights and categories must be carefully distinguished because considerably different effects on tribal culture may result. In terms of categories of tribal lands, the state may extend rights to any or none of the following.

1. Land traditionally exploited by the tribe
2. Land considered necessary to meet the future needs of an expanding or recovering population
3. Land actually occupied or actively exploited at a given time
4. Land with registered title

In addition to these land categories are the critical questions of whether customary communal tenure will be allowed, and how to deal with the problem of land transfers and alienation to outsiders. In theory, any tribal land could be considered totally inalienable and, therefore, the permanent possession of the tribe with no provisions for any acquisition by outsiders or the state. But most often governments have assumed responsibility for determining what tribal land can be alienated and for what purposes. It has also been common practice for governments to assume eminent domain over tribal lands in regard to certain categories of natural resources such as minerals, forests, and sometimes game, and to regulate tribal use of these resources accordingly.

The following sections examine general trends in government land policies as they relate to tribal peoples in different parts of the world. The policies of the United States concerning the Indians and Alaska natives are presented in most detail as a basis for comparison with the situation in other countries, but in most areas only a superficial survey is attempted. It will be obvious that despite the many divergent details, outstanding parallels throughout the world reside in the fact that governments have restricted the access of tribal peoples to their lands and have actively attempted to destroy customary patterns of land tenure.

The American Reservation System

The right of North American Indians to their lands was recognized in principle since the colonial period. For example, the British Royal Proclamation of 1763 stated that any lands that were not purchased or ceded to the crown would be reserved as Indian hunting grounds. This principle was reaffirmed by the new American government after the Revolution in the 1787 Ordinance for the Government of the Northwest Territory, which declared:

> *The utmost good faith shall always be observed towards the Indians, their lands and property shall never be taken from them without their consent; and in their property rights and liberty, they never shall be invaded or disturbed, unless in just and lawful wars authorized by congress.* (Fey and McNickle, 1970:56)

Such declarations were probably made in good faith, and were apparently taken seriously—at least while the Indians were numerically strong enough to constitute a threat and when there was some danger that they might seek support from foreign governments. As soon as these dangers were no longer a problem and when settlers and speculators began clamoring for new lands, these noble promises were quickly forgotten. There followed a steady reduction of the Indian land base through wars, removals, outright confiscations, and treaties that confined Indians on small reservations against their will.

The first major rejection of the policy of "utmost good faith" occurred with President Andrew Jackson's Indian Removal Act of 1830, which called for the removal of all eastern tribes to "permanent" Indian country in the Great American Desert west of the Mississippi, where it was thought that white men would never be able to settle. Some 90,000

Indians were actually removed, but not all tribes left their traditional homelands peacefully. The Florida Seminoles fought a war from 1836 to 1842 that cost the United States the lives of 1,500 soldiers and 20 million dollars to remove 4,000 Seminoles. The Cherokee of Georgia also presented a difficult case. They fought removal through the courts and obtained a favorable Supreme Court decision, but President Jackson refused to enforce it and the Cherokee had to surrender 2.8 million hectares to be distributed by lottery to Georgia's white population. Fourteen thousand men, women, and children were then herded into concentration camps and forced by federal troops to march to Oklahoma; 4,000 died en route. Unfortunately, not even their newly assigned land in Oklahoma was secure from further dispossession: much of it had to be surrendered in a short time as punishment after they sided with the South during the Civil War.

By 1840 a "permanent" frontier had been established by a line on the map and a string of forts running west of the Mississippi from Texas to Canada. Within this Indian country, which extended to the crest of the Rockies and served as a vast buffer zone between the United States and disputed territories in the far west, the Indians were to be allowed considerable freedom to enjoy their lands. For a short time it appeared that the government really intended to deal in the "utmost good faith." Regulations were passed prohibiting the entry of outsiders into Indian country without special permits and outlawing the sale of alcohol to the tribesmen. A few schools and training centers were to be established inside Indian country under the direction of the Bureau of Indian Affairs created in 1832, and troops were to be used to prevent intertribal conflicts. For the most part, however, the quarter of a million Indians in the area were to be left largely to their own devices. This scheme constituted what must have been the largest tribal "reserve" ever envisioned, and it even held some promise of success. But it was a regrettably short-lived experiment.

When Texas, the Oregon country, and the Southwest passed to American control in 1845, 1846, and 1848, respectively, the Indian country of the plains suddenly seemed to stand in the way of progress, and settlers began to stream across it in great numbers on their way farther west. The government quickly moved to negotiate new land agreements with the tribes, including rights of passage. At the government's invitation in 1851, a general council with thousands of Indians representing many plains tribes was convened at Fort Laramie. In exchange for promises of abundant gifts in the future, the tribes agreed to grant rights-of-way for the Oregon Trail and accepted specific tribal boundaries. This was only the beginning of what was already a familiar process to the eastern tribes. Shortly thereafter, states and territories were carved out of what had been

CHAPTER
FIVE

designated permanent Indian country, and all of the tribes were continually relocated on smaller and smaller reservations.

Land agreements were conducted in a similar manner to the transfers of political sovereignty described in an earlier chapter. While some writers will perhaps still defend the legality of the transactions and the good intentions of the government, there can be little doubt that coercion—if not outright deception—was often involved, and that the Indians lost millions of acres of their best lands against their will. In his account of the plains wars, Andrist (1969:8) acknowledges that, strictly speaking, most Indian land was alienated with Indian consent, but he summarized the conditions under which "consent" was granted as follows:

> It was given by tribes which had just been broken in wars,
> it was given by peoples who had been threatened or cajoled into
> signing, or misled about what they were agreeing to. It was often
> consent granted by a minority of the tribe's leaders who had been
> subverted or liquored up; the Commissioners were never squeamish
> about hailing the voice of a few as the voice of all if that was the best that
> could be had. So, when the Indians gave up their land by their own
> consent, they were usually consenting with a knee in their groin.

Reservations grew smaller and smaller and in many cases became totally inadequate to support their Indian populations by traditional means. Furthermore, they were often outside traditional homelands. The tribesmen were forced to live on sporadic and insufficient government doles of unfamiliar food, and they had to accept the confinement and new regulations imposed on them. From 1789 to 1849 reservations were actually run by army officers, and even after agents of the Bureau of Indian Affairs took charge, army posts were located on most reservations. Reservations were not always happy places, and it is little wonder that the government often had to resort to force to keep the tribesmen on the land assigned to them.

Dull Knife's band of 320 Northern Cheyenne endured what they considered to be the intolerable conditions of their reservation in Oklahoma Indian Territory for a year and a half. Then, in 1878, they attempted to return to their homeland in Montana. After a flight of more than 600 miles they were recaptured and imprisoned, but they still refused to return to their designated reservation. After being deprived of food and warmth for five days in subzero weather, they attempted to escape again but were surrounded by soldiers and shot down (Fey and McNickle, 1970:34-36; Andrist, 1969:320-330).

In 1946 the government finally acknowledged that Indian grievances over past land deals were still of sufficient magnitude and presented such unique problems that special legal machinery in the form of the Indian Claims Commission was created to deal with them. Previously, between 1881 and 1950, 118 Indian land cases had been presented before the United States Court of Claims, but only 34 of these cases actually recovered damages (Lurie, 1957:57). The new Indian Claims Commission was considerably more generous toward Indians in terms of the kinds of cases it would hear and the kinds of evidence that could be accepted. A specific category included "fraud, duress, unconscionable consideration, mutual or unilateral mistake" in the treaty-signing, as a basis for claim, or simply the failure of the government to pay as promised (Lurie, 1957:62). Some 247 cases were actually tried by the commission between 1950 and 1967 and 250 million dollars in damages was awarded as at least partial restitution for past wrongs.

In spite of these belated efforts at compensation, the govenment had already embarked upon policies that were equally destructive of tribal land rights even before the last Indian wars ended. Indian administrators had long assumed that tribal forms of land ownership constituted an obstacle to progress, and as early as the 1830s an Indian commissioner had maintained that "common property and civilization cannot coexist" (Fey and McNickle, 1970:72). Finally these views found expression in the General Allotment Act of 1887, which called for the subdivision of reservations into small plots to be assigned to individuals and held in trust for 25 years and then disposed of at the owner's discretion. "Surplus" land, remaining after the allotment, was purchased by the government and could also be disposed of at will. Allotment was often vigorously resisted by Indians, but to no avail, and its effects were devastating. During the period of most active allotment between 1887 and 1932 more than 60 percent of the 56.7 million hectares then in Indian hands was lost, and the tribes were left with only 20 million hectares of often marginal land (Fey and McNickle, 1970:84).

The integrity of reservation lands was again threatened by implementation of House Concurrent Resolution 108 of 1953, which declared it was the "sense of Congress" that federal supervision of certain Indian reservations should be ended or, as it was more popularly understood, reservations should be *terminated* as soon as possible. In this process (which did not differ significantly from allotment except that it was more drastic), many reservations were legally disbanded and their land and other assets divided among their members. Termination proceedings touched off serious controversies on several reservations between those anxious for a quick cash settlement and those who wished to retain their land and tribal status. Unfortunately, as in the past, the government was willing to proceed with or without Indian cooperation or approval. In addition to outright termination, Indian lands have been allocated by the Bureau of Indian Affairs in long-term *leases* to large-scale development corporations for projects such as strip-mining of coal and uranium mining.

The Alaska Natives Claims Settlement Act

> *All aboriginal titles, if any, and claims of aboriginal title in Alaska based on use and occupancy, including submerged land underneath all water areas, both inland and offshore, and including any aboriginal hunting or fishing rights that may exist, are hereby extinguished.* (ANCSA P. L., 92-203 Sec. 4b)

To clear the legal pathway for the construction of the Alaska pipeline following the dramatic discovery of oil at Prudhoe Bay in 1968, the United States Congress quickly put together formal legislation to permanently "extinguish" all aboriginal claims to the land. The act, passed in 1971 as the Alaska Natives Settlement Act (ANCSA) provided for the payment of 962.5 million dollars in direct cash and royalties from oil revenues to native corporations set up by the act (Arnold, 1978). The natives were also to receive title to some 162,000 square kilometers of land to be held by regional and village native corporations. In comparison with the land settlements received by Indians in the lower 48 states, the Alaska claims settlement might seem like a very generous arrangement. The natives, who in 1971 numbered approximately 78,500, or 25 percent of the Alaskan population, received roughly 17 percent of the total land area of Alaska, while the non-native private sector of the state was left with less than 1 percent of the land. State and federal holdings accounted for the remaining 82 percent. There were a few *catches*, however. The Alaskan natives were to be turned instantly into corporate executives and stockholders and were required to use their cash payments and the natural resources of their land holdings to extract cash profits from their native corporations. Furthermore, in twenty years (by 1991), the stocks in native corporations can then be sold to anyone and can, in effect, be bought up by outsiders. The corporation lands can, of course, be leased or sold as might be required to maintain profits. As of 1980 the native corporations were working hard to preserve traditional subsistence opportunities and protect their long-term interests, but it was still unclear what the outcome would be.

Reservations and Dispossession in South America

Throughout the Amazon regions of South America up to the present, tribal Indians have been driven from their lands by settlers and military action, and the "reservations" established for them have either not been seriously protected by government authorities, or they have been too small to allow continuation of traditional patterns. Thus, the situation closely resembles that in the United States. Like the Indian tribes of the American Great Plains, the Amazonian tribes utilize large areas of land, and, as hunters and shifting cultivators in many cases, they do not remain in a specific locality for more than two to three years. Their land rights have therefore been easily disregarded. The national laws that frequently guarantee Indian land rights on paper are often in reality only lightly enforced, and those who most need them are usually unaware of their existence or else lack the means of seeking their enforcement. In the face of continual dispossession, Amazonian Indians merely abandon their lands and withdraw into more remote areas.

In the 1850s Brazil's imperial government guaranteed the Indians' rights to the inalienable possession of lands needed for their survival. Under the republic, according to the constitutions of 1891, 1934, 1937, and 1946, this was modified to the extent that Indians were entitled to the possession of lands on which they were "permanently established" on the condition that they did not transfer it to others. In some states, lands were actually reserved for Indians under the supervision of the Indian Protection Service, but often the boundaries were simply not considered inviolable by state governments. In Rio Grande do Sul, for example, tribal reserves that in 1913 had amounted to nearly 81,000 hectares had been reduced to only 32,000 hectares by 1967 (Moreira Neto, 1972:319), through a variety of legal and extra-legal means.

The most ambitious Brazilian effort to "reserve" Indian land was begun in 1952, when some 85,000 square kilometers of virtually un-explored territory in Mato Grosso were provisionally declared off-limits to white colonization. However, the local government of Mato Grosso proceeded to let out 75 percent of that area in concessions to land speculators. When the boundaries were finalized in 1961, only some 22,000 square kilometers remained as an Indian reserve designated as the Xingu National Park, but its area was later increased to 30,000 square kilometers. For many years the Xingu Park was left virtually undisturbed as an example of Brazil's ideal Indian policy, but it also became a sanctuary for Indians who were being displaced by the frontier in adjacent areas, and it was eventually invaded itself (see pp. 210–212).

Previous legislative efforts to defend Brazilian Indian land rights were seriously undermined by the 1970 Federal Statute of the Indian. This law legalized the physical removal of Indians from their traditional lands for almost any ill-defined reason ranging from national security and higher national interests to public health concerns or to prevent dis-turbances occurring when settlers invade Indian lands. In effect, Indian rights to their lands no longer needed to be respected at all. Even though

CHAPTER
FIVE

Brazil's national Indian foundation (FUNAI) has designated millions of hectares as Indian parks and reserves on paper, since 1970 there has been little serious effort to prevent these areas from being invaded by powerful multinational development interests, highways, ranchers, and settlers (Davis, 1977; Presland, 1979). In 1980, the military took control of FUNAI and the most pro-Indian elements within the organization were removed, suggesting that the land situation would be even more desperate in the future (Davis, 1980).

The situation of Indian lands in the Peruvian Amazon has not been much better. Official land regulations totally disregarded the jungle Indians, who were merely pushed aside by settlers until 1957, when Supreme Decree No. 3 called for the establishment of native reserves in traditionally occupied areas. The size of reserves was not to be determined with regard to traditional subsistence requirements but, rather, according to a formula that allowed up to 10 hectares for each person over five years of age. The long-run policy objective was the introduction of private ownership to specific plots, because, according to the decree, the Indians *must* share in the benefits of progress and civilization. In 1974, Supreme Decree No. 3 was replaced by the "Law of Native Communities" and in 1975 by the "Forest and Wild Fauna Law," which call for the allotment of sufficient lands to native communities to meet their traditional subsistence needs (Chirif, 1975). However, implementation of these laws has been very slow, and it appears that in Peru, as in Brazil, Indian land rights are being overriden by corporate development interests (Cultural Survival Newsletter, 1980, Vol. 4(3):9-10).

Official Bolivian policy makes forest Indians the legal equals of any citizen; they are given no preferential treatment regarding land, even though their requirements are unique. They may legally claim title to lands they occupy, but they rarely do so, because the requirements of shifting cultivation do not encourage attachment to any small parcel of land. Consequently they are subject to dispossession whenever an enterprising colonist applies for a title. The state makes no provision for protecting larger tracts of land for Indian hunting grounds or for long-term reuse of swidden plots (Kelm, 1972:165-167).

In Colombia, an 1890 law provided for the establishment of Indian communal reserves (*resguardos*). However, this did not apply to uncivilized, non-Christian tribal groups, who were given no such rights and instead were placed under the legal guardianship of the Catholic missions delegated to civilize them. By 1961, however, Law 135 allowed reserves to be formed for uncivilized Indians, but unfortunately these have either not been established or they have been absurdly small; instead, tribal territories have been considered open for national expansion and colonization. For example, in the llanos in 1970, the Institute of Agrarian Reform reserved 2 hectares of arid savanna for each of 7,000 Guahibo Indians, while 3,000 to 40,500 hectares were allotted to each of approximately 60 colonists for agricultural development (Bonilla, 1972; Castillo-Cárdenas, 1972; Arcand, 1972).

In Venezuela, the Agrarian Reform Act of 1960 recognized Indian rights "to hold the lands, woods and waterways which they occupy or which belong to them in those sites where they customarily dwell" (Coppens, 1972), but Jimenez (1972:38) reports that this law is ineffective because no rules for its implementation have been established. According to Mosonyi (1972:48), Indian lands are steadily being appropriated by outsiders.

> *This process is going on all over the country and no one seems seriously concerned to put an end to it. It is only in the last few years that some Indian leaders have decided to request title-deeds and legal delimitation of their respective possessions from the appropriate tribunals. . . .*

Elsewhere in South America, reserves have been established in Chile and Argentina, but here, too, the allotment and individualization process has been applied. In 1940 only some 1,200 of 4.8 million hectares in Araucanian ownership remained under traditional tenure, and the tribal land base had been so reduced that most Araucanians found themselves facing a severe land shortage. The first Five-Year Plan in Argentina divided Indian lands into three categories (reservation, *reducción*, and *colonia*) that were actually stages leading to individual ownership on the same basis as other citizens (International Labour Office, 1953:308, 463). While the Inini Statute was in effect from 1930 to 1968, the Indians of French Guiana enjoyed a quite favorable land rights situation. Under the provisions of the statute, the Indians were left in undisturbed possession of 90 percent of the country. The territory was administered directly by the governor, but effective control remained with the Indians. After 1965 there was a move to convert the Inini area into regular French communes (Hurault, 1972). In other areas in the Guianas, the situation of Indian lands is equally precarious. In Surinam, Indians occupy crown lands and have no special legal protection. In Guyana, some reservations have been set up and an Amerindian Land Commission recommended further entitlements of Indian lands in 1969. However, by 1975 plans were under way to inundate the traditional lands of 4,000 Akawaio Indians with the Mazaruni hydroelectric project (Bennet, Colson, and Wavell, 1978), and the Land Commission recommendations had not been acted upon.

CHAPTER
FIVE

Tribal Land in Colonial Africa

The pattern of government acquisition of tribal land for the economic benefit of outside interests was unfortunately as common in Africa as in the New World, and sometimes even more blatant. The principal difference here was that very large tribal populations were involved, often far outnumbering the European colonists. However, except for a few outstanding exceptions such as in British-controlled West Africa, this did not hinder the alienation process.

In French-controlled West Africa the government declared that all lands for which the natives had no title actually belonged to the state. It then proceeded to dispose of such "unclaimed" lands by leasing them with full resource rights to European-owned concession companies for development purposes, while dispossessed natives were offered token "abandonment indemnities." In 1899, 70 percent of French Equatorial Africa was leased to only 40 such companies, with one company receiving 140,000 square kilometers. Natives were, of course, free to apply for titles, but they rarely did so (by 1945 fewer than 2,000 out of 16 million had applied), because they either did not feel the need for them or did not want to risk the community conflicts that private ownership would introduce (Suret-Canale, 1971:20, 255-261; Buell, 1928:1033).

The Congo Free State followed a similar course from 1885 to 1908 with its so-called *régime domanial,* which dictated that all "vacant" lands were claimed by the state. Vacant in this sense meant all land beyond the immediate vicinity of native villages and gardens. There were no provisions for tribal reserves or for any protection of native land rights beyond the islands of land actually occupied by villages at any given time, and natives were taxed for exploiting the state–owned resources in the forests surrounding their villages. This system was strictly enforced and consequently resulted in the incredible abuses described in an earlier chapter.

In areas of southern and eastern Africa considered particularly favorable for European settlement, reserves were usually set up to concentrate very large tribal populations on small poor quality tracts of land, which served as labor dormitories for the white farmers who cultivated vast holdings of the best land. This situation led to some incredible inequities, as the figures in Table 2 clearly show. It can be seen, for example, that while the natives of Southern Rhodesia constituted 95 percent of the total population, they were left with only a third of the land for their exclusive use.

The generally poor quality of African tribal reserves has frequently received comment. Writing of the Bantu reserves in southern Africa, Cole observed that they were generally poorer than the lands occupied by

Table 2
Amount of Land Reserved for Tribal Populations in Different Countries

	Native population as Percent of Total Population	Native Lands as Percent of Total Area
Bechuanaland[a]	99+	38
Swaziland[a]	98	48
New Guinea[b]	98	97
So. Rhodesia[c]	95	33
S.W. Africa[a]	87	25
South Africa[d]	80	12
Canada[e]	3	0.2
Chile[f]	2	0.6
United States[g]	0.3	1

[a]Cole (1952:6)
[b]Mair (1970:5, 146) population figures for 1960; "reserve" land here is actually nonalienated land as of 1967-68.
[c]Barber (1967:1, 7) figures for 1960.
[d]Jabavu (1934:287)
[e]International Labour Office (1953:68, 332) population as of 1949, land figures 1951.
[f]International Labour Office (1953:40, 307) figures as of 1940.
[g]International Labour Office (1953:333, 69) population as of 1940, land figures 1949.

Europeans and indeed had not attracted European attention. These reserves were also overcrowded and easily eroded, yet with wise management they were potentially productive (Cole, 1966:526-528). Wellington (1967) has noted how the reserves of Southwest Africa were purposefully located in the zones of lowest rainfall or, as a Herero chief complained in 1922, in deserts "where no human being ever lived before" (Wellington, 1967:279). In Kenya the reserves were structured to allow the Europeans, accounting for less than 1 percent of the population, to have full access to the agriculturally rich uplands that constituted 20 percent of the country and became known as the *white highlands* (Manners, 1967:283). This policy of European priority in the best lands was established early and was clearly spelled out by the colony's first commissioner, Sir Charles Eliot (1900-1904), in the following terms.

The interior of the protectorate is a white man's country,
and it is mere hypocrisy not to admit that white interests must be

*paramount, and the main object of our policy and legislation should be
to found a white colony.* (cited Lugard, 1965:324)

Eliot personally rejected the notion of large reserves because he felt
they would merely retard civilization and perpetuate barbarism and bad
customs. Instead he favored a policy of interpenetration for Kenya, which
would convert native villages into islands within European estates that
would serve as sources of labor. The natives were to have full rights to
lands they actually occupied, but here, as elsewhere, the concept of
unused land was interpreted to European advantage.

The cattle-herding tribes of Kenya fared particularly poorly under
these policies because of their nomadic habits, and like the North
American Indians they were forced to relocate frequently. The Masai
signed an agreement in 1904 in which they surrendered their finest lands
to the whites in exchange for a reserve that would endure "so long as the
Masai as a race shall exist," but seven years later they were forced to move
again (Soja, 1968:19). No reserves were really secure and any promises of
permanence were shattered by the Crown Lands Ordinance of 1915,
which "guaranteed" tribal land rights but allowed the governor to cancel
any part of a reserve if it were decided that the natives did not need it; any

FIGURE 11. *Masai man with his herds in Kenya. In 1904 the Masai were forced
to surrender their finest grazing lands.* (Irven DeVore, Anthro-Photo)

part could be excluded for railroads and highways or *any* public purpose. Kenya's tribal peoples in effect became tenants subject to dispossession at the whim of the government (Dilley, 1966:251-260).

Land Policies in Asia and the Pacific

In Asia and the Pacific region, almost the entire gamut of land policies are again represented. The harshest, most destructive policies occurred in Australia and areas under French, Japanese, and German control. Meanwhile in New Guinea, Fiji, and Micronesia (under American rule), substantial areas of land remained in native hands if not fully under native control. Throughout the Pacific the general trends noted elsewhere have been repeated. An initial period of relatively uncontrolled dispossession is followed by the establishment of reserves or at least stricter controls on the alienation process, and finally, individual title registration schemes are imposed that undermine communal tenure systems and result in further alienation.

Australia in some respects represents a special case because the entire area was occupied by hunter-gatherers and the government recognized neither the sovereignty nor the land ownership rights of these Aborigines. No land treaties or compensation payments were ever made to formalize their dispossession. Given the widespread practice in other areas of acknowledging native rights only in obviously occupied land, it is not surprising that the government declared all of Australia to be "unoccupied wasteland" and therefore state property. This was done in spite of the abundant testimony of early observers who were well aware of aboriginal land owenership and use practices. Anthropologists have even argued that every part of Australia was claimed by Aborigines and was exploited up to its maximum carrying capacity. According to Birdsell (1971:334), "there were no empty or unclaimed spaces." Australia had been occupied for perhaps 30,000 years before the arrival of Europeans, and this was plenty of time to develop very effective land tenure systems. The European invaders realized that these traditional systems conflicted with the system they wished to impose and chose to ignore them. The aboriginal reserves that were eventually established in Australia were almost afterthoughts left largely to the discretion of the local state governments. Such reserves were usually in the least desirable locations, remained government property, and were never considered to be for the exclusive, undisturbed use of Aborigines. Until the Aboriginal Land Rights Act (Northern Territory) of 1976 (see pp.181–182), the Australian government seemed convinced that ownership of land by Aborigines must be on exactly the same basis as for any other "citizen" of Australia—that is, by individual title (see discussion by Rowley, 1971, and Pittock, 1972)—and it stubbornly refused to acknowledge the legitimacy of aboriginal claims. The official position as of 1970 was clearly stated by the federal Minister for the Interior:

> *The Government believes that it is wholly wrong to encourage Aboriginals to think that because their ancestors have had a long association with a particular piece of land, Aboriginals of the present day have the right to demand ownership of it.* (cited Pittock, 1972:17)

The situation of aboriginal land rights began to change rapidly in 1972 with the election of a new government and the granting of some land holdings to Aborigines under the Land Rights Act. However, by 1980 the old government was again in power and it was clear that corporate mineral development would have priority over aboriginal claims.

In New Caledonia the French dealt with the natives in their typically straightforward manner. In 1855 the government assumed the exclusive right to handle land transactions involving natives and non-natives, and claimed all land that they considered to be unoccupied. In 1868 they introduced native reserves as a temporary measure pending full native acceptance of individual titles. As European planters became more interested in the island, the reserves proved to be too generous, and in 1876 a ruling known as the *Confinement Decree* was passed that, like the Indian Removal Act in the United States, called for the removal of natives and their relocation on smaller, often already occupied reserves. The removal process was resisted and had to be postponed until 1895, when it set off a rebellion that killed some 200 Europeans and 1,000 natives. When the rebellion was quelled, many of the defeated rebels were deported to small islands, and others were forced to agree to voluntary renunciations of their lands in exchange for promises of annuities to be paid to the chiefs. Some villages were moved as many as three times in a single year and were sometimes even burned down by military authorities who were overly eager that the land agreements be followed. By 1883 roughly 90 percent of the island had been taken out of native hands (Saussol, 1971).

In New Zealand the Maori were guaranteed by the 1840 treaty of Waitangi:

> . . . *the full, exclusive, and undisturbed possession of their lands and estates, forests, fisheries, and other properties which they may collectively or individually possess.* (cited Lindley, 1926:345)

As in America, the British respected in principle Maori rights of land ownership, but pursued a steady policy of land "purchase" by government land agents who unfortunately were not always scrupulously fair in their dealings. The main difficulty faced by the government agents was that of determining whether all individuals with claims to a given piece of land were indeed willing to sell and that they fully understood the transaction. It became obvious when fighting broke out in 1860 that the Maori felt that their land rights were in fact not being properly respected. The familiar problem, as Sinclair (1961:44) noted in a careful understatement, was that "the chief aim of land policy was to benefit the Europeans."

After most of the fighting had stopped in 1865, the government established a Native Land Court to continue the registration and alienation process in a more orderly manner. By 1940 the Maori had surrendered some 94 percent of their 1840 holdings in spite of (or perhaps *because* of) government "protection." Furthermore, thanks to the individualization policy, much of the land remaining in Maori ownership quickly became so fragmented as to be almost useless. This reduction in land base was particularly serious because the Maori population had been increasing since 1896 and had nearly tripled by 1940. More recently, the alienation process had slowed (only 4,600 hectares were transferred to Europeans in 1958-1959), and the government attempted to consolidate fragmented individual Maori holdings, but very little land remained under the traditional tribal system. The modern Maori have faced the unpleasant threat of an increasing population and a decreasing land base (New Zealand Official Yearbook, 1960:467-471; International Labour Office, 1953:301-302, 555-556).

Australian land policy in New Guinea markedly contrasts with the government's policy toward the Aborigine in Australia. When the protectorate was declared over Papua New Guinea in 1884, the natives were assured that "evil-disposed men will not be able to occupy your country, to seize your lands or take you away from your homes" (cited Mair, 1970:135). The native title was recognized here and in the Mandated Territory from the beginning, as in New Zealand, and here too the government assumed exclusive control of the alienation process. This time, however, there seemed to be genuine concern that enough land be reserved for native use to protect their future interests (and to preserve the labor supply), and relatively little land was actually alienated. By 1967-1968, only about 3 percent of the total land area of Papua and New Guinea had been alienated, but, of course, this figure includes much of the most valuable land, and in some areas the natives were forced into over-crowded reserves. The government also embarked upon a policy of registering individual titles because, as usual, it was believed that communal tenure would not offer a satisfactory basis for economic development. In its 1964-1965 Report, the Papua New Guinea administration expressed its policy aims as follows:

CHAPTER
FIVE

> *The ultimate long-term objective is to introduce*
> *throughout the Territory a single system of landholding regulated by*
> *the Territorial Government . . ., and providing for secure individual*
> *registered titles after the pattern of the Australian system . . . .*
> (Australia, Department of Territories, Report for 1964-65:43)

The Dutch were even more protective of native land rights in their half of New Guinea and did so little to encourage colonization that by 1953 little more than 2,000 hectares had been alienated. This changed after the Indonesians took control in 1963 and, in typical colonial fashion, claimed all unoccupied land for the state and proceeded to introduce Javanese settlers into once exclusively tribal areas (Crocombe and Hide, 1971:314-315).

In many of the smaller Pacific islands of Micronesia and Polynesia, where the land area is severely limited, colonization has usually been rigidly controlled. However, nearly everywhere governments have attempted to destroy communal tenure practices and replace them with individual tenure in hopes of facilitating cash-cropping activities and settling land disputes. Unfortunately, the result here, as elsewhere, has often been serious fragmentation of the land or its concentration in the hands of a few, even though alienation has not usually been a threat.

In both independent and colonial Asia there has been a general tendency not to create special reserves for tribal peoples. In India, Bangladesh, Thailand, Sarawak, and Sabah, forest areas are claimed by the state, and in several cases forest reserves have been created in which tribal peoples are allowed to remain only by special permission and under special conditions. The land regulations of 1947-1948 that were applied to the hill tribes of the North East Frontier Agency of India (NEFA) were unusually generous in that they allowed tribal communities full rights to the lands they normally cultivated in their shifting cycles and even recognized that villages might move within a general area without abandoning rights to the land (Elwin, 1959:65). In other areas of India tribal peoples have lost large amounts of land due to failure to register titles, or when their temporarily abandoned plots were claimed by settlers in spite of the special provisions for tribal and scheduled areas. In Bangladesh no lands are actually reserved for tribal peoples; instead, their use rights are "protected" and, as we have seen, are subject to government controls. The American administration in the Philippines specifically rejected the notion of tribal reserves, preferring instead to issue individual titles to tribal land. Later the independent Philippine government created some small reserves that were to be allotted to individuals as they became sufficiently assimilated (Keesing, 1934:163-

170); International Labour Office, 1953:550). In Indochina, the French claimed all hill tribe areas as crown lands and opened them for colonization. It was specified that areas actually claimed by tribal peoples could not be *purchased* by outsiders, but they could be *leased* for 99 years (Hickey, 1967:752). Thailand and Sarawak evidently make no special provisions for tribal lands, or at least have not done so until quite recently. Tribal peoples are presumably on equal terms in regard to land as other citizens. This "no special policy" policy is probably one of the simplest ways of accomplishing the usual goal of replacing tribal peoples and their tenure systems with what the government might consider to be more productive populations and ownership systems.

SIX
CULTURAL MODIFICATION POLICIES

Cultural realities can be changed rapidly by governmental action if . . .
massive, expensive, and highly organized coercive action is used.

R. Crocombe, 1971:380

Up to this point it has been shown how governments have destroyed the political autonomy of tribal populations and gained control of tribal lands. While these actions are in themselves certain to bring about profound "acculturation," the almost total transformation of tribal cultures is assured when these actions are combined with deliberate programs designed to eliminate all unique aspects of tribal culture and to bring about their *full* integration with civilization. Tribal peoples throughout the world have faced this situation, and given these forces for change it is surprising that any groups have managed to retain even their ethnic identities.

From their positions of coercive power and authority, government administrators, their agents, and missionaries methodically set about to destroy tribal cultural patterns in the name of progress, to make the natives more amenable to the purposes of the industrial state. Every area of tribal life from language to marriage customs and religion came under attack by various crusading agencies and individuals anxious to reform and improve them. Any native custom that seemed immoral, offensive, or threatening was instantly abolished by decree, while other customs that were considered barriers to progress were either abolished outright, or steps were taken to suppress them. Native offenders who continued the then-illegal customs were fined, jailed, or subjected to various forms of corporal or capital punishment until the new laws were respected. However, despite all the forces brought against them, many customs proved exceedingly difficult to eradicate and were often carried on covertly for years.

Forced cultural modification can be approached from many aspects, several of which have already been discussed or alluded to. This chapter describes the general attitude of governments and social scientists toward the subject, and surveys the range and intensity of cultural modification practices in different countries. (Economic development constitutes a special category of cultural modification and will be treated in a separate chapter.)

THESE ARE THE THINGS THAT OBSTRUCT PROGRESS

> *The political autonomy, economic habits, religious practices, and sexual customs of organized native groups, in so far as they threaten European control or offend Western notions of morality, must be abandoned.* (Reed, 1943:xvii)

Once the state embarks upon a policy of integrating a tribal people (and, as we have seen, this path is almost always taken), policy decisions must be reached regarding how to deal with the many diverse elements of tribal culture that do not mesh easily with industrial civilization. The opening quote suggests that, given enough force, governments could completely destroy any tribal society's cultural diversity with massive cultural modification programs. However, such a rapid course has generally not been economically desirable, and governments have usually been more selective in their destruction of tribal culture.

More than a hundred years ago, Herman Merivale (1861:502-503), in his lectures on colonization, provided some guidelines for government administrators interested in the control of native customs. Objecting to what he considered to be the misguided philanthropy of some individuals who would leave tribal peoples alone except in matters directly involving Europeans, he discussed tribal customs in terms of three categories: (1) "violations of the eternal and universal laws of morality"; (2) "less horrible," but still "pernicious" customs; (3) "absurd and impolitic" customs that were not directly injurious.

The first category included such practices as cannibalism, human sacrifice, and infanticide, all of which according to Merivale must be suppressed. As we shall see, most authorities have agreed that a category for "immoral" customs should be established, but there have been some very different interpretations about which customs belonged in it. Merivales's second category was even less clearly defined. It included a variety of cultural traits that were considered to be "incompatible with civilization," many of which he felt should also be suppressed, although others felt they would best be eliminated by gradual enlightenment rather than by outright force. Merivale's ethnocentric approach to the problem was quite apparent in his general conclusions.

> *It will be necessary, in short, that the colonial authorities should act upon the assumption that they have the right in virtue of the relative position of civilized and Christian men to savages, to enforce abstinence from immoral and degrading practices, to compel outward conformity to the law of what we regard as better instructed reason.* (Merivale, 1861:502-503)

This basic directive has been implicitly followed up to the present by government authorities throughout the world, although the "law" of "better instructed reason" has not always held the same meaning, and the question of which cultural traits should be deliberately modified is still being debated in some cases.

In general, headhunting and all forms of tribal feuding and warfare have been suppressed, along with cannibalism (including endo-cannibalism, the ritual eating of a people's own dead), infanticide, euthanasia, execution, and whatever was interpreted to be slavery. These traits all fall under the "inhuman or grossly immoral" category (Lindley, 1926:374), even though many, such as warfare and execution, are often actually institutionalized by states. It seems reasonable to assume that such traits are prohibited more because they represent challenges to state authority rather than because they are universally recognized as immoral. A good case could in fact be made in support of many of the above "immoral" traits on quite moral grounds. Euthanasia, for example, is now being openly advocated by some physicians. It is also instructive to note how the category of prohibited customs has been expanded to include almost every conceivable trait of tribal cultures. For example, in New Zealand by 1844, anything done by the Maori that could be considered "inconsistent with good order and with the progress of civilization" was likely to be prevented by government authorities (Snow, 1921:204). In practice, throughout the British Commonwealth tribal peoples were legally subjects of the crown and were expected to behave accordingly.

They could retain their traditional cultures as long as they were compatible with "justice, humanity and *good government*" (Lindley, 1926:375, emphasis mine).

Many aspects of tribal kinship and social organization have been attacked as crimes against public order, shocking and injurious, cruel, or simply as obstacles to progress. A partial list of such traits that have been condemned at various times would include payment of bride price, infant betrothal, the levirate (a man marrying his brother's widow), polygamy, secret societies, kinship duties in general, and the extended family. The latter has been particularly criticized as an inappropriate "drag on economic development" and "a serious obstacle to economic progress" (Bauer and Yamey, 1957:64, 66), but it is doubtful that direct efforts have ever been made to abolish it.

The Indian government attempted to soften its policy of assimilation by taking care not to disturb traditional tribal customs, as long as they were considered to be quite proper (Iyer and Ratnam, 1961:227). In the North East Frontier Agency, where greater liberality toward tribal cultures was followed than in India proper, it was standard practice for government administrators to prohibit the usual traits that offended against "law and order or the universal conscience of mankind," but here this came to include anything that was clearly "impoverishing" the population as well as "cruel" forms of animal sacrifice (Elwin, 1959:224, 250-251).

French policy toward cultural modification was summarized by the French authority on colonial science, René Maunier (1949), who explained that anything incompatible with French economic interests must go.

> *Let us say that the French must—or think they must— abrogate the customary law of the colonies when it threatens to interfere with security or prosperity.* (Maunier, 1949:501-502)

This approach was combined with an assimilation theory that attempted to replace everything native with things French, and gained for the French the title of "cultural imperialists," for "the wholesale attempt to impose an outside culture upon another people" (Buell, 1928:77). This was, of course, no different in fact from the native policies of every other major nation, but at that time the French were very blatant and at least seemed to be less sympathetic toward native cultures than, for example, were the British.

In the American dependencies, government directives regarding native culture were fully as ambiguous and open-ended as in other areas. A circular issued in 1932 by the Philippine Bureau of Non-Christian

Tribes urged government officals to respect cultural practices that were "not contrary to law, morals, and good customs," but reaffirmed that tribesmen were still to be assimilated as rapidly as possible (Keesing, 1934:33)

According to Schapera (1934:x-xii), by the 1930s South Africa was following the *adaptationist* policy as the most reasonable and economical means of "facilitating the transition to assimilation." This policy assumed that where necessary, tribal culture might be allowed to persist, but administrators and missionaries did not always agree on this point. Native customs actually were recognized by the courts if they were not "repugnant to elementary ideas of justice and humanity" or *"illegal!"* (Schapera, 1934:x-xii, emphasis mine). Here as elsewhere, this policy gave local officials considerable room for independent action, and attitudes toward tribal culture varied widely even among the country's scholars. In his discussion of the "native problem," the South African economist W. H. Hutt (1934:195-237) called for sympathetic understanding of native culture, but stresses that assumptions regarding the necessity or permanence of any traits should be avoided. His conclusion on the matter was that probably the entire native culture would have to "go."

> *Fortunately there is now almost universal agreement that the "cattle cult," animal sacrifices, the doctoring of land [magic], and many other obviously effete primitive customs and taboos must go. What is not so readily admitted is that with them must also go the native mode of life and probably the language which was adapted to that life.* (Hutt, 1934:209-210)

In New Guinea the Germans prohibited whatever they considered to be antisocial, while the Australian mandate government declared on the *positive* side that its policy would be to *improve* the moral and physical environment of village life, and to introduce "healthy forms of amusement." Reed observes that it resulted in the natives' being forced to abandon everything threatening or offensive to Europeans; it extended to the extreme that in the 1930s a native who used "obscene" language could end up in court (Reed, 1943:xvii, 138-139, 176-177). By the late 1960s the Australian administration in Papua New Guinea was still prohibiting certain religious practices thought to be "repugnant to the general principles of humanity," illegal, or "not in the best interest of a child." There were also official complaints that cultural diversity presented "obstacles to orderly social change" and that "adherence to custom can hinder progress" (Australia, Department of Territories, Report for 1967-1968:3, 8, 10-11, 19).

The cultural modification policies of the independent, modernizing nations have sometimes been more sweeping in their destruction of tribal culture than the earlier colonial authorities, particularly where they have followed the ruthless prescriptions of development experts such as Heilbroner, who recommended the following measures to help transform "tradition-bound" societies.

> *Nothing short of a pervasive social transformation will suffice: a wholesale metamorphosis of habits, a wrenching reorientation of values concerning time, status, money, work; and an unweaving and reweaving of the fabric of daily existence itself.* (Heilbroner, 1963:53)

It seems that anything that could remotely be considered to stand in the way of progress might be slated for elimination by the new leaders of developing nations acting on the advice of development specialists. One such expert who has written widely on the development problems of Africa and Asia lists a number of "nonadaptable" African tribal institutions, such as tribal organization, matrilyny, and shifting cultivation, which he feels are unsuitable in a modernizing society and presumably should be abandoned (Hunter, 1967:72). In a similar manner Goulet (1971:326) lumps chattel marriages along with infanticide as incompatible with human rights and positively harmful impediments to development, and he therefore considers them to be expendable cultural traits. Almost in the same breath he observes that the African value system based on cattle might also be "doomed to disappear." Paradoxically, Goulet earlier complained that in such matters social engineers lacked "clear universal directives" and faced "perplexing questions" over "which cultural peculiarities are to be allowed and which eliminated" (Goulet, 1971:268-270). Such problems are unavoidable when individuals attempt to program a way of life for people in alien cultures.

SOCIAL ENGINEERING: HOW TO DO IT

> *When a change that is to be applied to the common man, usually a village peasant, has been agreed upon by a member of the ruling elite and the overseas specialist, the problem is how to convince this common man to accept the new ideas without using force.* (Arensberg and Niehoff, 1964:68)

*It is no easy task for an outsider to get people to change
their pattern of doing things.* (Arensberg and Niehoff, 1964:87)

Designating what aspects of a tribal culture to eliminate and selecting
suitable replacements are relatively simple problems compared with the
difficulties of actually executing such decisions. During the early period
of colonial expansion governments allowed most of their cultural
modification work to be carried out by "natural" frontier processes, or
they resorted to direct military or police force to suppress "illegal"
customs, while the remaining unsuitable customs were attended to by
missionaries. Naked force has certainly been widely applied against
tribal cultures and continues to be used even at the present time because
of the speed and apparent efficiency of its results. The Uganda
government, for example, recently abolished a bothersome hunting-and-
gathering culture virtually overnight when they loaded the entire
population of Ik into trucks and drove them out of their homeland
(Turnbull, 1972). More commonly, direct coercion has been brought to
bear against specific aspects of a traditional culture that have been
declared illegal. Maunier (1949:504) explained the French approach to this
kind of legal abolition or "civilization by legislation" as follows: "Such
and such an act may be absolutely, totally, unreservedly, forbidden."
Later in this chapter, numerous examples of such use of direct force in
culture change are presented, but indirect force or "social engineering"
will be discussed first because it has recently become far more common
and deserves special treatment.

In the postwar decolonization period, with its emphasis on self-
determination of peoples, the use of force in culture change has generally
been frowned upon by international agencies and social scientists
concerned with basic human rights. While the 1948 United Nations
Declaration of Human Rights does not specifically mention forced culture
change programs, it does state in Article 22 that everyone is entitled to the
realization of the "cultural rights indispensable for his dignity and the
free development of his personality," and forced change could certainly
threaten such rights. This interpretation was affirmed, enlarged upon,
and made directly applicable to tribal peoples by the International
Covenant of Human Rights, adopted by the UN General Assembly in
1966, which states unequivocally in its convention on civil and political
rights that:

> *In those states in which ethnic, religious or linguistic
> minorities exist, persons belonging to such minorities shall not be
> denied the right, in community with the other members of their group,
> to enjoy their own culture, to profess and practice their own religion or
> to use their own language.*

CHAPTER
SIX

Any program of directed culture change imposed upon a "target" population against their wills would almost unavoidably violate these rights, and *in principle* at least such programs are usually rejected by social engineers. In 1968 the Permanent Council of the International Congress of Anthropological and Ethnological Sciences acknowledged that force was still being widely used and unanimously passed a resolution on forced acculturation that called upon governments to respect the Declaration of Human Rights.

Applied anthropologists have in general rejected the use of any change techniques that the target or recipient population might interpret as coercive, in part because as Goodenough (1963:16) explained, "we have scruples against attempting to impose blueprints on others," but perhaps more importantly because it was long realized that force did not always achieve permanent results. Even Maunier (1949:513) warned that force often generated resistance and caused undesirable traits to go underground. Goodenough was concerned with the same problem and felt that from a strictly "practical" viewpoint, successful "reform" could not depend on external force, because "the truth is that to accomplish purposive change in another usually requires the other's cooperation." Cultural modification then becomes "helping others to reform themselves." Goodenough specifically rejected the notion that force might still be involved even when it may not be directly perceived by the target group, and he stated flatly that his book outlining how change agents can gain the "cooperation" of their targets was not a book on "how to get other people to do what you want and like it" (Goodenough, 1963:16-17). A closer look at the general techniques of social engineering as it developed in the early postwar period suggests otherwise.

Mead, in her discussion of culture change in Manus Island, New Guinea, was convinced that tribal peoples there were quite eager for change, and she likewise seemed unwilling to recognize how force could possibly be involved. As she stated:

> *We do not conceive of people being forcibly changed by other human beings. We conceive of them as seeing a light and following it freely.* (Mead, 1961:19-20)

Such firm conviction that if cooperation is gained, force is not involved is perhaps understandable in change agents who were convinced of the desirability of the changes sought. Indeed, to many change experts, the ends appeared to justify the means, regardless of the likelihood that outsiders might make ethnocentric judgments concerning "benefits," and in spite of the unpredictability of the long-run effects of change. This reckless attitude seems to be expressed in the formal code of ethics adopted by the Society for Applied Anthropology in 1963, which spoke of the need for respecting the "dignity and general well-being" of target peoples, but which was silent on the specific issue of the use of force and actually appeared to condone it under the proper circumstances. Action that might adversely affect the "lives, well-being, dignity and self-respect" of targets was considered unethical, *unless* efforts are made to *minimize* such adverse side effects, and *unless* such action was thought to be beneficial (Anonymous, 1963-1964). In other words, as long as your intentions are good, whatever techniques achieve the desired results most effectively will be acceptable.

The indirect manipulation or engineering of tribal peoples is not an invention of applied anthropologists, but it has been employed probably as long as direct force. Maunier advised French colonial authorities that it was generally more advantageous to "conditionally" eliminate undesirable customs through such measures as taxation, licensing, or other forms of control. The secret was to make the change imperceptible.

> *If reform is necessary, it ought to be carried out after preparation and with due consideration, leaving the subject people under the illusion that their old traditions will be maintained, even if they are in fact being gradually, unobtrusively, progressively, modified—as is necessary. That seems to be sound psychology.*
> (Maunier, 1949:513)

Elsewhere Maunier observes that there are actually "thousands of ways" of achieving culture change against the real wishes of the natives. In addition to the general method of regulating without directly abolishing customs, Maunier described what could be called the *enlightenment* approach, in which "reform" was sought by convincing argument, example, and education—all aimed at showing how inferior native ways were and how advantageous it would be for the natives to abandon them in favor of superior French ways. The formal education approach will be examined more closely in another section, but here it can be pointed out that the creation of dissatisfactions as a stimulus for change has been widely recommended by modern change experts. Goulet suggests that traditional peoples must be shocked into the realization that they are living in abnormal, inhuman conditions as psychological preparation for modernization (Goulet, 1971:25-26). In Goodenough's view:

> *The problem that faces development agents, then, is to find ways of stimulating in others a desire for change in such a way that the desire is theirs independent of further prompting from outside.*

CHAPTER
SIX

> *Restated, the problem is one of creating in another a sufficient*
> *dissatisfaction with his present condition of self so that he wants to*
> *change it. This calls for some kind of experience that leads him to*
> *reappraise his self-image and reevaluate his self-esteem.*
> (Goodenough, 1963:219)

Applied anthropologists have no special secret weapons for achieving culture change: their recommendations, as they evolved during the 1960s, were usually in the form of commonsense advice, or sound psychology, based on an understanding of the culture to be modified and embodying proven methods of persuasion. For example, in addition to the obvious tactic of tampering with self-images, change agents were advised to:

1. Involve traditional leaders in their programs
2. Work through bilingual, acculturated individuals who have some knowledge of both the dominant and the *target* culture
3. Modify circumstances or deliberately tamper with the equilibrium of the traditional culture so that change will become imperative
4. Attempt to change underlying core values before attacking superficial customs

The change agent was furthermore advised to gain the respect and confidence of the people; to manipulate traditional attitudes toward status and prestige to his advantage; to make certain that modifications sought are actually possible; and to time them carefully (Goodenough, 1963; Arensberg and Niehoff, 1964; Foster, 1969; Jones, 1965). The judicious employment of material rewards or "benefits" was perhaps one of the strongest of change strategies because these may be offered to the target group "when it performs in a manner prescribed by the agent of change," not unlike pigeons being taught to peck at appropriately colored disks (Jones, 1965).

While anthropologists trained and advised change agents, they themselves could work directly in change programs where they could use their specialized knowledge of social structure, value systems, and the functional interrelatedness of culture to identify both the "barriers" to change and the "progressive forces" within a specific target culture (Foster, 1969:120).

Clearly, the change strategies just outlined did not rely on the *direct* use of force, but in terms of the larger context of most change programs, coercion was almost always implicit. Change *was* being deliberately initiated by outsiders. In the final analysis, blueprints *were* being handed down from above, by individuals and agencies in the dominant culture who were making the basic policy decisions for a submissive target culture that ultimately had no power to resist. The critical problems here are that not only are basic human cultural rights being threatened, but the changes themselves, while they may have been well intentioned, all too often were tragically destructive. What is really being questioned here is what Foster has called the "rationale" for *directed* culture change programs:

> *that technical experts can and should evaluate the practices of other people and decide which ones should be modified.*
> (Foster, 1969:136)

When "other people" are people with a radically different culture, and when they are ultimately powerless to resist such change programs, perhaps the rationale needs to be reconsidered.

The following sections present specific examples of cultural modification policies in action against tribal peoples in different parts of the world. Education policies in colonial settings and American Indian schools are briefly examined, and both direct and indirect change strategies are illustrated with cases involving government attempts to destroy shamanism and ceremonial, desert pastoral nomadism, the East African cattle complex, and swidden agriculture.

Education for Progress

> *People must learn to be scientific and progressive in outlook instead of living by ancestral laws and long-tried rules of thumb.* (Jones, 1965)

In many countries schooling has been the prime coercive instrument of cultural modification and has proven to be a highly effective means of destroying self-esteem, fostering new needs, creating dissatisfactions, and generally disrupting traditional cultures. As representatives of the prestige and power of the dominant culture, teachers deliberately assume positions of authority over students, overshadowing parents and traditional tribal leaders. But even more important, schooling conflicts with the basic education that children gain from participation in their own cultures. Tribal cultures generally require mastery of an elaborate and highly specialized knowledge of the natural environment, as well as special training in folklore, religion, ritual, technology, and other skills. The years that children are required to spend studying the dominant

CHAPTER
SIX

culture's textbooks are in direct competition with the normal enculturation process. Furthermore, schooling deprives the traditional community of the important contribution that children often make to the subsistence economy. Cunnison (1966:40-41) reports that children of Sudanese tribal nomads who spent as little as two years in schools returned to their homes without the skills needed of cattle herders, but that they also became physically too "soft" to readapt to the demands of traditional life.

Under colonial conditions, schooling was often a very direct means of cultural modification. According to Buell (1928:55), in French colonial schools two basic subjects were taught. The first was *morale*, which aimed at instilling French ideals of "good habits, cleanliness, order, politeness, respect, and obedience." *French* was the second subject and the principal language of instruction, while in some areas all use of native language in schools was forbidden by decree. Lessons included "simple ideas of France and the French people," and advancd students were instructed in the meanings of such terms as justice, respect, altruism, charity, pity, and compassion—all of which were presumed to be unfamiliar concepts. The most important lesson was "the need of loyalty to France" and the importance of cooperating with French interests. Schoolchildren were taught to despise their own traditions and cultures in a surprisingly direct and ethnocentric manner, as illustrated by the following excerpt from a French reader designed in 1919 for use by French West African school-children.

> *It is . . . an advantage for a native to work for a white man,* *because the Whites are better educated, more advanced in civilization* *than the natives, and because, thanks to them, the natives will make* *more rapid progress . . . and become one day really useful men. . . .* *You who are intelligent and industrious, my children, always help the* *Whites in their task. This is a duty.* (Moussa et Gi-gla, Histoire de deux Petits Noir, cited Buell, 1928:63)

In the government schools of Italian East Africa, tribal children were taught discipline, respect, and obedience—to Italian authority. With amazing ethnocentrism, teachers also proceeded to teach tribal boys arts and crafts and how to farm, while girls were taught how to cook native food! Italian textbooks, described as "didactic aids adapted to the attitudes and capacities of the natives," contained such choice readings as:

> *I am happy to be subject to the Italian government and I* *love Italy with the affection of a son.*

or simply,

> *Help me, oh God, to become a good Italian!* (cited De
> Marco, 1943:36, 40)

For many years in the United States the government delegated the formal education of Indian children to missionaries such as Stephen Riggs, whose general attitude to Indian culture was well summarized by his 1846 statement that, *"As tribes and nations the Indians must perish and live only as men!"* (his emphasis, cited Berkhofer, 1965:7). Boarding schools were considered one of the best means of destroying Indian culture because here even very young children could be almost permanently separated from the influences of their parents. Mission teachers imposed haircuts, Western dress, new English names, and rigid schedules on their charges, and they emphasized religion and manual labor.

A similar approach to missionary boarding schools is still being applied in South America. For example, the Salesian boarding school of La Esmeralda, which was opened in 1972 in Venezuela for the Yanomamo and Makiritari Indians, was apparently being operated with very little regard for the traditional culture. Children were kept within the school's walled-in compound, often against their wills. Their hair was cut, their clothing was changed, and they were given Spanish names. Outside observers reported that the children complained of the restrictions, lack of food, homesickness, ridicule of their traditions, and being beaten. They also frequently attempted to run away (Lizot, 1976).

Eliminating Shamanism

Leaders in traditional religion and specialized knowledge such as tribal curers and shamans have often been singled out for special attention by both missionaries and government authorities because they seem to represent direct challenges to Western medicine and Christianity, and because they have sometimes come to symbolize the traditional culture in opposition to progress.

Perhaps one of the strongest anti-shaman campaigns was that carried out by the Soviet Union in the Soviet Far East, where shamans were classified along with other tribal leaders (or ruling cliques) as wealthy "exploiters" and "parasitic groups" who "battled bitterly against the new regime and actively attempted to sabotage its projects" (Levin and Potapov, 1964:10, 497-498). In the official view, shamans played an extremely negative role among the tribal people, in part because they made "wasteful" animal sacrifices and clearly were the principal exponents of an "outdated religious ideology," but also because they apparently did lead the resistance to Soviet schools, medical centers, "culture-bases," and collective farms. One shamanistic activity that must have been particularly frustrating for Soviet authorities was the continuing effort of the shamans to regulate the tribe's resource exploitation practices by enjoining hunting and fishing on certain days and even totally prohibiting the killing of some animals. Clearly, in Soviet eyes, shamans were a "reactionary, counter-revolutionary force" (Kosokov, 1930:70, cited Kolarz, 1954:76).

An offensive was launched against the shamans in which they were arrested and exiled or forced to publicly renounce their activities. The local representatives of the "League of Militant Godless" were enlisted to gather information on shamans and to generally conduct antireligious propaganda among the tribes. As part of the campaign, efforts were also made to replace shamans with what Kolarz (1954:79-80) refers to as the "Lenin-Stalin Cult." The government circulated poems and folk-tales among the tribal population in which Lenin and Stalin were represented as all-powerful solar deities capable of defeating all evils, in hopes of overshadowing the role of shaman. The extravagant nature of these tales is well represented by the following quote from *Sun of the People,* a story that refers to Stalin and was designed for the hunting and fishing Nanai.

> *Nobody can equal the strength of that hero [Stalin]. His eyes see everything that goes on on earth. His brain knows all that people think. His heart contains the happiness and the woe of all peoples. The depth of his thought is as deep as the ocean. His voice is heard by all that inhabit the earth. Such is the greatest of the very greatest in the whole world.* (cited Kolarz, 1954:80)

What shaman could compete with that kind of power and authority?

Shamans and the practice of tribal religions in general also came under similar attacks in other parts of the world. Speaking of Bantu shamans in South Africa, Schapera (1934:33-34) stated that their influence was unhealthy, and that they constituted a "powerful obstacle to progress" because of their "almost fanatical" conservatism. He felt that the best way to eliminate their influence and the general belief in witchcraft and magic would be through "the effective teaching of scientific principles."

In nearby Rhodesia, witchcraft and certain forms of divination have been outlawed since the Witchcraft Regulations of 1895 and the Witchcraft Suppression Act of 1899. The latter act, which was still being vigorously enforced in the 1960s, provides punishments of up to seven years of imprisonment and/or 36 lashes for anyone proven to be "by habit and repute a witch doctor or witch finder" (Witchcraft Suppression Act,

Articles 4 and 8), or for the use of charms to locate lost or stolen articles. The law also declares that anyone receiving money for any "exercise of so-called witchcraft or the use of charms," or who gives any instruction or advice on the subject, will be punished for fraud (Crawford, 1967).

In New Guinea, native curers are often regarded as illegal and are not infrequently prosecuted for practicing their art. Medical doctors sometimes attempt to shame and embarrass them by using modern drugs and may even impose medical attention on unwilling patients who sometimes have had to be literally dragged into operating rooms because of their fear of foreign practitioners (Ryan, 1969:41).

Every Ceremony Must Go

Conspicuous ceremonial activities or particularly unusual customs have very often been candidates for elimination, because even if they were not contrary to universal morality, they were certain to be considered obstacles to progress.

In the United States from 1884 to 1933, there were laws forbidding "pagan" Indian ceremonies that the Indian Bureau felt would inhibit the spread of Christianity. The sun-dance ceremony of the Plains Indians, which was their highest expression of tribal unity and identity, was specifically outlawed, presumably because it involved immoral physical ordeals. In 1926 the leaders of Taos Pueblo in New Mexico were actually jailed for participating in illegal religious ceremonies described as pagan, horrible, sadistic, and obscene. Efforts were even made to prevent Pueblo youth from being initiated in traditional tribal fashion (Collier, 1947:233-234, 256).

The French acted with characteristic thoroughness in areas under their jurisdiction. In the Marquesas in the 1850s, tattooing, singing, dancing, and performance of the traditional religion were abolished at one sweep (Maunier, 1949:500-501). The Dutch treated ceremonies more cautiously than the French. In the Celebes, ceremonies "which could be vested with a Christian mantle" could remain, but this sometimes required some special engineering such as allowing certain ceremonies to take place at different dates, renaming them, etc. (Kruyt, 1929:7-8).

In New Guinea missionaries took it upon themselves to speed culture change by destroying "pagan" ceremonial art and burning down spirit houses (Ryan, 1969:68). Missionaries in Assam forbade singing, dancing, and the wearing of all distinctive ornaments by their Naga converts, while government schools went even further by not allowing their pupils to wear flowers in their hair (Elwin, 1939:512; 1959:196,220). In the Naga case, the missionary rationale for their action was simple, as Elwin explains:

CHAPTER
SIX

*As religion plays a part in every Naga ceremony and as
that religion is not Christianity, every ceremony must go.* (Elwin,
1959:220)

While missionary efforts to clothe natives are notorious, it is often
forgotten that government efforts in the same direction have often been
just as vigorous and even harder for tribal people to ignore. For example,
a local government order in Burma in 1957 prohibited hill tribesmen from
wearing their traditional red cane belts, and specified how wide their
loincloths were to be, as well as the length of women's skirts (Lehman,
1963:211). By Royal Decree in 1881, the Spanish attempted to force
Philippine hill tribesmen in northern Luzon to wear breeches and coats in
the presence of government officials (Keesing, 1934:67-68). It has also
been common practice for government edicts to require the distribution
of clothing to native labor forces and to insist that it be worn.

Even the simple dignity of burial according to the forms prescribed
by their traditional cultures has sometimes been denied tribal peoples. In
1918 and 1922 the American administration in the Philippines passed
laws requiring the tribesmen to bury their dead in proper fashion in
approved cemeteries. In order to eliminate lengthy processes of smoking
and tending of the bodies, regulations specified that burial must take
place within 48 hours (Keesing, 1934:238-239). Practices involving platform burials or secondary burial have almost always been prohibited.
Even the normally broad-minded Dutch authorities refused to allow
tribal peoples in the Celebes to clean the bones of their dead (Kruyt,
1929:6). Tribal peoples in New Guinea have protested bitterly when
medical researchers and government coroners have desecrated their dead
against their wishes, and as recently as 1968 riot police were called out to
prevent native "interference" with official autopsies (Ryan, 1969:41).

It may seem incredible that any society would accept so much
interference in their lives, but after government control has been firmly
established over a tribal population there is little alternative but
conformity, at least with conspicuous customs. However, *before*
government authority is complete the situation is quite different. For
example, in Assam a British survey party and escort totaling some 80 men
was massacred by the Wancho in 1875 after the people had been ridiculed
for their peculiar burial practices and when a chief's tomb was desecrated
(Elwin, 1959:250). In New Guinea in 1904, ten missionaries were killed in
a single incident when they attempted to outlaw polygyny (Ryan,
1969:65). It seems that formerly autonomous tribal peoples did not always
welcome interference even *after* control was established, and that they
managed to keep many aspects of their cultures alive covertly in the face
of constant government efforts at suppression.

Settling Nomads

> *In the corridors of international agencies and the desert*
> *capitals, the cry goes up, "How do we settle the nomads?"*
> (Cunnison, 1967:10)

The pastoral nomads of North Africa, the Middle East, and Southwest Asia have evolved a highly successful ecological adaptation to extremely arid conditions and for thousands of years have maintained a relatively stable symbiotic relationship with their sedentary "civilized" village neighbors (Spooner, 1973). Few tribal groups in other parts of the world have made such a satisfactory adjustment to both civilization and their natural environment. However, in recent years this adaptation has been increasingly threatened because governments have set about to solve what they consider to be the nomad problem by abolishing the nomadic way of life. The "problem" of the nomads is that their very mobility makes it difficult for governments to impose controls over them, and that they seem to place tribal loyalties above national loyalties. Furthermore, there are sometimes misleading official complaints that nomadism is wasteful and that nomads infringe on the rights of settled farmers. Perhaps closer to the truth, some writers have explained that nomadism constitutes a "challenge to the orderly mind" of the government administrator eager to do something to improve the "wretched" living conditions of nomads (Brémaud and Pagot, 1962:320). Cunnison (1967:9) boils all the charges against nomads into one: "incompatibility with the aims of a modern state and the modern world." This means, of course, that most states refuse to compromise and will not recognize either the special contribution that nomads make to the national economy or their special needs. Actually, nomads efficiently exploit vast areas of desert in the only way that the peculiar ecological conditions of many of these areas will probably ever allow, and in the process nomads are often actually better fed and wealthier than village agriculturalists.

Governments have generally followed the "solution" to the nomad "problem," which calls for converting all nomads into sedentary villagers. In some countries this had been expressed as clear government policy, such as in Syria, where the 1950 Constitution declared "the government shall endeavor to sedentarize all nomads" (Article 158). A certain degree of continuous sedentarization has probably always been a necessary part of the nomadic adaptation, and has even included some nomadization of the sedentary population, but in the last few decades the process has been drastically accelerated by deliberate government action. Certainly the pacification of the desert, which ended intertribal feuding and raids, has served to weaken tribal political organization, but would not in itself destroy the nomadic way of life. More significant have been government settlement schemes involving outright propaganda programs on the virtues of settled life, and the drilling of wells, land allotments, and schooling. These direct measures have been facilitated by the roads and trucks that have replaced camel caravans, and by the oil companies that have made extensive use of nomad labor. Governments are fighting powerful ecological and cultural forces, however, and it is possible to assume that they will not be entirely successful without the use of even greater coercion. As recently as 1960 nearly 7 million people in the Sahara, Arabia, and Southwest Asia were estimated to still be following the nomadic life (Capot-Rey, 1962; Awad, 1962; Barth, 1962). Since then that figure has undoubtedly been considerably reduced.

Nomadism in general (and the Arab Bedouin form in particular) has been highly romanticized in the Western world, but fortunately this has not prevented all anthropologists from speaking in defense of the nomadic way of life. Some social scientists, however, have certainly supported the prevailing government policies of assimilation. For example, Awad, who in 1960 participated as chairman of UNESCO's executive board in the UN-sponsored international symposium on "The Problem of the Arid Zone," in no way questioned the need to settle nomads, and reported optimistically that converting them to a sedentary life was not impossible, although he cautioned that the process would be slow and that "no initiative can be expected from the nomads themselves." He felt that the initiative must come from the governments concerned, and he recommended that the end should be achieved as rapidly as possible whether the motives were humanitarian, political, economic, strategic, or administrative (Awad, 1962:336). Interestingly, other participants in the symposium, such as Capot-Rey and Barth, felt that total elimination of the nomadic way of life was undesirable and would result in the impoverishment of the people involved. Along with Cunnison (1967), they made the radical suggestion that governments might attempt to cooperate with the nomads.

Combating the Cattle Complex

Closely paralleling the drive to settle the desert nomads are the efforts of East African governments to end the semi-nomadism of their tribal cattle-herders and to convert them into settled village farmers or isolated ranchers with "improved" herds. In many of these cultures, subsistence, kinship organization, politics, religion, folklore, and personal identity and worth all center on cattle (Netting, 1977). This overwhelming value placed on cattle extends to the point that the loss of a favorite cow might be cause for suicide. Much to the frustration of administrators, African cattle-herders are almost totally self-sufficient and find that very little from the outside world is of any use to them. This, of course, makes it difficult to replace their cattle values with equally compelling money values, and in general makes their overall life-style very difficult to modify. While administrators complain of the poor quality of tribal cattle, careful anthropological research has repeatedly emphasized that African pastoralists are interested in cattle for *subsistence* purposes and not for marketability. Their herds are designed to support as many people as possible, and the system is not an inefficient, irrational, and wasteful use of natural resources as many development experts and government planners ethnocentrically suppose. It is simply a specialized economic system based on principles in complete opposition to those underlying cattle raising in an industrial society (Dyson-Hudson and Dyson-Hudson, 1969). Any highly successful economic system is bound to be persistent.

The Karimojong of northeast Uganda represent a specific case of one such East African cattle-herding society that has been subjected to intensive government directed pressure to abandon their nomadic life-style and modify their basic cattle complex. According to Dyson-Hudson (1962), real pressure for change began for the Karimojong in 1921, when the British established a civil administration after several years of military patroling during which "chiefs" had been appointed. In rapid succession, missionaries, a poll tax, and controls on population movement were introduced, and administrative boundaries were drawn in total disregard for traditional cultural groupings. Perhaps most seriously, the tribe was prohibited from using its normal dry-season grazing areas without special permission from the district commissioner, and anyone making unauthorized moves was subject to a fine of four head of cattle or imprisonment. Movements between settlements, which had helped distribute the population, were prohibited, and the administration itself freely moved commmunities about to suit its own purposes. The people often openly defied the new orders in spite of the punishments that were meted out, and in 1923 they even speared to death one of the government-appointed chiefs who had attempted to prevent their annual cattle movements. Restrictions on cattle and population movements were followed by measures to reduce the number of cattle and "improve" their quality to suit them for the market. The administration urged the Karimojong to sell their cattle and raise cash crops instead. As a further inducement, entire regions traditionally used as pasturage were closed to the Karimojong and opened to use by the neighboring tribes, cattle markets were organized, and special inoculation programs were initiated. These actions only caused further resentment and the Karimojong responded by hiding their herds and refusing to sell. They

CHAPTER
SIX

were particularly disturbed when some of their inoculated cattle died, and correctly assumed that their way of life was being attacked by a government that "eats our cattle."

On the basis of his study of the Karimojong, Dyson-Hudson concludes (along with numerous other observers) that pastoral societies are "generally slow and difficult to change." By 1958, after facing nearly 40 years of deliberate cultural modification policies, the 60,000 Karimojong had managed to maintain their basic value system intact, even to the extent that they still engaged in cattle raiding against neighboring groups.

In nearby Kenya the government-sponsored Konza Scheme was designed in 1947 as a pilot program to convert the nomadic Masai into settled ranchers but also failed to overcome traditional pastoral values. Ten families were settled on individually fenced plots that were provided with wells, dams, and dipping tanks, but they refused to sell their cattle, retained their social ties with their nomadic kin, and within ten years had completely undermined the scheme (Allan, 1965:322-324)

More direct action was taken by Tanzania, an independent country with an avowed goal of blending socialism and African culture. Perhaps recognizing the difficulties of changing pastoralists when the basic cattle complex remained intact, they attempted to force the Barabaig to stop herding cattle and to settle down as gardeners. The government program included a ban on traditional dress and forced "reeducation" of tribal youth, and was pushed so vigorously that George Klima, who recently conducted anthropological research in the area, concluded that:

> *All of these changes and more will eventually destroy the traditional life-ways the Barabaig have created over the centuries. Another island of cultural diversity will have disappeared into oblivion.* (Klima, 1970:112)

Unfortunately, the result of such modification policies has meant far more than merely the loss of cultural diversity, but as will be shown in Chapter 8, it also brings social, economic, and environmental disaster.

Weaning from the Axe

Shifting, or swidden agriculture, has come under government attack almost as frequently as pastoral nomadism. To administrators it appears to be a wasteful process, but in most tropical forest environments under aboriginal conditions it has proven to be a very sound and stable form of adaptation where shallow soils and heavy rainfall place severe limitations on agricultural activities. Like nomads, shifting agriculturalists tend to be

FIGURE 12. *A young Batangan man of Mindoro planting his swidden plot.
Under traditional conditions shifting cultivation may often be the only ecologically
sound form of agriculture in many areas, but this practice has been almost
universally condemned by government officials.* (Pennoyer)

independent, self-sufficient peoples, characterized by frequent
population movements, and their entire cultures are often neatly integrated with their agricultural cycles. None of these features fits neatly
with the interests of government planners.

The Baiga of India, who have been described by Elwin (1939),
exemplify the kinds of pressures that governments have used in many
countries to destroy the swidden life-style. In 1868, in the interests of
both civilizing the Baiga and opening their forests for commercial
exploitation, the government declared that the Baiga had no occupancy
rights in their forests and completely forbade shifting cultivation in
certain zones. To enforce the new laws, crops were destroyed, and since
hunting and fishing were also important components of the Baiga
subsistence system, they too were declared illegal by the Game Act, which
prohibited even the killing of hares. The bows and arrows that the Baiga
were not allowed to carry were confiscated and burned by officials, while
outsiders who could purchase licenses were, of course, allowed to hunt
within Baiga territory. In Elwin's estimation, forbidding shifting

cultivation was equivalent to taking food directly from Baiga mouths and thus constituted a direct assault on their entire culture. Under some administrators the policy was softened to a gradual "weaning" from the axe because, as an official report complained in 1893, the Baiga insisted on clinging "like a spoilt child to their axe and fire" (cited Elwin, 1939:119). Axes were taxed and the Baiga were permitted to continue their traditional farming practices only in carefully selected reserve zones considered to be totally useless for any other purposes. Even within these reserves, attempts were made to make the Baiga take up sedentary plow agriculture on individually allotted plots, and outsiders were brought in to farm reserve land as examples for the Baiga. These efforts were supplemented by attempts to actually remove Baiga tribesmen and scatter them in with sedentary villagers, where they could be supplied with plows, seed, land, and bullocks. Some successes were claimed, but many Baiga chose to flee rather than give up their traditional culture. Weaning from the axe also caused the population to plummet from some 1,500 individuals in 1891 to a low of 600 in 1939, and those who survived faced poverty and destitution.

SEVEN
ECONOMIC DEVELOPMENT

In other words, it is now held that economic development can be induced or even imposed, the goals being determined by governments who become responsible for the coordination and planning deemed necessary to attain them.

Mountjoy, 1967:28

Given the fundamental importance of economic patterns in all cultures, and considering the extreme contrasts between tribal and industrial economies, the economic incorporation of tribal cultures into the world market economy is a critically important phenomenon. A tribal culture may surrender its political autonomy, but can still continue to be an essentially tribal culture if it is allowed to retain its self-sufficient, subsistence economy and if it remains unexploited by outsiders. From the moment the distinctive features of a tribal economic system begin to be replaced by the characteristic traits of a modern cash economy, that culture truly begins *to cease being a tribal culture*. This is also the point at which the *price of progress* begins to accrue.

It is widely assumed that the economic development of tribal peoples is *development* in the usual meaning of the word, that is, "a process of *natural* evolution or growth." But, in fact, outside coercion and deliberate manipulation have usually been necessary both to destroy the tribal economy and to carefully channel its conversion into a market-oriented economy. *Development* is a comfortably ethnocentric term, resting on assumptions of progress and inevitability, but it might better be replaced by a more accurate and less ethnocentric term such as *transformation*.

CHAPTER
SEVEN

In many areas of the world the initial breakdown of tribal economies began under the coercive pressure of the policies of colonial governments designed to develop native labor resources or to promote cash cropping for the benefit of the colonists. These efforts were successful in initiating widespread migratory wage-labor and many forms of marginal production for the market economy, but most tribal cultures still managed to retain many of their traditional features, including partial self-sufficiency and low levels of consumption. Following World War II, government pressures on tribal economies were greatly intensified as a result of a new worldwide campaign for rapid economic growth. Under the technical and financial assistance of the leading industrial countries, nations everywhere attempted to raise their GNPs and initiate self-perpetuating economic growth. Professional development experts including economists, anthropologists, sociologists, geographers, agriculturalists, and other specialists from various countries and the United Nations all turned their attention to tribal peoples, who, because of their "backward" cultures, were considered to be major obstacles to national and international economic goals. Elaborate programs were divised to bring unwilling tribal peoples fully into national economies, to further raise their agricultural productivity and per capita cash incomes, and to promote whatever socioeconomic transformations they deemed necessary to achieve these goals.

In this chapter the primary concern is to examine the attitudes of governments and development writers toward this kind of economic development directed at self-sufficient tribal peoples. Emphasis is given to the strategies employed and the obstacles encountered. The purpose is to demonstrate that tribal peoples have not always been enthusiastic recipients of industrial economic values and techniques, but rather that their participation in the world market economy has often been brought about by government-supported compulsion, persuasion, and deliberately altered circumstances. The *consequences* of this economic transformation will be examined in the following chapter.

FORCED LABOR: HARNESSING THE HEATHENS

The natives must be induced to work. (Report to the League of Nations for 1923, Australian Trust Territory of New Guinea, cited Reed, 1943:179)

Throughout Africa, Asia, and the Pacific the economic pursuits of European colonists depended almost entirely upon native labor, but as these new areas were opened, government administrators and colonists soon realized to their dismay that tribal peoples were neither willing nor eager to labor for the white man. Undisturbed tribal cultures *really are* well-integrated, self-contained, satisfying systems, and their members cannot be expected to suddenly begin working for the material rewards of a totally alien culture without some form of compulsion.

Direct compulsion in the form of forced or corvée labor was openly indulged in by many governments. In British colonies it was common practice to demand an annual period of labor from tribal villagers, sometimes for up to a month of road construction work. In the Dutch Celebes nearly two months of labor per year were required of tribal peoples. This was considered to be a tax and was justified in terms of its effectiveness for dealing with *cashless* tribal economies.

The force involved in the recruitment of labor by the "blackbirders" has already been described, but here it may be noted that when New Guinea was being opened for settlement after the Queensland labor trade had subsided, it was not unknown for both German and Australian government officers to engage in their own kidnapping of labor recruits. Reed assures us that this was done primarily in cases of undisturbed villages that refused to supply recruits and where kidnapping seemed to be the only way of "breaking the ice." We are told that *trickery* was used more often than force, and that the procedure would only resemble slavery if done too often. In some instances small groups of highland Papuans were even flown by the government to work in coastal plantations, but this operation was not very successful because the tribesmen soon wanted to return home and suffered high mortality rates in the strange environment. In its 1923 Report to the League of Nations, the Australian mandate government of New Guinea defended such labor policies with the novel argument that if they were not forced to work, the natives were likely to die out from lack of exercise!

The French made liberal use of forced tribal labor in both Africa and Indochina. The Fifteen-Year Plan for the economic development of French West Africa received a major boost by a decree in 1926 creating a conscript labor force that allowed three years of labor per man toward the construction of highways, railroads, irrigation works, and other development projects. Such measures became necessary when the native population proved unwilling to volunteer for year-round labor at incredibly low wages, sometimes thousands of miles from home, and in the face of high mortality rates. The extent of this corvee labor force was truly staggering. For example, in 1923 nearly 5 million man-days of free labor were reportedly employed in Senegal. Conditions were so poor in some areas that annual death rates in the labor forces sometimes ran as high as 60 percent (Buell, 1928:937-1044). Elsewhere in Africa, forced labor was used extensively by the Congo Free State, where a 1903 decree called for 40 hours of labor a month from each native in exchange for a token wage.

At best, corvée labor was a traumatic introduction for tribal peoples to the benefits of labor in the market economy; at worst it was an inhuman and destructive form of slavery. However, clear evidence for the apparent necessity of the procedure can be seen in the fact that forced labor was not officially outlawed by the world community until 1957—long after it had served its purpose. In that year the International Labour Office formally abolished forced or corvée labor in member nations, regardless of whether it was justified as a means of education, labor discipline, or economic development.

LEARNING THE DIGNITY OF LABOR: TAXES AND DISCIPLINE

> *Under all circumstances the progress of natives toward civilization is only secured when they shall be convinced of the necessity and dignity of labour; and therefore I think that everything we reasonably do to encourage the natives to work is highly desirable.*
> (Joseph Chamberlain, 1926 speech to the House of Commons, cited Wellington, 1967:250)

Even where direct corvée labor was not practiced, tribal people were still coerced into the labor force by other means, and were often subjected to rigid discipline so that they would not fail to learn the dignity of labor. The most popular and effective form of indirect compulsion was taxation. There were head taxes, poll taxes, even dog taxes, all payable only in cash, which in turn was obtainable only through labor or cash cropping. In many cases the primary purpose was not to obtain revenue for the state directly. Rather, it was to create an artificial need for money, and to thereby force reluctant tribesmen to either seek labor in the mines, on the farms and plantations of the colonists, or in the towns, or else to take up cash cropping. This is clearly indicated by official government statements and by contemporary observations, but is also confirmed by the manner in which these taxes were applied. For example, in Australian New Guinea the head tax did not apply to anyone who had already signed up as an indentured laborer. South African scholars certainly had no doubts about the purposes of the various taxes that their government directed at the Bantu. Hutt (1934:212-213) observed in 1934 quite matter-of-factly that:

> *The poll tax and hut tax to which natives are subjected have been used as a means of forcing them into the European economic system.*

He felt that the more backward a given tribe proved to be, the greater the pressure must be in order to overcome their reluctance to join the labor force. The poll tax itself was initiated around 1900 and demanded the equivalent of up to two months of annual labor for all adult male tribesmen over the age of eighteen. A jail sentence awaited those who failed to pay up. Significantly, this tax applied only to natives, and recognized their adulthood three years earlier than that of Europeans, but it was defended as a relatively mild and effective device.

> *As the natives were often reluctant to leave their homes, a little gentle pressure was brought to bear upon them by the intro-duction of a poll tax. This measure quite effectively stimulated their desire for earning the white man's money.* (Eiselen, 1934:71)

Merely forcing tribesmen to obtain some kind of cash income was not sufficient to convert them into full-time regular employees, because all too frequently they responded to these pressures by becoming unenthusiastic "target workers" who returned to their villages when they had earned enough to pay their taxes or to purchase a few specific items. Further "instruction" was needed in the dignities of labor, and sympathetic governments readily provided concerned European planters and miners with laws allowing various forms of corporal punishment to correct the "negligence" and "ignorance" of their native employees. In German Southwest Africa, the Imperial Ordinance of 1896 prescribed imprisonment in irons and other forms of corporal punishment for natives if their employers found them guilty of "continued neglect of duty and idleness" or "unwarranted desertion" from their places of work. Deaths resulting from such "fatherly correction" were not considered to be murder by German law, but it was recognized that the natives might not understand such subtle distinctions (Wellington, 1967:230-231). In German New Guinea, European plantation owners could obtain a special disciplinary license permitting them to administer floggings to their native employees "for sufficient cause." Under the Australians, punishments for labor offenses were strictly a government prerogative and officially took place only after trial in the district courts, which

CHAPTER
SEVEN

> The Chief Registrar of Natives,
> NAIROBI.
> N.A.D. Form No 54/..... .
>
> **COMPLAINT OF DESERTION OF REGISTERED NATIVE.**
>
> Native's Certificate No.........................Name.......................................,..
>
> The above native deserted from my employ..
>
> He was engaged on..................................... .on......................days verbal contract
> *(date)*   *(date)*
> ....months written contract
>
> at...
> *(place)*   *(Contract No.)*
> I wish to prosecute him for this offence and hereby agree to appear to produce evidence to give evidence
> if and when called upon.
>
> ....
> *Signature of Employer.*
>
> *Address* ....
>
> ....
>
> *Date*...............................

FIGURE 13. *While learning "the dignity of labor," in Kenya in 1922, it was a crime for a tribal person to quit work without authorizaiton.* (W. McGregor Ross 1927, *Kenya From Within*. London: George Allen & Unwin Ltd.)

actually seemed overwhelmingly dedicated to this problem. Reed reports that in 1937-1938 nearly half of all district court cases involved handing out two-week jail sentences to natives accused of deserting or neglecting their duties (Reed, 1943:143, 177).

All of these measures have been stoutly defended as fulfilling the necessary responsibilities of a civilized guardian over his childlike ward. The American legal authority Alpheus Snow (1921:163) pointed out that natives simply lack the acquisitive drive characteristic of civilized man, and doing virtually anything that will correct this mental deficiency is permissible and even a moral duty of the state.

CREATING PROGRESSIVE CONSUMERS

> *... the Australian Government's expenditure on general administration, social services and education helps to raise consumption levels and thus assists the growth of local commercial enterprises.* (Australia, Department of Territories, Report for 1967-1968:24)

One of the most significant obstacles blocking native economic "progress" was the ability of the natives to find satisfactions at relatively low and stable consumption levels, and the fact that their cultures were basically self-sufficient. Fully independent tribal peoples with viable economies often expressed little desire to obtain any foreign manufactured goods except those of immediate practical utility such as metal axes, knives, and mirrors. Demand for these simple, utilitarian articles often initiated certain changes in tribal life but did not mean a rejection of traditional culture. Therefore, this demand was often not powerful enough to assure full "progress." Outsiders quickly realized that if tribal peoples could somehow be made to reject the material satisfactions provided by their own cultures and if they could be successfully urged to desire more and more industrial goods, they would become far more willing participants in the cash economy.

Raising tribal consumption levels was not as simple as it might seem. As pointed out previously, acquisitiveness is not a universal trait, and tribal cultures have developed numerous means of limiting the overaccumulation of material goods. Special pressures were necessary to overcome these built-in defenses against alien material goods and standards of value. The first and most obvious pressures for increased consumption of foreign goods were brought about by disturbances in tribal socioeconomic organization that accompanied the uncontrolled frontier and the end of tribal political autonomy. Forced labor, depopulation, reduced land base, loss of traditional food sources, and taxation all helped create a dependency on external goods. When these factors were combined with the ready availability of such goods—whether given out by missionaries and government welfare posts or offered by traders—increasing demand was almost certain to follow. Certainly, government development projects that have pushed new communication networks into formerly isolated tribal areas and have encouraged or even subsidized the work of commercial agents have contributed to increased demand for manufactured goods. It seems doubtful, however, that the mere *availability* of these goods, in the absence of the disturbances accompanying this availability, would in itself be sufficient to create significant demand for them. Many proponents of the demonstration effects theory would argue just the opposite—attributing the disturbance and demise of tribal cultures largely to their demands for the superior goods of industrial civilization. But it would seem equally valid and certainly less ethnocentric to assume that these new demands are more *symptomatic* of tribal disruptions that were already in progress, rather than their immediate causes.

Since the establishment of administrative control, governments have been able to manipulate conditions to unobtrusively stimulate new needs almost at will through such means as community development programs and formal schooling. Schools have served the double function of creating new needs and preparing individuals for their roles as consumers. Illich (1970) has argued that this double function is one of the primary purposes of schools, even in highly industrialized societies.

PROMOTING TECHNOLOGICAL CHANGE

Governments around the world have been engaged in a massive effort to replace traditional tribal crops, livestock, and productive techniques with what development experts consider to be *superior* crops, livestock, and techniques. What makes this phenomenon so different from "natural" diffusion is that the recipients, or target peoples, are not generally allowed to pick and choose what suits them. Choices are made by distant officials who are primarily concerned with increasing the production of a certain region. The task of implementing those decisions is delegated to local administrators, extension agents, and applied anthropologists who must present tangible results within specified program timetables. Not only are the choices made by outsiders who have their own goals in mind, but the technologies themselves are usually the products of totally foreign environments and cultures and in many cases must still be considered *experimental* even in their countries of origin.

Accepting novel technologies in most cases must mean a total abandonment of traditional economic self-sufficiency, and this is not always an easy change to promote. Many of the innovations are, in fact, tailored specifically to the needs of the world market. Accepting them very often means also accepting a variety of other related innovations and an ever-increasing dependence on the world economy. Growing a miracle hybrid grain may require expensive applications of purchased chemical fertilizers and pesticides, and the grain seed itself may need to be purchased again each year. Cash crops may also undermine self-reliance in other less obvious ways. In many areas under the influence of government-directed agricultural development programs, all the productive land in entire regions may be transformed from subsistence farming to production of a nonfood cash crop. Such a transformation means, of course, that people who were formerly feeding themselves directly must now purchase their food from external sources by selling their crops. In less extreme cases, some subsistence farming may be carried on, but substantial amounts of imported food still must be purchased. An often unforeseen hazard in cash cropping is that it is often difficult to return to full self-sufficiency if crops fail or if world-market prices fall—and tropical mono-crops are particularly vulnerable to both of these problems.

The frequent resistance to technological change on the part of traditional peoples can thus be readily appreciated. The uncertain benefits of new crops and techniques must be carefully weighed against the certain loss of both economic independence and reliable subsistence pursuits, as well as against the *unknown* hazards involved in any experiment with complex cultural and natural systems. Unfortunately, governments have pushed innovations with little appreciation of the problems involved. In many areas, new crops have been imposed by direct force. New Guinea, for example, resorted to a Compulsory Planting Ordinance in 1919, requiring villagers to plant a specified number of coconut palms under penalty of fines or jail sentences. Coffee planting was forced by both the Spanish in the Philippines and the Dutch in the East Indies, and forced planting was common practice in many other colonial countries. More recently, reluctant tribal peoples have been cajoled and harassed by eager agricultural extension agents and have been plied with free seeds and special subsidies, in order to overcome their fully justified caution.

In the following sections, three specific case studies illustrate the argument presented in the preceding sections. The first case involves the initial efforts of Dutch colonial administrators to force a fully self-sufficient, autonomous tribal population into the world-market economy. In the second case, the Azande Scheme, a colonial government is shown using a massive and highly coercive development scheme designed to introduce a new cash crop after the establishment of administrative control and initial involvement with a cash economy. The final example is an extended treatment of the basically noncoercive methods employed by the American administration of Micronesia to introduce American standards of consumption to a subsistence-oriented population where local resources will clearly not support such developments. While these three examples by no means represent the full range of development strategies, they do illustrate several major trends.

Dutch Colonial Development in the Celebes

A brief case study of how Dutch colonial administrators prepared the way for the "healthy" development of the Toradjas, tribal peoples of the Poso district in central Celebes, is an example of classic colonial development techniques designed to push an unwilling population into the world economy. According to Kruyt (1929:1-9), when mission efforts began in 1892 the Toradjas were deemed completely incapable of progress without outside intervention. Kruyt found and described several of the basic stabilizing features of tribal societies in full operation among the Toradjas. He concluded that because of these features, "development and progress were impossible"—the Toradja were "bound to remain at the same level." Toradja society was totally cashless and there was neither desire to earn money nor unfulfilled needs for which it might be required. Wealth-leveling mechanisms, such as reciprocal kinship obligations, religious sacrifices and feasting, and special values on generosity, helped maintain the balance.

Mission work in this relatively undisturbed setting proved a dismal failure. The Toradjas were entirely self-satisfied and quite uninterested in converting to any new religion, in sending their children to the mission schools, or in planting coconuts and coffee as cash crops. Obviously, drastic measures were required to break through their "wall of conservatism." In 1905 the Netherlands Indies government brought the Poso region under administrative control, using armed force to crush all attempts at resistance. In rapid succession, headhunting was stopped, a head tax was imposed, roads were built with conscript labor, and the entire Toradja population was forcibly removed from their traditional hilltop homes where they had grown dry rice, and were relocated along the new roads in the lowlands where they were persuaded to grow wet rice for their own good.

The Toradjas were understandably resentful and bewildered by these actions, especially when their mortality rates suddenly soared and they found themselves being punished continually by the administration for offenses which they did not understand. They turned to the missionaries for help, became "converted," and began sending their children to school. Eventually they were cultivating their own coconut and coffee plantations and began to acquire the appropriate new *needs* for such goods as oil lamps, sewing machines, and "better" clothing. Within twenty years the self-sufficient tribal economy had been totally replaced by deliberate government action.

The Zande Development Scheme

The Zande Development Scheme, which has been described in detail by Reining (1966), represents a truly massive economic development effort aimed at raising the cash income and agricultural productivity of a subsistence-oriented native population after the usual colonial development techniques proved too slow and ineffective. The scheme deserves special attention as a pioneer effort at the *directed* economic transformation of tribal society, and as an illustration of how even well-intentioned development plans may often be executed with coercion and little regard for the real wishes of their "targets."

ECONOMIC
DEVELOPMENT

Prior to extensive European intervention the Azande were a large population of shifting cultivators and hunters living in the isolated southwest corner of the Sudan in basically self-sufficient, dispersed homesteads and recognizing the political authority of local chiefs.

The termination of Azande political autonomy in 1905 and the initial administrative assaults on their subsistence economy followed the familiar pattern. To establish "law and order," the British disbanded warrior groups, collected firearms, outlawed the manufacture or possession of shields, and, according to the Azande, banned the smelting of iron. The traditional authority of chiefs was limited, and they were converted into government agents under indirect rule.

After civil administration began in 1911 the entire population was relocated along roads constructed by conscript native labor. Ostensibly, the move was designed to prevent people from living in tsetse fly zones, but it was also intended to facilitate administration. This first major disturbance of the traditional ecological balances was quickly followed by other "improvements." In the interest of conservation, the Azande were forbidden to locate their swiddens in the most favored locations in the gallery forests along the streams, and traditional hunting techniques were seriously restricted or forbidden. Participation in the cash economy was stimulated by a head tax introduced in the 1920s. At that point deliberate efforts at economic development were pushed no further, although the importation of manufactured goods by licensed traders and missionary education were encouraged. Further development seemed frustrated by the region's exteme isolation and total lack of significant natural resources for the world market. In spite of the disturbances already introduced, the Azande remained largely self-sufficient subsistence farmers. They had developed a taste for a limited range of consumer goods offered by the traders, but they were content to obtain these by selling wild honey, beeswax, and wild peppers. They remained uninterested in augmenting this meager cash income by migratory wage labor because, it was said, they were too fond of their own country, and did not want to leave it. When prices on their limited salable resources fell or when the price of the foreign goods rose too high, they readily returned to their traditional goods. According to Reining, they had not yet passed the point of no return in their economic involvement with the industrial economy, and could easily have reverted to full self-sufficiency. Unfortunately administration planners had other ideas.

In the late thirties the government began to favor expanded economic development—regardless of cultural and environmental "barriers"—and experiments were begun with cotton as a possible cash crop for the Azande. In 1938, J. D. Tothill, an agricultural development specialist, was appointed to conduct research and make policy recommendations. Within five years his views were presented to the administration in the form of a memorandum entitled "An Experiment in the Social Emergence of Indigenous Races." He called for the conversion of the Azande into "happy, prosperous, literate communities ... participating in the benefits of civilization" through the cultivation of cotton and the establishment of factories to produce exportable products on the spot (cited Reining, 1966:143). His plans found support in the government although, of course, no one thought of consulting the Azande themselves, and in 1944 the civil secretary urged the governor-general's council to approve an intensive economic development policy for the entire southern Sudan. Blaming the region's "backwardness" on "tribal apathy and conservatism," he made an appeal to the wardship principle as a justification for renewed efforts, and stated with familiar ethnocentrism:

We have a moral obligation to redeem its [the southern Sudan] inhabitants from ignorance, superstition, poverty, malnutrition, etc. (cited Beshir, 1968:55)

By 1946 a modified scheme for the total economic transformation of the Azande was under way. A small industrial complex was quickly built that included spinning, weaving, cotton oil, and soap mills, an electrical power station, a water system, and a dairy. All of these industrial plants were to be operated by 1,500 Azande workers, who would be trained and supervised by Europeans and northern Sudanese. Telephone lines, improved motor roads, and concrete bridges soon spread across the landscape.

The scheme was envisioned and entirely directed by British planners, and the Azande, who had not been consulted at any point, were called upon to furnish labor for the initial construction at the rate of approximately 1,000 men a month for nearly seven years. Every man in the district was required to work at least one month per year for pay of from $.85 to $1.30 a month! The administration decided that the cotton planting could be most efficiently regulated by introducing a carefully laid out, geometrically precise, settlement pattern that would allow the Azande to live in an "accessible and rational manner, not as beasts in the wilderness." Consequently, over a five-year period 50,000 Azande families—nearly the entire district population of some 170,000 people—were removed from their roadside locations (where they had been placed 30 years earlier), and distributed along a grid of sixteen-hectare individual household plots covering thousands of square kilometers of dry scrub forest. Plots were arbitrarily assigned by a clerk escorted by police, with no regard for individual Azande desires to live near their kin, and restrictions were imposed against any future moves.

The key to the entire scheme was the growing of cotton, but this presented some difficulties because the Azande were not interested in growing cotton. Deliberate efforts were made to train Azande merchants and to supply them with consumer goods, because planners believed that what the Azande lacked was a "realization of what money can do for them." It was felt that as soon as the Azande had learned to desire money they would become eager cash croppers. However, along with these deliberate attempts to increase consumerism, direct compulsion was felt to be necessary. This compulsion took the form of forcing anyone who refused to plant or properly cultivate cotton to do a month of public works labor on the roads as punishment. When yields declined as a result of low prices, and dissatisfaction occurred over food shortages that were caused by this new stress on normal subsistence activities, the number of cotton "defaulters" and the frequency of punishment increased accordingly.

In the face of this degree of direct compulsion, and with a social-engineering scheme of this magnitude, it seems incredible that the planners were motivated by the best intentions, but this definitely seems to be the case. In 1948 the chairman of the project's board of directors reiterated in a special memorandum that the underlying purpose of the Zande Scheme was "to bring progress, prosperity, and the reasonable decencies and amenities of human existence to the Azande" (cited Reining, 1966:156). Herein, of course, lay the difficulty. Outsiders applied their own ethnocentric judgments on what should constitute progress, prosperity, decency, and amenities, and then proceeded to impose this blueprint on a totally different culture, assuming that the noble ends justified the apparently drastic means. While the scheme was in progress, the administration operated under the incredible illusion that the traditional culture was actually being respected, while it was in fact being eliminated. According to the district commissioner's platitudes: "The object throughout has been to interfere as little as possible with the people's own way of life" (cited Reining, 1966:108).

Overall, it appears that the Zande Scheme did succeed somewhat in raising production, income, and consumption levels. These successes were apparently illusory, however, because as soon as the independent Sudanese government was instituted, a new team of development experts was called in to submit further recommendations for the entire southern Sudan. Their report, submitted in 1954 to the Development Branch of the Ministry of Finance and Economics, concluded that *greater* agricultural output was needed to provide *steady improvement* in the standard of living. What was needed was new crops, improved techniques, mechanization, better marketing, etc. By 1960 an all-new Ten-Year Development Plan was under way.

CHAPTER
SEVEN

In 1965, some twenty years after the first development project was begun and halfway through the Ten-Year Plan, a Sudanese journalist, Mohammed Said (1965:141), reported enthusiastically that the standard of living in Zandeland was higher; consumption of sugar had doubled in just nine years; there were no naked people left; Azande women were dressed in the fashionable northern Sudanese way; and everyone had bicycles and lived in clean houses equipped with beds and mattresses. And Mohammed Said reported that, best of all, there were now swarms of children everywhere! A more cynical observer might well have wondered who would be setting the development goals for the burgeoning next generation and how long Zandeland's shallow lateritic soils and the Azande themselves could support their newly attained standard of affluence.

Purchasing Progress and Dependency in Micronesia

Micronesia represents another outstanding example of the close relationship between government policy and the transformation of a traditional subsistence economy. In contrast to the Zande Scheme, in which overt coercion was an integral part of development strategy, in Micronesia the transformation has been readily accomplished without coercion. Instead, it was accomplished by a lavish distribution of material rewards by a wealthy government, and by massive spending on administration, education, and special development programs. By the late 1960s, many Micronesians who only a few years earlier were participants in presumably satisfying traditional cultures, and who were literally self-sufficient in food and material needs, were consuming costly imported goods in the American style. The Micronesian subsistence economy was undermined in favor of dependence on a cash system in a specific manner that is perhaps unique but that dramatically magnifies the general processes involved in the "development" of traditional economies around the world.

The Micronesian environment imposes several rigid limitations on economic activity, one of the most obvious being the severe limitation on land area, combined with vast distances and extreme isolation. There are approximately 2,000 islands with a total combined land surface of only 1,864 square kilometers, scattered over 7.7 million square kilometers of ocean—an area roughly the size of the United States. Many of these islands are low coral atolls, and agricultural potential on even the larger islands is limited. A further complication is the fact that the region is swept regularly by devastating typhoons. This seemingly unpromising environment has been populated by a rich variety of self-sufficient cultures for perhaps a thousand years and has been in contact with the "civilized" world for some 450 years. Spain, Germany, Japan, and the United States have successively claimed political control over the islands, but thanks to the area's isolation and since relatively few of Micronesia's limited resources have found a place on the world market, the traditional economies have been only slightly disturbed by foreign influences until recently. There were some efforts under the German administration, beginning in 1899, to promote copra plantations, but major efforts at economic development did not occur until the Japanese took control in 1914.

Under the Japanese, the typical colonial pressures were applied to bring the natives into the economy. All "unoccupied" land was claimed by the government and the best areas were thrown open for Japanese colonists or developed as sugar plantations. "Vulgar" native dances and kava drinking were suppressed; over half the native children were placed in schools to learn Japanese and "ethics"; all males over age sixteen were required to pay a head tax; and subsidies were offered for the planting of coconuts. In spite of these inducements, the natives still proved to be unwilling laborers. The economic development that did occur during this period was centered on the larger islands and was undertaken largely by the Japanese colonists, who outnumbered the native Micronesians by 1937. Except for a general increase in copra production the outlying islands were relatively undisturbed (Clyde, 1935; Nishi, 1968).

World War II brought large-scale devastation to Micronesia because many of the islands had been fortified by the Japanese and bitter fighting was necessary to dislodge them. The United States Navy assumed administrative control in 1945 and the pattern for large-scale intervention in the lives of the people was soon reestablished. In 1946, within a few months after gaining control, the navy launched a major survey of Micronesia's economic potential in order to guide the military administration in the formulation of policy. The survey was undertaken by 23 specialists from the United States Commercial Company, a branch of the Foreign Economic Administration, and included anthropologists, geologists, nutritionists, geographers, economists, botanists, and agronomists. According to Oliver, who edited a summary of the final report, the astonishing objective of the survey was:

> the sobering one of attempting to prescribe a way of life for people who have no effective voice in deciding their own destinies.
> (Oliver, 1951:vi)

There was a clear recognition of the fact that the administration was assuming ultimate power over the lives and welfare of the indigenous population and would, in effect, shape their cultures after whatever pattern the administrators chose. The report contains a curious mixture of caution over the dangers involved in manipulating other cultures, and of blatantly ethnocentric and even contradictory recommendations. It was noted that the traditional cultures were still very much intact, and that they represented "more or less delicately balanced adaptations to specific sets of environmental and historical factors and could be badly unbalanced by unwise forced changes" (Oliver, 1951:8). It was stressed that the population should be helped to return to its prewar economic self-sufficiency, and that the government should not attempt to attract natives to settle in administrative centers for government convenience, because this was contrary to their traditional ecological patterns and would threaten their self-reliance. The report even indicated that some of the more isolated areas might not even need permanent administrators.

It seems obvious in retrospect that at this point the administering authorities had a clear opportunity to permit a resumption of an essentially indigenous way of life, free even of the modifications introduced by the Japanese. The aboriginal cultures were familiar with the disruption and devastation of typhoons, and were therefore equipped with traditional patterns for dealing with the kinds of problems presented by the war's destruction. Some segments of the population undoubtedly missed the foreign luxuries made possible by massive Japanese colonization, but everywhere proven traditional patterns of subsistence and technology were being resumed. Even people who had become familiar with motor-driven boats were repairing and rebuilding their sailing canoes. Inspired by premature speeches and naval authorities promising "liberty," the people of Ponape returned enthusiastically to their traditional subsistence activities and feasting. According to Bascom (1965:15), who conducted anthropological research on Ponape, such speeches caused the natives to ignore their copra plantations and served only to "retard" economic development.

It quickly became apparent that the policy makers were not considering a return to cultural autonomy: rather, these cultures were to be remade and reformed, this time according to *American* ideals.

After just four months of field work, the team of experts of the United States Commercial Company Economic Survey proceeded to lay the groundwork for policy decisions that would completely transform cultures that possessed the accumulated knowledge of a thousand years of successful adaptation to a unique and complex environment. All of this was to be swept aside and replaced by foreign cultural patterns that policy makers assumed would provide a more satisfying way of life. With colossal ethnocentrism, reinforced by almost total ignorance of the complexities of Micronesian culture, these "experts" made judgments in the light of their own misplaced values and recklessly proceeded to prescribe a way of life for an entire people.

The basic assumptions of the survey team were apparent in the report, which spoke of economic reform and the need to establish an expanding economy and an expanding population (Oliver, 1951). The native people were described as impoverished because they were not enjoying the standards of consumption of luxury goods established by the Japanese, and it was repeatedly emphasized that these foreign goods were now necessities. A taste for such exotic foods as rice, flour, canned meat, and cheese had been cultivated among the conscript labor forces at military camps. Since some of these men were now anxious to continue eating these foods, *they were to be supplied*—regardless of their expense or inappropriateness. One member of the survey later advised that new *needs* should be deliberately promoted: "Acquaintance with new ideas should be encouraged and desires to try new articles or products should in general be facilitated" (Bascom, 1965:53). Apparently no one recognized the incompatibility between self-sufficiency and dependence on foreign foods and consumer goods.

According to the team's report, traditional Micronesian gardening practices were undeveloped by American standards, and native food was monotonous and bland and not well balanced, even though no signs of nutritional deficiency could be found. The report stated that the people were not eating enough fruit, and that for their own benefit they should learn to grow vegetables, "in spite of the present native resistance to a vegetable diet" (Oliver, 1951:13-19). It was felt that agricultural advisers should be provided to teach the population "elementary practices of horticulture," even though it should have been obvious that perhaps the natives might have more to teach the advisers about such basics as plant varieties and their special requirements, soil conditions, growing seasons, etc. Along with dietary changes, new crops, and new gardening techniques, the experts recommended that, where possible, every family should be provided with a cow, two pigs, and as many chickens as they wanted. This was surprising in view of the fact that the traditional economy was already solidly based on ample *marine* protein sources. Pigs and chickens were certainly not needed (and there was actually little to feed them), while cattle, having pasturage requirements, were absurdly out of place in an area as short of land as Micronesia.

The report piously affirmed, almost as a self-evident truth, that economic change in Micronesia was inevitable, implying that the natives were bringing it on themselves and that it could therefore not be prevented.

CHAPTER
SEVEN

> *Micronesians will, for better or worse, continue to expand*
> *their participation in western systems. In the kind of world we live in,*
> *that is inevitable, and no one but a nostalgic antiquary would imagine*
> *otherwise.* (Oliver, 1951:85-86)

Curiously, however, it was ominously warned that the "inevitable" changes "must occur gradually and voluntarily" (Oliver, 1951:8). Administrators were advised not to use *force;* rather the people were to be *directed*, not compelled, into proper economic patterns. As the report explained:

> *Much can be accomplished positively if natives are led*
> *rather than pushed into channels which are intended for their*
> *economic benefit.* (Oliver, 1951:91)

In spite of this strange double-talk, Oliver explicitly noted in his conclusions that the Micronesians would probably not "be permitted the absolute freedom of choice to decide their own destinies." It was obvious that the government was deciding what was to be inevitable and that it was deliberately setting about to create the conditions under which the inevitable new economic style would almost certainly be chosen. In one of the most remarkable passages in a report full of paradoxes, the team of experts recommended that Micronesians should be made to think they were choosing freely even though they really were not.

> *Attempts to bring about economic reform in conformance*
> *with western modes of living, before the natives are ready to make the*
> *changes, would undermine their faith in our avowed intentions.*
> *Natives should be given the opportunity of learning about and*
> *considering cultural alternatives, but the desire for change should*
> *come from within the society. No penalties in any form should be*
> *invoked for refusal to accept a proposed change over which they were*
> *told they had a free choice.* (Oliver, 1951:91)

When the administration of Micronesia was transferred in 1951 to civilian authorities of the United States Department of the Interior (under the United Nations Trust Territory agreements), the newly appointed high commissioner proclaimed to the natives that "your existing customs, religious beliefs, and property rights will be respected," but this proved to be as misleading as the navy's promise of liberty (Proclamation No. 2, Annual Report on the Administration of the Territory of the Pacific Islands, 1953:79-80, hereafter abbreviated as TTR—Trust Territory Report). In the same proclamation, the high commissioner also promised an administration based on "applied science," and the tone of the annual administrative report for 1951-1952 leaves no doubt that *respect* was being pushed aside by the need for *advancement*. While there was talk of "gradual evolution," and it was claimed that "no pressure has been used to force the people to discard their customs in favor of western institutions," there were complaints that the "divisive effect of ethnocentricity must be overcome," and that a more democratic form of government with a broader outlook was being carefully created through "well nurtured growth ... education and civil guidance by administrative officials" (TTR, 1953:13-14). The "ethnocentrism" to be overcome was, of course, the native belief in the superiority of their own institutions, not the ethnocentrism of government officials who, after all, were dealing in applied science to further a natural evolutionary process.

In the economic field, subsistence activities were to be fostered, but it was felt that the "fullest possible development of land resources" was impeded by traditional land tenure practices. The official program for Micronesian economic advancement followed the lines recommended by the 1946 survey and overflowed with extravagant promises and American values. Everything was to be improved—more and better, better and greater. Production would be increased, new practices and superior crops would be introduced, and the environment would be dealt with *more effectively* (TTR, 1953:26-31). In effect, a thousand years of Micronesian cultural development was declared obsolete, and applied science was to miraculously replace it. In the eyes of the administration the traditional culture was simply standing in the way of a better life.

Within two years the administration's development strategy was taking shape. The territory's natural isolation would be ended by the introduction of radio communication and a modern air and sea shipping network. The reluctance of Micronesians to discard their traditional cultures would be overcome by large doses of administrative advice and education, while the natural limitations on economic growth imposed by the restricted resource base would be circumvented by the massive importation of American dollars in the form of wages for indigenous government employees. In 1953, fully 15 percent of the total native population of 57,000 was enrolled in schools. This figure included 1,300 high school and college students who were preparing for government employment and acquiring first-hand experience in American standards of consumption at schools in Guam, Hawaii, and the United States mainland. By 1954 the success of the program was already becoming apparent in the fact that more than 1,200 Micronesians were securely on the administration's payroll, 200 cars were in native hands, and 1.3 million dollars' worth of imports was now flowing into the islands. A

FIGURES 14 and 15. *Traditional houses in Yap, Micronesia (above). A new tourist hotel on Yap (below) was made possible by an overwhelming outpouring of American dollars for Micronesian development.* (Price)

government operating budget of nearly 6 million dollars annually was needed to support these activities, but only 1.6 million dollars could be obtained in revenue from local resources—the remainder was appropriated as a direct subsidy from the federal government (statistical tables TTR, 1954, 1955).

The motivation for this policy of creating dependency seems to have resulted largely from the government's desire to strengthen its dominance in the region in order to retain it as a strategic military resource, rather than from any real need for the area's other meager resources.

By 1958 the administration was even prouder of the success of its development strategy. Native houses were now more substantial, power boats were being purchased more widely, and some 500 private vehicles, 275 radios, and various other electric appliances could now be pointed to as evidence of an increased standard of living. Unfortunately, however, some isolated pockets of cultural resistance still remained. *Improvement* in the remote islands was slower and less evident. More education and greater effort were needed.

> *In such remote areas the basic problem is one of educating the local inhabitants to the need for or desirability of improvement and the development of local means to accomplish such improvements.*
>
> *Further improvement of living standards can be accomplished throughout the Territory.... The policy and programs of the Administration are planned and intended to develop an awareness and understanding of community needs and the desirability of improvement, and to develop local community resources and means to a maximum extent to achieve the improvement desired.* (TTR, 1959:90-91)

For ten years the pace of development input from the administration increased steadily but gradually, until the annual budget stood at approximately 7.4 million dollars. Micronesians were now consuming over 60 dollars worth of imported goods per capita annually, while exports of island resources remained at approximately their prior levels. It was obvious that the value of exports had reached something of an absolute ceiling even by the mid-1950s, but *apparent* economic growth continued as more and more natives were placed on the government payroll and more capital improvements were made. Clearly, dependency was growing and the native culture was being gradually overwhelmed in a tide of dollars and foreign consumer luxuries. If at this point the world price of copra had fallen, and if the government payroll had been drastically reduced, several thousand impoverished Micronesians would have been left to fend for themselves. It was hoped that enough of the traditional culture would have survived in the outlying islands to have made possible a return to self-sufficiency. The government, however, had no intention of reducing its development efforts, and actually had even greater things in store.

In 1962 the government suddenly more than doubled its spending in Micronesia to facilitate more rapid development and to "meet the needs of the Micronesian people." Official reports explained that this represented a major shift in the administration's commitment to Micronesia (TTR, 1973:41), but this was a careful understatement. A truly massive, all-new development machine was actually being cranked into motion, fueled by a seemingly endless stream of American dollars. By 1965 government spending had tripled the pre-1962 annual levels and was still climbing, until the projected 1973 budget reached an incredible 78.6 million dollars—more than eleven times the pre-1962 levels! Between 1962 and 1972 the administration spent a total of some 397.4 million dollars, much of this directed toward what was called an accelerated *emergency* program to upgrade and speed development of essential public services, including schools, transportation, communication, and power plants. The results of some of this money could be seen immediately in the educational plant, where by 1972, 80 percent of the public elementary schools met American standards—approximately 80 square meters of working space and concrete and metal to replace coral floors and thatch.

In a dramatic rejection of earlier policy emphasizing self-reliance, the territory was opened to U.S. capital investment by presidential decree in 1962 to stimulate new economic activity for the "maximum economic and cultural benefit of all Micronesians" (TTR, 1964:49-50, 1973:54). Progress based on local resources and capabilities was no longer adequate.

> *The government recognizes that outside capital and expertise, particularly for large-scale, sophisticated enterprises, are needed for maximum efficiency and profit.* (TTR, 1973:54)

The subsistence economy was now out.

> *The Administration continues to seek means to promote development of the economy of Micronesia so that it will become geared to a world money economy and thus, its subsistence aspects will become supplemental.* (TTR, 1973:45)

An enormous tide of exotic material wealth was beginning to engulf the islands, but the official administration position was that these changes would be good and they would be *voluntarily chosen*. According to the 1972 report to the United Nations, the "Administering Authority":

> *encourages Micronesians to voluntarily integrate into their own culture useful features of other civilizations to enable them to*

lead more meaningful and rewarding lives in today's changing world.
(TTR, 1973:93)

Predictably, the "useful features" were all drawn from American civilization and represented the material trappings that Americans considered essential for a "more meaningful and rewarding" life. In a remarkable exercise in self-deception, the administration observed that it would permit only those foreign investments that would contribute to the territory's overall economic well-being "without adversely affecting the existing social and cultural values and ethnic conditions of the district" (TTR, 1973:54).

Solid evidence of progress suddenly began to appear throughout the territory in direct proportion to government spending and foreign investment. Jetports sprang up on Truk, Ponape, and Majuro, and by 1972 Continental Airlines was operating tourist hotels on three islands. Nearly 7,000 private motor vehicles were now spilling over 960 kilometers of roads, and 26 million dollars' worth of imported food, clothing, gasoline, machinery, and other consumer goods were pouring in. There were 415 licensed commercial business outlets where there had been only 54 in 1958. Electrical power plants were in place or being installed that would have a total capacity of 30,000 kW; 22 movie houses were in operation, one television and eight radio stations were broadcasting, and an estimated 50,000 radios were in private homes and cars.

A multitude of special programs and new institutions were needed to channel native participation in these developments. A massive effort at the recruitment, placing, and training of future civil servants was soon under way to help swell the government payrolls even further. In 1972 there were already over 5,700 native employees in the government receiving some 18 million dollars in salaries, and more than 600 natives were enrolled in special training programs designed to increase incomes. These programs were sponsored by the United States federal government under Public Service Careers and Public Employment Programs; the United Nations; the South Pacific Commission, and the World Health Organization. Credit unions, the Small Business Administration loan program, and the Economic Development Loan Fund were all "making it easy to borrow money for useful purposes." Useful purposes included such diverse, but thoroughly American, enterprises as the establishment of cattle ranches, laundromats, jewelry and upholstery shops, car rentals, and the purchase of outboard motors and motorcycles. In 1972 the Economic Development Loan Fund alone had made over a million dollars' worth of direct and guaranteed loans, while 3 million dollars' worth of applications were pending.

CHAPTER
SEVEN

To help overcome the last remnants of resistance in the remaining backward areas, in 1966 the Peace Corps was called in for community development work. In their peak year, 700 volunteers were on duty teaching English, organizing self-help programs, advising on business matters, promoting increased agricultural production, and spending money. As an underdeveloped, impoverished region, Micronesia also qualified for a number of federal War On Poverty programs, and soon there were federally funded Community Action programs, Head Start programs, Economic Opportunity Office programs, special scholarships, workshops, and a bewildering array of other "opportunities," plus a Neighborhood Youth Corps and a special Grant-in Aid program. As a final touch, the most isolated communities were visited every year by Santa Claus, the supreme cultural hero of American materialism, who air-dropped free consumer goods on needy children, courtesy of the U.S. Navy and Air Force based on Guam.

EIGHT
THE PRICE OF PROGRESS

---

*In aiming at progress . . . you must let no one suffer by too drastic a measure,
nor pay too high a price in upheaval and devastation, for your innovation.*

Maunier, 1949:725

Economic development and progress have, until recently, always been
considered to be unquestionably beneficial goals that all societies should
want to strive toward. The social advantages of progress—as defined in
terms of increased incomes, higher standards of living, greater security,
and better health—are thought to be positive, *universal* goods, to be
obtained at virtually any price. While it may often be acknowledged that
tribal peoples must sacrifice their traditional cultures to obtain these
benefits, it is generally felt by government planners that this is a small
price to pay for such obvious advantages.

In earlier chapters evidence was presented to demonstrate that
autonomous tribal peoples have not actually chosen progress to enjoy its
advantages, but that governments have pushed progress upon them to
obtain tribal resources, and not primarily to share with the tribal peoples
the benefits of progress. It has also been shown that the price of forcing
progress on unwilling recipients has involved the deaths of literally
millions of tribal people, as well as their loss of land, political sovereignty,
and the right to follow their own life-style. This chapter does not attempt
to further summarize that aspect of the cost of progress, but instead
analyzes the specific effects of the participation of tribal peoples in the
world market economy. In direct opposition to the usual interpretation, it

is argued here that the benefits of progress are often both illusory and detrimental to tribal peoples.

PROGRESS AND THE QUALITY OF LIFE

One of the primary difficulties in any attempt to assess the benefits of progress and economic development for any culture is that of establishing a meaningful measure of both benefit and detriment. It is widely recognized that *standard of living,* which is currently the most frequently used measure of progress, is an intrinsically ethnocentric concept relying heavily upon indicators that clearly lack universal cultural relevance. Such factors as GNP, per capita income, capital formation, employment rates, literacy, formal education, consumption of manufactured goods, number of doctors and hospital beds per thousand persons, and the amount of money spent on government welfare and health programs may actually be quite irrelevant measures of actual *quality* of life for autonomous or even semi-autonomous tribal cultures. In Micronesia, as recently as its 1954 report, the Trust Territory government indicated specifically that since the population was still largely satisfying its own needs within a cashless subsistence economy, "money income is not a significant measure of living standards, production, or well-being in this area" (TTR, 1953:44). Unfortunately, within a short time the government began to rely on an enumeration of certain imported consumer goods as indicators of a higher standard of living in the islands, even though many tradition-oriented islanders felt that these new goods symbolized a definite lowering of the quality of life.

A more useful measure of the benefits of progress might be based on a formula for evaluating cultures devised by Goldschmidt (1952:135). According to these less ethnocentric criteria, the important question to ask is: does progress or economic development increase or decrease a given culture's ability to satisfy the physical and psychological needs of its population, or its stability? This question is a far more direct measure of quality of life than are the standard economic correlates of development, and it is universally relevant. Specific indication of this *standard* of living could be found for any society in the nutritional status and general physical and mental health of its population, the incidence of crime and delinquency, the demographic structure, family stability, and the society's relationship to its natural resource base. A society with high rates of malnutrition and crime, and one degrading its natural environment to the extent of clearly threatening its continued existence, might be described as at a lower standard of living than another society where these problems did not exist.

FIGURE 16.   *Trash litters a lagoon in Micronesia. Quality of life often suffers as economic development accelerates.* (Price)

Careful examination of the acculturation data, which compare, on these specific points, the former condition of self-sufficient tribal peoples with their condition following their incorporation into the world market economy, leads almost invariably to the conclusion that their standard of living is *lowered*, not raised, by economic progress—and often to a dramatic degree. This is perhaps the most outstanding and inescapable fact to emerge from the years of research that anthropologists have devoted to the study of culture change and modernization. In spite of the best intentions of those who have promoted change and improvement, all too often the real results have been poverty, longer working hours, and much greater physical exertion, poor health, social disorder, discontent, discrimination, overpopulation, and environmental deterioration—all this combined with the destruction of the traditional culture.

DISEASES OF DEVELOPMENT

> *Perhaps it would be useful for public health specialists to start talking about a new category of diseases. . . . Such diseases could be called the "diseases of development" and would consist of those*

CHAPTER
EIGHT

pathological conditions which are based on the usually unanticipated
consequences of the implementation of developmental schemes.
(Hughes and Hunter, 1972:93)

Economic development seems to increase the disease rate of affected
peoples in at least three ways. First, to the extent that development is
successful, it makes developed populations suddenly become vulnerable
to all the diseases enjoyed almost exclusively by "advanced" peoples.
Among these are diabetes, obesity, hypertension, and a variety of
circulatory problems. Second, development disturbs traditional
environmental balances and may dramatically increase certain bacterial
and parasite diseases. Finally, when development goals prove
unattainable, an assortment of poverty diseases may appear in
association with the crowded conditions of urban slums and the general
breakdown in traditional socioeconomic systems.

Outstanding examples of the first situation can be seen in the
Pacific, where some of the most successfully developed native peoples are
found. In Micronesia, where development has progressed more rapidly
than perhaps anywhere else, between 1958 and 1972 the population
doubled, but the number of patients treated for heart disease in the local
hospitals nearly tripled, mental disorder increased eightfold, and by 1972
hypertension and nutritional deficiencies began to make significant
appearances for the first time (TTR, 1959, 1973, statistical tables).

In Polynesia, where these general trends are even more obvious, the
progressive acquisition of modern degenerative diseases was rigorously
documented by an eight member team of New Zealand medical
specialists, anthropologists, and nutritionists, whose research was
funded by the Medical Research Council of New Zealand and the World
Health Organization. These researchers set out to investigate the health
status of a genetically related population at various points along a
continuum of increasing cash income, modernizing diet, and
urbanization. The extremes on this acculturation continuum were
represented by the relatively traditional Pukapukans of the Cook Islands
and the essentially Europeanized New Zealand Maori, while the busily
developing Rarotongans, also of the Cook Islands, occupied the
intermediate position. In 1971, after eight years of work, the team's
preliminary findings were summarized by Dr. Ian Prior, cardiologist and
leader of the research, as follows:

We are beginning to observe that the more an islander takes
on the ways of the West, the more prone he is to succumb to our
degenerative diseases. In fact, it does not seem too much to say our
evidence now shows that the farther the Pacific natives move from the

quiet, carefree life of their ancestors, the closer they come to gout,
diabetes, atherosclerosis, obesity, and hypertension. (Prior, 1971:2)

In Pukapuka, where progress was limited by the island's small size
and its isolated location some 480 kilometers from the nearest port, the
per capita income was only about 36 dollars and the economy remained
essentially at a subsistence level. Resources were limited and the area was
visited by trading ships only three or four times a year, and thus there was
little opportunity for intensive economic development. Predictably, the
population of Pukapuka was characterized by relatively low levels of
imported sugar and salt intake, and a presumably related low level of
heart disease, high blood pressure, and diabetes. In Rarotonga, where
economic success was introducing town life, imported food, and
motorcycles, sugar and salt intakes nearly tripled, high blood pressure
increased approximately ninefold, diabetes two- to threefold, and heart
disease doubled for men and more than quadrupled for women, while the
number of grossly obese women increased more than tenfold
proportionately. Among the New Zealand Maori, sugar intakes were
nearly eight times that of the Pukapukans, gout in men was nearly double
its rate on Pukapuka, and diabetes in men was more than fivefold higher,
while heart disease in women had increased more than sixfold. The Maori
were, in fact, dying of "European" diseases at a greater rate than the
average New Zealand European.

Government development policies designed to bring about changes
in local hydrology, vegetation, and settlement patterns and to increase
population mobility, and even programs aimed at reducing certain
diseases, have frequently led to dramatic increases in disease rates
because of the unforeseen effects of disturbing the preexisting order.
Hughes and Hunter (1972) published an excellent survey of cases in
which development has led directly to increased disease rates in Africa.
They conclude that hasty development intervention in relatively
balanced local cultures and environments has resulted in "a drastic
deterioration in the social and economic conditions of life."

Traditional populations in general have presumably learned to live
with the endemic pathogens of their environments, and in some cases
they have evolved genetic adaptations to specific diseases, such as the
famous sickle-cell trait, which provided an immunity to malaria.
Unfortunately, however, outside intervention has entirely changed this
picture. Sleeping sickness suddenly increased in many areas of Africa
and even spread to areas where it did not formerly occur, due to the
building of new roads and migratory labor, both of which caused
increased population movement. Large-scale relocation schemes, such as
the Zande Scheme, had disastrous results when peoples were moved

from their traditional disease-free refuges into infected areas. Dams and irrigation developments inadvertently created ideal conditions for the rapid proliferation of snails carrying schistosomiasis (a liver fluke disease), and major epidemics suddenly occurred in areas where this disease had never before been a problem. DDT spraying programs have been temporarily successful in controlling malaria, but there is often a rebound effect that increases the problem when spraying is discontinued, and the malarial mosquitos are continually evolving resistant strains.

Urbanization is one of the prime measures of development but it is certainly a mixed blessing for most former tribal peoples. Urban health standards are abysmally poor and generally worse than in rural areas for the detribalized individuals who have crowded into the towns and cities throughout Africa, Asia, and Latin America seeking wage employment out of new economic necessity. Infectious diseases related to crowding and poor sanitation are rampant in urban centers, while greatly increased stress and poor nutrition aggravate a variety of other health problems. Malnutrition and other diet-related conditions are, in fact, one of the characteristic hazards of progess faced by tribal peoples and are discussed in the following sections.

The Hazards of Dietary Change

The traditional diets of tribal peoples are admirably adapted to their nutritional needs and available food resources. Even though they may seem bizarre, absurd, and unpalatable to outsiders, they are unlikely to be improved by drastic modifications. Given the delicate balances and complexities involved in any proven subsistence system, change always involves risks, but for tribal people the effects of dietary change have been catastrophic.

Under normal conditions, food habits are remarkably resistant to change, and indeed people are unlikely to abandon their traditional diets voluntarily in favor of dependence on difficult-to-obtain exotic imports. In some cases it is true that imported foods may be identified with powerful outsiders and are therefore deliberately sought as symbols of greater prestige. This may lead to such absurdities as Amazonian Indians choosing to consume imported canned tunafish when abundant high-quality fish is available in their own rivers. Another example of this situation occurs in tribes where mothers prefer to feed their infants expensive and nutritionally inadequate canned milk from unsanitary, but *high status*, baby bottles. The high status of these items is often deliberately promoted by clever traders and clever advertising campaigns. Aside from these apparently voluntary changes, it appears

FIGURE 17.   *A Batangan woman of Mindoro, Philippines, with empty Pepsi-Cola bottle. Dietary change is a critical aspect of culture change in general, and for tribal peoples it often results in lower health and nutritional status.* (Pennoyer)

that more often dietary changes are forced upon unwilling people by circumstances beyond their control. In some areas, new food crops have been introduced by government decree, or as a consequence of forced relocation or other policies designed to end hunting, pastoralism, or shifting cultivation. Food habits have also been modified by massive disruption of the natural environment by outsiders—as when sheepherders transformed the Australian Aborigine's foraging territory, or when European invaders destroyed the bison herds that were the primary element in the Plains Indian's subsistence patterns. Perhaps the most frequent cause of diet change occurs when formerly self-sufficient peoples find that wage labor, cash cropping, and other economic development activities that feed tribal resources into the world market economy must inevitably divert time and energies away from the production of subsistence foods. Many developing peoples suddenly discover that, like it or not, they are unable to secure traditional foods and must spend their newly acquired cash on costly, and often nutritionally inferior, manufactured foods.

Overall, the available data seem to indicate that the dietary changes that are linked to involvement in the market economy have tended to *lower* rather than raise the nutritional levels of the affected tribal peoples. Specifically, the vitamin, mineral, and protein components of their diets are often drastically reduced and replaced by enormous increases in starch and carbohydrates, often in the form of white flour and refined sugar.

Any deterioration in the quality of a given population's diet is almost certain to be reflected in an increase in deficiency diseases and a general decline in health status. Indeed, as tribal peoples have shifted to a diet based on imported manufactured or processed foods, there has been a dramatic rise in malnutrition, massive increase in dental problems, and a variety of other nutrition-related disorders. Nutritional physiology is so complex that even well-meaning dietary changes have had tragic consequences. In many areas of Southeast Asia, government-sponsored protein supplementation programs supplying milk to protein-deficient populations caused unexpected health problems and increased mortality. Officials failed to anticipate that in cultures where adults did not normally drink milk, the enzymes needed to digest it were no longer produced and milk *intolerance* resulted (Davis and Bolin, 1972). In Brazil, a similar milk distribution program actually caused an epidemic of permanent blindness by aggravating a preexisting vitamin A deficiency in a very dramatic way (Bunce, 1972).

Teeth and Progress

> There is nothing new in the observation that savages, or peoples living under primitive conditions, have, in general, excellent teeth. . . . Nor is it news that most civilized populations possess wretched teeth which begin to decay almost before they have erupted completely, and that dental caries is likely to be accompanied by peridontal disease with further reaching complications. (Earnest Hooton, 1945:xviii)

It has long been recognized by anthropologists that undisturbed tribal peoples are very often in excellent physical condition. And it has often been noted specifically that dental caries and the other dental abnormalities that so plague modern industrialized societies are conspicuously absent or rare among tribal peoples who have retained their traditional diets. The fact that tribal food habits may well contribute to the development of sound teeth, while modernized diets may do just the opposite, was dramatically illustrated as long ago as 1894 in an article in the *Journal of the Royal Anthropological Institute* that described the results of a comparison between the teeth of ten Sioux Indians and a comparable group of Londoners (Smith, 1894:109-116). The Indians were examined when they came to London as members of Buffalo Bill's Wild West Show, and were found to be completely free of caries and in possession of all their teeth, even though half the group were over 39 years of age. Londoners' teeth were conspicuous for both their caries and their steady reduction in number with advancing age. The difference was attributed primarily to the wear and polishing caused by the traditional Indian diet of relatively coarse food and the fact that they chewed their food longer, encouraged by the absense of tableware.

One of the most remarkable studies of the dental conditions of tribal peoples and the impact of dietary change was conducted in the 1930s by Weston Price (1945), an American dentist who was interested in determining what caused normal healthy teeth. Over a six-year period between 1931 and 1936, Price systematically explored tribal areas throughout the world to locate and examine the most isolated peoples who were still living on traditional foods. His fieldwork covered Alaska, the Canadian Yukon, Hudson Bay, Vancouver Island, Florida, the Andes, the Amazon, Samoa, Tahiti, New Zealand, Australia, New Caledonia, Fiji, the Torres Strait, East Africa, and the Nile. The study brilliantly demonstrated both the superior quality of aboriginal dentition and the devastation that occurs as modern diets are adopted. In nearly every area where traditional foods were still being eaten, Price found perfect teeth with normal dental arches and virtually no decay, while caries and abnormalities increased steadily as new diets were adopted. In many cases the change was sudden and striking. Among Eskimo groups subsisting entirely on traditional food he found caries totally absent, while in groups eating a considerable quantity of store-bought food approximately 20 percent of their teeth were decayed. This figure rose to more than 30 percent with Eskimo groups subsisting almost exclusively on purchased or government supplied food, and reached an incredible 48 percent among the Vancouver Island Indians. Unfortunately for many of these people, modern dental treatment did not accompany the new food, and their suffering was truly appalling. The loss of teeth was, of course, bad enough in itself, and it certainly undermined the population's resistance to many new diseases, including tuberculosis. But new foods were also accompanied by crowded, misplaced teeth, gum diseases, distortion of the face, and pinching of the nasal cavity. Abnormalities in the dental arch appeared in the new generation immediately after the change in diet, while caries appeared almost instantly even in adults.

Price reported that in many areas the affected peoples were quite conscious of their own physical deterioration. At a mission school in

Africa he was asked by the principal to explain to the native schoolchildren why they were not physically as strong as children who had had no contact with schools. On an island in the Torres Strait the natives knew exactly what was causing their problems and resisted—almost to the point of bloodshed—government efforts to establish a store that would make imported food available. The government prevailed, however, and Price was able to establish a clear relationship between the length of time the government store had been established and the increasing incidence of caries among a population that aboriginally showed an almost 100 percent immunity to them.

In New Zealand, the Maori, who in their aboriginal state are often considered to have been among the healthiest, most perfectly developed of peoples, were found to have "advanced" the furthest. According to Price:

> *Their modernization was demonstrated not only by the high incidence of dental caries but also by the fact that 90 percent of the adults and 100 percent of the children had abnormalities of the dental arches.* (Price, 1945:206)

Malnutrition

Malnutrition, particularly in the form of protein deficiency, has become a critical problem for tribal peoples who must adopt new economic patterns. Population pressures, cash cropping, and government programs all have tended to encourage the replacement of traditional crops and other food sources that were rich in protein with substitutes high in calories but low in protein. In Africa, for example, protein-rich staples such as millet and sorghum are being replaced systematically by high-yielding manioc and plantains, which have very insignificant amounts of protein. The problem is further increased for cash croppers and wage laborers whose earnings are too low and unpredictable to allow purchase of adequate amounts of protein. In some rural areas agricultural laborers have sometimes been forced systematically to deprive nonproductive members (principally children) of their households of their minimal nutritional requirements to satisfy the need of the productive members. This process has actually been documented in northeastern Brazil following the introduction of large-scale sisal plantations (Gross and Underwood, 1971). In urban centers the difficulties of obtaining nutritionally adequate diets are even more serious for tribal immigrants, because costs are even higher and poor quality foods are more tempting.

One of the most tragic, and until recently largely overlooked, aspects of chronic malnutrition is that it can lead to abnormally undersized brain development and apparently irreversible brain damage; it has been associated with various forms of mental impairment or retardation. Malnutrition has been linked clinically with mental retardation in both Africa and Latin America (see, for example, Mönckeberg, 1968), and this appears to be a worldwide phenomenon with very serious implications (Montagu, 1972).

Optimistic supporters of progress will surely say that all of these new health problems are being overstressed, and that the introduction of hospitals, clinics, and the other modern health institutions will certainly overcome or at least compensate for all these difficulties. However, it appears that uncontrolled population growth and economic impoverishment will probably keep most of these benefits out of reach, and the intervention of modern medicine has at least partly contributed to the problem in the first place.

ECOCIDE

"How is it," asked a herdsman ... "how is it that these hills can no longer give pasture to my cattle? In my father's day they were green and cattle thrived there; today there is no grass and my cattle starve." As one looked one saw that what had once been a green hill had become a raw red rock. (Jones, 1934)

Progress not only brings new threats to the health of tribal peoples, but it also imposes serious new strains on the ecosystems upon which they must depend for their ultimate survival. The introduction of new technology, increased consumption, lowered mortality, and the eradication of all traditional controls have combined to replace what for most tribal peoples was a relatively stable balance between population and natural resources, with a new system that is totally imbalanced. Economic development is forcing *ecocide* on peoples who were once careful stewards of their resources. There is already a clear trend toward widespread environmental deterioration in tribal areas, involving resource depletion, erosion, plant and animal extinction, and a disturbing series of other previously unforeseen changes.

After the initial depopulation suffered by most tribal peoples during their engulfment by frontiers of national expansion, most tribal populations began to experience rapid growth. Authorities generally attribute this growth to the introduction of modern medicine and new health measures, and the termination of intertribal warfare, which lowered mortality rates, as well as to new technology, which increased food production. Certainly all these factors played a part, but merely lowering mortality rates would not have produced the rapid population growth that most tribal areas have experienced if traditional birth-spacing mechanisms had not been eliminated at the same time. Regardless of which factors were most important, it is clear that all of the natural and cultural checks on population growth have suddenly been pushed aside by culture change, while tribal lands have been steadily reduced and consumption levels have risen. In many tribal areas the resource base has already been pushed beyond its carrying capacity and serious environmental deterioration due to this overuse has set in. In countless other areas it is certain that that point is approaching quickly as resources continue to dwindle relative to the expanding population and increased use.

Swidden systems and pastoralism, both highly successful economic systems under traditional conditions, have proven particularly vulnerable to increased population pressures and outside efforts to raise productivity beyond its natural limits. Research in Amazonia demonstrates that population pressures and related resource depletion can be created indirectly by official policies that restrict swidden peoples to smaller territories. Resource depletion itself can then become a powerful means of forcing tribal people into participating in the market economy—thus leading to further resource depletion. For example, Bodley and Benson (1979) show how the Shipibo Indians in Peru were forced to further deplete their forest resources by cash cropping in the forest area to replace the resources that had been destroyed earlier by the intensive cash cropping necessitated by the narrow confines of their reserve. In this case, certain species of palm trees that had provided critical housing materials were destroyed by forest clearing and had to be replaced by costly purchased materials. Research by Gross (1979) and others shows similar processes at work among four tribal groups in central Brazil and demonstrates that the degree of market involvement increases directly with increases in resource depletion.

The settling of nomadic herders and the removal of prior controls on herd size have often led to serious overgrazing and erosion problems where these had not previously occurred. There are indications that the desertification problem in the Sahel region of Africa was aggravated by programs designed to settle nomads. The first sign of imbalance in a swidden system appears when the planting cycles are shortened to the point that garden plots are reused before sufficient forest regrowth can occur. If reclearing and planting continues in the same area, the natural patterns of forest succession may be disturbed irreversibly and the soil can be impaired permanently. An extensive tract of tropical rainforest in the lower Amazon of Brazil was reduced to a semi-arid desert in just 50 years through such a process (Ackermann, 1962). The soils in the Azande

FIGURE 18. *This area in Botswana was formerly thornbush desert; now it is devastated by overgrazing related to government intervention which modified traditional cultural patterns.* (R. Lee, Anthro-Photo)

area are also now seriously threatened with laterization and other problems as a result of the government-promoted cotton development scheme (McNeil, 1972).

The dangers of overdevelopment and the vulnerability of local resource systems have long been recognized by both anthropologists and tribal peoples themselves, but the pressures for change have been overwhelming. In 1948 the Maya villagers of Chan Kom complained to Redfield (1962) about the dangerous shortening of their swidden cycles, which they correctly attributed to increasing population pressures. Redfield told them, however, that they had no choice but to go "forward with technology" (Redfield, 1962:178). In Assam, swidden cycles were shortened from an average of twelve years to only two or three within just twenty years, and anthropologists warned that the limits of swiddening would soon be reached (Burling, 1963:311-312). In the Pacific, anthropologists warned of population pressures on limited resources as early as the 1930s (Keesing, 1941:64-65). These warnings seemed fully justified, considering the fact that the crowded Tikopians were prompted by population pressures on their tiny island to suggest that infanticide be legalized. The warnings have been dramatically reinforced since then by the doubling of Micronesia's population in just fourteen years between 1958 and 1972, while consumption levels have soared.

The environmental hazards of economic development and rapid population growth have become generally recognized only within the past few years, and unfortunately there is as yet little indication that the leaders of the now developing nations are seriously concerned with environmental limitations. On the contrary, governments are forcing tribal peoples into a self-reinforcing spiral of population growth and intensified resource exploitation, which may be broken only by disaster.

DEPRIVATION AND DISCRIMINATION

> *Contact with European culture has given them a knowledge of great wealth, opportunity and privilege, but only very limited avenues by which to acquire these things.* (Crocombe, 1968)

Unwittingly, tribal peoples have had the burden of perpetual relative deprivation thrust upon them by acceptance—either by the people themselves or by the governments administering them—of the standards of socioeconomic progress set for them by industrial civilizations. By comparison with the material wealth of fully industrial societies, tribal societies become, by definition, impoverished. They are then forced to transform their cultures and work to achieve what many economists now acknowledge to be unattainable goals. Even though in many cases the modest GNP goals set by development planners for the developing nations during the "development decade" of the sixties were often met, the results were hardly noticeable for most of the tribal people involved. Population growth, environmental limitations, inequitable distribution of wealth, and the continued rapid growth of the already industrialized nations have all meant that both the absolute and the relative gap between the rich and poor in the world is steadily widening. The prospect that tribal peoples will actually be able to attain the levels of resource consumption to which they are being encouraged to aspire is remote indeed.

Tribal peoples feel deprivation not only when the economic goals they have been encouraged to seek fail to materialize, but also when they discover that they are powerless, second-class citizens who are discriminated against and exploited by the dominant society. At the same time they are denied the satisfactions of their traditional cultures, because these have been sacrificed in the process of modernization. Under the impact of major economic change family life is disrupted, traditional social controls are often lost, and many indicators of social anomie such as crime, delinquency, suicide, emotional disorders, and despair may suddenly increase. The inevitable frustration resulting from this continual deprivation finds expression in the cargo cults, revitalization movements, and a variety of other political and religious movements that have been widespread among tribal peoples following their disruption by industrial civilization.

NINE

THE SELF-DETERMINATION REVIVAL

Our plea to the world is to help us in our struggle to find a place in the world community where we can exercise our right to self-determination as a distinct people and as a nation.

The Dene Declaration (Watkins, 1977)

The previous chapters have presented a rather gloomy picture. Throughout, tribal peoples have appeared largely as passive victims, except for episodes of armed resistance. It might, therefore, be easily assumed that their situation is entirely hopeless. Indeed, many observers have confidently predicted the impending total extinction of tribal peoples, but such a judgement would be quite premature. Almost imperceptibly, during the 1970s tribal peoples who had experienced nearly overwhelming external pressures against their traditional cultures began forging new political structures that would help promote a viable accommodation with the national states surrounding them. Ideally, such an accommodation would be characterized by "self-determination" which would safeguard tribal ways of life from outside interference. As native people define it, self-determination would mean a return to full local political, economic, and cultural autonomy. As we shall see, this need not mean isolation from the metropolitan world, but rather that tribal peoples would be allowed to control affairs on their own terms within their own territories. As the preceeding chapters have shown, self-determination of this kind is precisely what has been lost in the push for progress in most parts of the tribal world. Regaining control of their destinies while retaining the vital elements of tribal culture is a difficult struggle, but it is being fought with surprising vigor by a newly emerging "indigenous peoples" movement. The term *indigenous peoples* is introduced here because it is used extensively by those who are involved in the struggle. The term itself will be examined in detail in following sections.

The present self-determination revival by indigenous peoples raises several critical issues such as: Who are indigenous peoples? What are their objectives? How can they be realized? Perhaps the most important questions center on the self-identity of indigenous peoples, and the nature of their social, political, and economic institutions. These issues are especially important today, because many conflicting groups are clamoring for recognition, control over resources, and self-determination. This conflict creates a situation in which the uniqueness of indigenous peoples may continue to be overlooked and their claims may be ignored. The present chapter will consider these questions in some detail, while the following chapter will examine how indigenous peoples are being supported by their nonindigenous allies.

WHO ARE INDIGENOUS PEOPLES?

The most obvious answer to the question, "who are indigenous peoples?" is that they are who they say they are. However, the consciousness of sharing a common identity is only now developing among indigenous peoples. Furthermore, indigenous peoples have sometimes been justifiably reluctant to define themselves, since in the past "legal" definitions have been used by governments to divide and manipulate them. A resolution was passed in 1977 by the second general assembly of the World Council of Indigenous Peoples (WCIP) declaring that only indigenous peoples could define indigenous peoples. There is no doubt that indigenous peoples know who they are, and they know they are unique. Unfortunately, the few formal definitions they have offered have not always been adequate. The official definition used by the WCIP states:

> *Indigenous people shall be people living in countries which*
> *have populations composed of different ethnic or racial groups who are*

*descendants of the earliest populations which survive in the area, and
who do not, as a group, control the national government of the
countries within which they live* (WCIP information leaflet).

This is basically a political definition that says nothing about special cultural characteristics, nor does it easily distinguish indigenous people from any national ethnic minorities who are "native" to a country. By this definition, if indigenous peoples were to be recognized as independent sovereign nations, controlling their own national governments, they would suddenly cease to be indigenous peoples. Regardless of these difficulties, there is no doubt that the term "indigenous peoples" is now the most widely accepted global term for the distinctive groups we are concerned with here. There are other generic terms that have gained wide regional acceptance by some indigenous peoples, but that are rejected in other parts of the world. The term *Indian* or *Indio* is now widely accepted in the Americas, but the Eskimo peoples now prefer to call themselves *Inuit*, and have never considered themselves to be Indians. The term *tribal* is accepted by many native peoples in Amazonia and the Philippines, but may be rejected elsewhere.

Of course, the real issue is not the label used, but the underlying common identity among indigenous peoples. When leaders from diverse cultures meet each other for the first time, they are overwhelmed by the fact that they share the same basic culture in spite of their often conspicuous, but superficial, differences. As will become apparent in the case studies later in this chapter, indigenous peoples throughout the world are independently saying exactly the same things when they describe the elements that make them different from the dominant societies surrounding them. The first shared trait that is invariably mentioned is their relationship to the land. As Julio Carduño, a Mexican Indian leader, declared at the First Congress of South American Indian Movements held in Cuzco in 1980:

> *Perhaps what most unites us is the defense of our land.
> The land has never been merchandise for us, as it is with capitalism,
> but it is the support for our cultural universe* (Carduño, 1980:112-
> 113, my translation).

We have noted repeatedly in other chapters that land is communally held by indigenous peoples. The land cannot be sold, even though there may be many different systems for regulating individual access. Native leaders often state that their land system is highly equitable and that no exact parallel to it exists in any industrial nations, socialist countries included. Indigenous peoples are also united in opposition to technologies and development projects that they consider destructive and unnecessary. They consider themselves more sensitive to the need to protect their land from environmental deterioration than those who would take the land from them. This view was presented by Julio Carduño at the Cuzco conference in the following terms:

> *There can be no economic interest superior to the necessity of preserving the ecosystem; we do not want a bonanza today at the cost of a desolate future* . . . (Carduño, 1980:120-121, my translation).

There are other shared features of the social and political systems of indigenous peoples that present sharp contrasts to other national systems, minority groups, or political parties. Leaders of the emerging indigenous peoples' self-determination movement see their own societies as classless, community-based, egalitarian, and close to nature. On the other hand, they see the societies around them as highly stratified, centralized, individualistic, anti-nature, and highly secular. These opposing constellations of traits do, in fact, pinpoint the most crucial differences that anthropologists recognize between the idealized tribal cultures and modern nation states (see, for example, Redfield, 1953 and Diamond, 1968.) Some anthropologists might argue that no society was ever really egalitarian and that all contemporary tribal societies have irrevocably lost whatever ideal features they may have once possessed, but today's indigenous leaders do not agree.

Certainly, not all indigenous peoples accept the idealized view of their traditional culture, nor do they necessarily all support the self-determination movement. Many individuals may find the personal rewards potentially available in the dominant society to be more attractive than the traditional tribal lifestyle. It is significant, however, that those who are prominent in the self-determination movement have usually had extensive experience and opportunities in the dominant society but have rejected it in favor of their own culture, which they consider to be superior. An example of this attitude was recently demonstrated by a Bolivian Indian leader when he attempted to explain to a journalist in Amsterdam why the Indian movement rejected Marxism. To make his point, he outlined general differences between Indian and western social systems and discussed the advantages of Indian methods of wealth and power regulation, concluding:

> *We think that this (Indian method) is an original way of solving the problem of individual wealth accumulation and political power at the same time, but it seems absurd to westerners. We want to conserve our institutions not only because they are ours, but also*

because we consider them just (Portugal, 1980:177, my
translation).

Objectives of the New Movements

In the past government officials, missionaries, anthropologists, and other
experts have endlessly debated the best policies for indigenous peoples.
The usual solution was to recommend integration into the dominant
society, perhaps blending "the best of both worlds." The natives
themselves were seldom consulted, because either no one thought the
natives knew what was good for them, or no one was seriously concerned
about their real desires. However, it is now apparent that indigenous
leaders of the self-determination movement do have a clear conception of
who indigenous peoples are. They also know what needs must be
accommodated if their cultures are to remain a viable alternative to the
perceived deficits of industrial civilization. The specific objectives of
different indigenous groups may vary widely according to local
conditions, as will be seen in the case studies that follow, but
self-determination is the common theme, and control over traditional
lands is always an overriding objective.

There have been many cases in which indigenous peoples would
approach government officials with well-reasoned proposals which
would permit their cultural autonomy and continued well-being.
However, such proposals have seldom been accepted. For example, in
1975 representatives from 34 Guajibo communities in the Colombian
llanos presented the government with a formal petition for the
establishment of a reserve measuring 20,000 square kilometers for the
40,000 Guajibo, the traditional residents of the region. They argued that
not only did they know how to take care of the land, but that they also had
a rightful claim to it, unlike the twenty colonists who had illegally moved
in. They also rejected a previous recommendation for a series of small
Guajibo reserves, because such fragmentation would facilitate their
eventual destruction (Unidad Indigena, 1975, I(1):4). In 1976 the Inuit
Tapirisat (Eskimo) of Canada presented the Canadian government with a
proposal for the establishment of a special territory to be known as
Nunavut, which means our land in the Inuit language. *Nunavut* would
consist of the nearly 2 million square kilometers of traditional Inuit land
which was never surrendered by treaty, where they continue to be the
dominant inhabitants. The Inuit wanted full ownership of some 648,000
square kilometers and exclusive hunting and fishing rights over the
remainder. As the majority population, they proposed that they should
control the regional government as well as the regulation of any resource
development of *Nunavut*, which would insure their primary objective of

self-sufficiency. In both the case of the Guajibo and the Inuit, the governments involved have refused to respond favorably. However, the point is clear—indigenous peoples do know what they want, but there is a real problem in realizing their objectives.

In rare cases, indigenous peoples have successfully been able to *force* governments to accept their proposals. In 1925 the Kuna Indians were able to take advantage of the relative political and military weakness of the Panamanian government and declared themselves an independent nation. The Kuna fought a brief armed rebellion before the government finally compromised with them in 1930, and accepted the Kuna plan for the establishment of a highly autonomous Kuna reserve (Falla, 1979a). This reserve still exists today as the *Comarca Kuna,* and the lands within it continue to be communally held by the 28,000 resident Kuna who carefully restrict use of their resources by outsiders (Falla, 1979b). The Kuna run their own internal affairs and send three representatives to the national assembly. The *Comarca Kuna* constitutes what is, in effect, a province within Panama, but it remains a uniquely Kuna, highly traditional, and self-sufficient area. The objectives they achieved are basically the same as those being sought by the Canadian Inuit and Dene peoples. These groups are engaged in a strictly political struggle with the Canadian government.

THE POLITICAL STRUGGLE

In many respects, the problems confronting indigenous peoples are political power problems—indigenous peoples are being destroyed because they lack the political power to adequately defend themselves and to press for their demands. Unfortunately, the obvious solution of seeking political power is not as easy as it might seem. In the past, nonstate peoples have sometimes consolidated in self-defense against invading states, transforming themselves into states, only to lose their unique features in the process. Fortunately, stateless societies have devised many ingenious ways of regulating political power. Today, indigenous peoples are designing political structures that permit the consolidation of a power base to successfully confront states without sacrificing their egalitarian and communal characteristics. On the other hand, tribal societies are often numerically weak and face the difficult task of combining with ethnically different, often hostile, neighboring groups. To further complicate matters, they must win allies in the dominant society. Regardless of the difficulties, in recent years there has been a steady emergence of regional, national, and international indigenous political organizations which have been working with increasing success for the self-determination of indigenous peoples.

Genuine native political organizations can accomplish many critical tasks. Perhaps the most important task is the double role of keeping the traditional heritage strong and that of organizing often widely dispersed and demoralized peoples into a united force to confront the common external threat. Acting in concert, they can press their demands with much greater visibility and effectiveness. Simply bringing local cases to national and international attention is an important function, since many of the most serious assaults on native peoples are illegal, according to national legislation and widely recognized international agreements. Under the embarrassing glare of international publicity, national governments have, in certain cases, been forced to take action on behalf of native peoples. It is also likely that most of the recent improvements that have taken place in official policies have been a direct result of the steadily increasing political power of indigenous peoples.

The unifying role of native political organizations is often carried out by holding periodic local and regional assemblies where common problems are discussed and resolutions passed. Many organizations have increasingly come to rely on their own published newspapers, magazines, and newsletters. In a few cases, groups have operated their own radio broadcasting systems and have gained control over their own formal educational institutions. Native political organizations vary widely in the details of their structures and exist at different levels. Some may be small, local groups representing single homogeneous ethnic groups. Others are regional federations, perhaps united on the basis of a more remote cultural heritage. In many countries there are now national-level indigenous peoples organizations, and more recently, a World Council of Indigenous Peoples (WCIP) has been formed.

While the basic objectives of these new political organizations are remarkably similar throughout the world, the context of the political struggle varies considerably from country to country. This makes it difficult to generalize about strategies and prospects. In order to give a clearer picture of the complexities of this ongoing struggle, case studies will be presented in the following sections illustrating examples from Ecuador, Colombia, Canada, Australia, and the Philippines. These cases by no means exhaust the field—there are many other important indigenous political organizations, particularly in North, Central, and South America, that will not be discussed. The cases examined, however, do provide a reasonable sample of the problems that indigenous organizations face and how they are dealing with them. In the South American examples, that are examined, Indian political organizations confront powerful local elites who are often closely allied with civil and military forces within national governments. These forces are often openly hostile to the acquisition of political power by any native groups. Here, the indigenous struggle can easily be understood as part of a larger class struggle, although the Indians generally do not regard themselves as part of the class system and are often suspicious of alliances with leftist groups. In the Canadian and Australian examples, the governments may be supportive of native political organizations, but they also have a conflicting interest in encouraging large corporations to extract resources from tribal lands. Here however, there is no pronounced class struggle and there may be considerable popular support for native peoples. The Philippines example represents a case where emerging tribal organizations face a hostile dictatorship which is allied with multi-national corporations. Meanwhile, the country is divided by a strongly polarized national class system and ongoing armed liberation movements.

THE SHUAR SOLUTION

> . . . a culture that evolves by itself and finds in itself new solutions for new problems, is more alive than ever (my translation, Federación de Centros Shuar, 1976:130).

The Shuar are a Jivaroan speaking, forest-dwelling group in Ecuador, who by their own estimate numbered over 26,000 people in 1975. Traditionally they were self-sufficient cultivators and hunters, living in dispersed extended families. They are widely famous as "head-hunters" and for their successful resistance to foreign domination since the arrival of the Spanish in 1540. The Shuar still retained control over much of their traditional territory, and their basic culture remained viable well into the present century. However, by 1959 they were outnumbered by colonists and were rapidly losing their most valuable subsistence lands. Their entire way of life was threatened with disintegration.

At this point the Shuar in the most heavily invaded areas set about developing what they called an "original self-solution" to the crisis. They concluded that their situation had been irrevocably altered by circumstances, but felt that they could still make a satisfying adjustment. The basic objective was to retain control over their own futures—they sought self-determination. They realized that the key to self-determination lay in retaining an adequate community land base, which would require effective participation in the government colonization program. If the Shuar sought individual land titles, only a few would succeed, given the pro-colonist bias in the entitlement process. In the end the Shuar community would be destroyed. The solution was the creation in 1964 of a fully independent, but officially recognized, corporate body—a federation, based on regional associations of many local Shuar communities. The federation became a legal entity, the *Federación de Centros Shuar*, that as of 1978 contained some 20,000 members organized into 160 local centers and 13 regional associations (Zallez & Gortaire, 1978). According to the federation's official statutes, the basic objectives of the organization are to promote the social, economic, and moral advancement of its members, and to coordinate development efforts with official government agencies. There are elected officials with carefully specified duties, and five specialized commissions to deal with such matters as health, education, and land.

The Federation quickly opted for a system of community land titles through the appropriate government body IERAC (*Instituto Ecuatoriano de Reforma Agraria y Colonización*), and promoted cooperative cattle ranching as the new economic base. Cattle ranching was especially important because land was titled on the basis of actual use and the legitimate requirement for pastureland was greater than for other forms of land use. The Federation obtained financial and technical assistance from various national and international agencies; by 1975, 95,704 hectares were securely in community titles. By 1978, the cattle herd had grown to more than 15,000 head and had become the primary source of outside income.

With the approval and support of the Ecuadorian ministry of education, and with the cooperation of the Salesian mission, the Federation has developed an education system suited to local needs and supportive of the traditional culture. Much of the instruction utilizes the Shuar language and Shuar teachers. In order to minimize the family disruption caused by boarding schools, and to spread educational opportunities as widely as possible, the Federation established its own system of radio-broadcast bilingual education beginning in 1972. The program has successfully reduced the elementary school role of the mission-operated boarding schools, and these have now been converted into technical schools for advanced training. The Federation has operated its own radio station since 1968, broadcasting in both Shuar and Spanish. In addition, since 1972 it has published a bilingual newspaper, *Chicham*, the official organ of the Shuar Federation.

The Federation solution is in many ways unique in Amazonia. The Shuar are the only native group to have retained such effective control over its own future. The initiative for the major adaptive changes that have occurred in the Shuar system as well as the administration of the entire program has been carried out by the Shuar themselves. Of course, the Federation itself was a response to uninvited outside pressures, and its early formation was facilitated by the Salesian missionaries who had been in the area since 1893, but there is no doubt that the Shuar have created a distinctly *Shuar* solution to the problem. The Federation has not yet become fully self-sufficient, but it has drawn on a very broad base of financial support so that no single outside interest has been able to assert undesired influence. Technical volunteers from many countries have been recruited on a temporary basis, but they have not dominated any programs.

The Shuar are very proud of the Federation and of the clear gains they have made. They recognize that they have had to make enormous changes in their culture, but they feel that they are still Shuar. Certainly, many traditional patterns have been abandoned with few regrets, and many material elements are disappearing or have been converted to the tourist trade. But the Federation has succeeded in strengthening the Shuar language and cultural identity, and in securing a viable resource base. The Shuar are actively promoting selected qualitites which they feel represent the essence of their culture and which clearly distinguish them from their non-Indian neighbors. These qualities include: communal land tenure, cooperative production and distribution, a basically egalitarian economy, kin-based local communities with maximum autonomy, and a variety of distinctive cultural markers.

The Federation has not existed without problems. Understandably, the colonists have resented its successes. In 1969, the Federation's central office was burned down, presumably by colonists, and Federation leaders have been jailed and tortured for crimes for which they were never convicted (Zallez and Gortaire, 1978:78, see also IWGIA Newsletter No. 20-23, 1978-79). While the government officially recognizes and cooperates with the Federation, actual support for their programs has been sporadic, and outside interests have consistently been favored by government agencies over the needs of the Shuar. The government has also forcefully attempted to prevent the Shuar from promoting the political organization of other Ecuadorian Indians and generally seems opposed to the idea of Ecuador becoming a multiethnic nation (see Whitten, 1976). The Federation has also been criticized by leftist organizations for accepting aid from capitalists, while at the same time some missionaries have accused Federation leaders of being communists. In the long run, the Federation faces other problems as well. Economic differentiation related to cattle ranching and the gradual emergence of an educated and salaried elite may be difficult to contain within the traditional egalitarian ideal to which the Federation still aspires. Furthermore, the present land base, which is broken up into discontinuous islands, may prove in a short time to be inadequate for the needs of a growing population.

INDIAN UNITY IN COLOMBIA

*Without unity we will never have the force to defend our
land and the future of our children (Unidad Indigena, 1975 1(1):1).*

Since 1971 at least five major regional Indian organizations have
emerged in Colombia. As with the Shuar in Ecuador, the primary focus of
all of these organizations has been to fight for control of traditional Indian
lands, for traditional forms of organization, and for their language and
culture. These new organizations include: *CRIC*, the Regional Indian
Council of the Cauca in the southern Andean region; *UNDICH*, the Union
of Chocó Indians of the western lowlands; *COIA*, the Arhuaco Indian
Congress of the Sierra Nevada of northern Colombia; *CRIVA*, the
Regional Indian Council of the Vaupes in the forested eastern lowlands;
and *UNUMA* of the eastern llano Guajibo peoples. The activities of these
organizations, as well as other more localized groups, are covered by a
nationally distributed newspaper, *Unidad Indigena*. In the short time that
these organizations have existed they have effectively raised Indian pride
in their own identity, promoted widespread awareness of common
problems, and they have presented realistic proposals to the government
from a position of considerable strength. Significant gains have been
made in some areas, but very serious opposition has also been aroused.
The example of *CRIC* will be discussed in some detail because it was the
earliest to organize in Colombia and has become a model for other
groups.

The Colombian department of Cauca in the southwest corner of
Colombia contains one of the densest Indian concentrations in the
country. Reliable figures are unavailable, but there may now be over
200,000 Chibcha-speaking Paez and Guambiano Indians in a department
that counted a total population of over 600,000 people in 1968. This is a
mountainous region of large coffee plantations, where in 1970 80 percent
of the agricultural land was held by a mere 14 percent of the landowners
(DANE, 1978:106–107, table 41). The Indians were conquered by the
Spanish in the sixteenth century and were allocated communally held
reservations or *resguardos* and their own form of internal self-government,
the *cabildo* system. The reservations were to be permanently removed
from the land market, and it seems that the Indians enjoyed a relatively
secure existence in spite of the colonial oppression that they faced in the
form of labor and tribute payments. However, in the nineteenth century,
the reserves began to be invaded by colonists and the government
initiated termination proceedings. Throughout the present century,

many reserves have been eliminated entirely and the protesting Indians have been crowded into smaller and smaller reserves which, in many cases, have become totally inadequate to their needs. The Indians fought protracted legal battles for the defense of these fragmented lands, but little was actually achieved.

The picture began to change dramatically in 1971 when 2,000 Indians from ten different reserves held a mass meeting and organized CRIC (*Consejo Regional Indigena del Cauca*) to coordinate the Indian struggle throughout the Cauca region. The new organization was formed as a federation, and the governing body consisted of representatives from each of the reserves. Annual congresses were convened and by 1973, 45 local reserves had joined. CRIC's original objectives were specified in the following seven points (Cartilla del CRIC No. 1, cited Corry, 1976:43-47, see also IWGIA Newsletter 1980, No. 24:19-26), which remain the basis of its program:

1. To recuperate the reservation lands
2. To increase the size of the reservations
3. To strengthen the Indian Councils (*cabildos*)
4. To stop the payment of illegal land rents
5. To make known the laws concerning Indians and to insist on their proper application
6. To defend the history, language, and customs of the Indians
7. To form Indian teachers to teach in the Indian language in ways which are applicable to the present situation of the people

In an unequivocal answer to those who might suggest that they have been too heavily acculturated by 400 years of reservation life to still be considered Indians, they emphatically state, "We are Indians, and we believe that it is good to be an Indian" (Corry, 1976:43). The Cauca Indians certainly have much in common with the local peasantry, and indeed both see the large landowners as enemies, but the Indians are quite specific about what makes them unique. They of course point to their ancestry, language, dress, and customs, but they also emphasize their economic egalitarianism:

> . . . *we are Indians because we believe that the things of the world are made for everyone. It is like saying that since we are all equal, the means of living should also be equal. . . . Because of this, we believe that the land, just as the air, the water and all the other things which keep us alive should not be only for the few. The land should not be owned, but should be communal. . . . This is why we like the reservations. Because there, the lands must all be shared out between all the members of the community* (Cartilla del CRIC No. 1, cited Corry, 1976:43).

The primary struggle has, of course, been over land. The CRIC strategy has been to reorganize the councils that have been terminated and to campaign for the restoration of the old reserves or for the extension of existing reserves by legal appeals through INCORA (*Instituto Colombiano de la Reforma Agraria*), the government agrarian reform office. When legal means fail, the Indians nonviolently occupy the lands they claim and begin to cultivate them. Arrests usually follow, but in many cases their legitimate claims are recognized. Within three years 5,000 hectares had been recovered and the "rents" charged Indians on lands illegally expropriated from them were eventually abolished.

The early successes of CRIC resulted in countermeasures from the local power structure. At first the landowners threatened CRIC leaders and attempted to control the *cabildos*. When these measures failed, the government moved to block Indian assemblies. Finally, in 1974, assassinations began and critical areas of the Cauca were militarized. Key CRIC leaders were arrested under the pretext that CRIC was a subversive organization linked to the M-19 terrorist group. By 1979, 30 CRIC leaders had been murdered and at least 40 more, including the CRIC president, were imprisoned. However, CRIC has received continuing support from international organizations concerned with the rights of indigenous peoples, and it continues to exist despite the political terrorism.

THE DENE NATION: LAND, NOT MONEY

The Dene Indians of the Canadian Northwest Territories are one of the best examples of the self-determination revival in North America. These Athapaskan-speaking peoples, who number about 17,000, are scattered through some 725,000 square kilometers of the great Mackenzie Valley (McCullum and Olthuis, 1977:40). In this area, just as their ancestors did for thousands of years before them, they continue to rely on moose, caribou, and fish for much of their subsistence. Since approximately 1790, when they began to be drawn into the fur trade, their economic self-reliance was gradually reduced. However, their egalitarian regional economy, based on kinship reciprocity, remained strong. When the world fur market declined after the second world war, the government responded to the "crisis" by attempting to push the Dene into full dependence on the stratified, highly individualistic wage-labor economy. In order to receive their welfare checks and to keep their children in school, the Dene were encouraged to settle in towns. This sedentary life made traditional subsistence pursuits more difficult (Asch, 1977). By the late 1960s, Dene society and culture was showing obvious signs of stress, but even more serious threats loomed when in 1968 oil was discovered at Prudhoe Bay in Alaska. The Canadian government immediately proposed converting the Mackenzie Valley into an "energy corridor" for pipelines to move arctic oil and gas to consumers in the United States and southern Canada. The Dene then had real fears that their entire way of life was in jeopardy.

In 1970, under the slogan "Land and Unity," the Dene formed the Indian Brotherhood of the Northwest Territories, combining all the scattered tribes into a single political organization capable of mounting an effective struggle for recognition of their rights to the land and an independent existence. Their first major political act, in 1973, was the filing of a legal caveat with the Territorial court that registered their prior claim to the land in order to block any further development without their approval. They were able to demonstrate that the treaties of 1899 and 1921, which supposedly cancelled their land rights, were fraudulent, and they obtained a favorable ruling on the caveat. The pipeline companies and the Department of Indian and Northern Affairs were appalled at the decision, which was finally overturned by the Supreme Court in 1976 on a technicality, but it did serve to clearly demonstrate the validity of the native claim.

The Dene political movement gradually began to take shape. In 1974, more than 250 native people from throughout the Mackenzie Valley met at Fort Good Hope. They had before them the unfortunate example of the Alaska natives, who had been forced to accept the poorly conceived Native Claims Settlement Act of 1971 in order to clear the way for the Alaska pipeline. At Fort Good Hope the Dene agreed emphatically that they wanted their rights recognized, not extinguished—they wanted "land not money." Their position was clarified the following year at a second assembly of 250 Dene at Fort Simpson, at which a formal *Dene Declaration* was drawn up. In this eloquent statement, the Dene pointed out that they were a majority within the Northwest Territories, yet they had not been allowed to control their own future. They declared themselves to be a distinct people and a "nation." They also called for recognition of their right to self-determination as native peoples within the Canadian nation. They were not, of course, seeking independent nation-state status. Their proposal was reasonable in terms of the Canadian constitution (Russell, 1977), but they were immediately accused of being separatists, racists, or "socialists."

In order to fully document their claim to the land, in 1974-76 the Dene carried out an extensive two-year research project into their own land use practices. They interviewed one third of the Dene hunters and trappers from throughout their territory and plotted on large scale maps the areas they actually utilized. This work revealed a maze of trails and traplines in an area that, to outsiders, would look like only wilderness. This demonstrated beyond any doubt that the Dene were indeed still a hunting people. Whether considered in terms of the numbers of people involved, the cash value of the resources obtained, or the actual contribution to the diet, traditional use of the land was absolutely vital for the Dene (Nahanni, 1977; Rushforth, 1977).

In spite of the mounting native resistance to the proposed pipeline, the major companies pressed ahead with their plans. In order to satisfy all the legal requirements that stood in the way of final approval of the pipeline, the Canadian government commissioned a formal study of the project and its possible implications for the north. The inquiry was conducted by British Columbia Supreme Court Justice Thomas R. Berger, who took the unprecedented step of seeking direct testimony and written documents from the Dene people. For several months in 1975-76 he visited every major town and settlement in the Mackenzie Valley, and heard from nearly a thousand people. In his final report, issued in 1977, Judge Berger expressed strong support for native self-determination and argued that the pipeline should be delayed for at least ten years to allow sufficient time for a just settlement of native claims. The Dene had presented a compelling case.

In fact, the government was taking seriously the Dene demand for self-determination. In 1976 the Minister of Indian Affairs asked the Dene to prepare a formal position paper so that negotiations on their land claim could begin. In this "Agreement-in-Principle," the Dene appealed to international law and United Nation's declarations in support of their right to self-determination. They listed 16 principles as a basis for negotiations, including the following:

1. The Dene have the right to recognition, self-determination, and ongoing growth as a People and as a Nation.
2. The Dene, as Aboriginal People, have the right to retain ownership of so much of their traditional lands, and under such terms, as to ensure their independence and self-reliance, traditionally, economically and socially ... (Watkins, 1977).

The Agreement-in-Principle claimed that it was the Dene's place to define themselves, and thereby avoided the divisiveness of a formal definition of who they were. They stated simply, "The Dene know who they are." Who the Dene are is implicit in their concept of self-determination. Self-determination for the Dene means, following the Dene system and not the dominant system of southern Canada. As George Barnaby, vice president of the Indian Brotherhood of the Northwest Territories, recently explained, the Dene system means a cooperative community life based on sharing, joint decision making, and communal land ownership (Barnaby, Kurszewski, and Cheezie, 1977:120-121).

LAND RIGHTS AND THE OUTSTATION MOVEMENT IN AUSTRALIA

What is happening is an Aboriginal revival, a reversal—if you like—of frontiers. No longer is the government pushing Aboriginals back. It is Aboriginals who today are pushing Governments back (Australia, DAA 1977, Aboriginal Affairs Minister, R. I. Viner, Perth, 1977).

Australian Aborigines have refused to either die out or to be assimilated. Today they are struggling with increasing success to gain legal control over their lands, and they are abandoning government settlements in favor of traditionally oriented communities in the bush. The catalyst for the present revival was the full-scale assault in the mid-1960s by multinational mining corporations on the aboriginal reserves in Arnhem Land and the Cape York Peninsula. These regions in the Northern Territory and Northern Queensland contained large populations of Aborigines who still lived on their ancestral lands. Unfortunatly, the land also contained outstanding bauxite deposits. The Aborigines were totally opposed to mining because they knew it would mean destruction of their traditional economy and of their sacred sites, as well as a total disruption of their societies. However, the government approved the mining projects, completely disregarding aboriginal protests. Ultimately, the mining did proceed, but the Aborigines did not give up. Their resistance attracted the attention of Aborigines and white supporters throughout the country and resulted in a major land rights political struggle.

In 1968 the Yirrkala people of the Gove peninsula in Arnhem land initiated legal proceedings in order to establish their aboriginal claim, arguing that the government and the mining companies had illegally appropriated their lands. In 1971 the court finally ruled against them, but this decision only served to draw attention to the blatant injustice of official Australian policies toward aboriginal land claims, which intensified the opposition to those policies. Aborigines began to organize public demonstrations on an unprecedented scale to demand changes in the law. Early in 1972 an "Aboriginal Embassy" was established in a tent in front of the parliament building in Canberra. It was torn down by police, only to be reerected, and remained for six months as an irritating symbol to the government of their injustices to Aborigines. Finally, in December of 1972 the Labour party came to power on a pro-Aborigine platform, and genuine changes in official policy began to take shape.

The first concrete action on the part of the new government was the establishment in 1973 of an Aboriginal Land Rights Commission under Justice Woodward to determine how to implement a just land policy. The Woodward Commission reports, which came out in 1973 and 1974, strongly recommended that Aborigines in the Northern Territory be given title to their reserved lands and that they be able to prohibit mining on those lands. It also recommended that the Aborigines be allowed to claim unalienated crown lands outside of the established reserves if they could demonstrate traditional ties, and called for the establishment of Aboriginal-run Land Councils to implement the new policies. Officially there was at last to be an end to injustice, repression, and the old assimilation policy. According to the new prime minister, the primary objective of the new policy would be:

> to restore to the Aboriginal people of Australia their lost
> power of self-determination in economic, social and political affairs
> (cited Pittock, 1975:30).

The labour government did propose a progressive aboriginal land rights bill, but before it could be approved they were thrown out of office and replaced by a much more cautious government which proceeded to rewrite and significantly weaken the land rights bill. Angered over the modifications, Aborigines organized a National Aboriginal Land Rights Conference in Sydney in August of 1976 where they presented a formal declaration outlining their conditions for a satisfactory land right settlement as follows:

1. Acknowledgement that all Aborigines, wherever they live, share a claim to land, which was totally the Aborigines' land prior to the arrival of White settlers who stole it from them.
2. That to remedy this injustice, Aborigines must be granted freehold control of all lands they rightfully claim, and total compensation for those lands previously taken away.
3. That the return of all lands to the Aboriginal people must include total control of minerals, forests, fishing, coastal waters, and all other aspects of the land, together with the right to control their own destiny on the land (pamphlet, National Aboriginal Land Rights Conference, Sydney, 1976).

CHAPTER
NINE

FIGURE 19. *Malak Malak claimants erect a sacred site sign on the Kilfoyle waterhole in the Daly River land claim area, 1979* (Arthur B. Palmer Northern Land Council Darwin Australia)

When the Aboriginal Land Rights (Northern Territory) Act of 1976 finally became law in January 1977, it rejected most of the above demands. However, this act still represented at least a partial victory for Aborigines and can be seen as a major concession coming from a government that for nearly 200 years has stubbornly refused to recognize the legitimacy of any Aboriginal land claims. There is now a legal basis for defending existing reserves and for extending them in some cases. Under the Act, the Aborigines organized representative land councils in the Northern Territory and they have worked vigorously to help local communities document their land claims. The councils have negotiated with mining companies and the government to minimize the detrimental impact of development projects on their lands. Unfortunately, under the present terms of the Land Rights Act, state and territorial governments retain considerable control over the administration of Aboriginal land and the Aborigines cannot prevent mining that is considered to be in the "national interest." The two Aboriginal land councils in the Northern Territory are officially recognized and are supported by a percentage of the royalties from mining on reserve lands. Aborigines in Queensland

FIGURE 20. *Yirrkala men from Eastern Arnhem Land preparing a dog (dingo) hero dance for land at the formation of the Kimberley Land Council, Noonkanbah Western Australia, 1978.* (Arthur B. Palmer Northern Land Council Darwin Australia)

and Western Australia have also now organized their own unofficial land councils, and they are pressing for legal control over their lands as well.

As some control over the land has been gradually regained, and as the government has softened its official emphasis on assimilation as the only alternative, Aborigines have begun to reassert their traditional culture and independence in a dramatic way. The most visible manifestation of this revival is the "Outstation Movement." By 1978, throughout the country there were 148 outstations, decentralized communities, where small groups of Aborigines were reestablishing the traditional life on their own ancestral lands away from the crowded, dependent conditions of the missions and government posts (Australia, Department of Aboriginal Affairs, 1978). These new communities have sought to be maximally self-sufficient, and wherever possible they rely heavily on wild food resources, but many still receive support from the government and maintain radio and transportation links with central stations. The important thing is that in the outstations Aborigines are again in control of their daily life, and they are securely on their own lands to which they have profound spiritual bonds. The advantages of life in the outstations have been seen immediately in terms of improved health conditions, but the Aboriginal social system is also gaining renewed strength and there has been an enthusiastic revival of ceremonial life. So far this new movement has been so successful that in some areas half of the Aboriginal population has already moved to outstations.

PHILIPPINE TRIBALS: NO MORE RETREAT

Today there are over four million tribal people in the Philippines, representing some 40 major groups, who seek to maintain their independent identities. Many of these groups have successfully retained their independence by gradually retreating into the mountains, but now, after more than 400 years of colonial domination, they have nowhere else to go. They are being forced to adopt new forms of self-defense because their final refuges are being invaded by powerful national and international interests. The tribal peoples are strong numerically, as they constitute some ten percent of the total national population, but they are widely scattered and separated by differences of language and culture, making a common defense difficult. However, in response to new external threats to their survival, they have begun to bury their internal differences and are mounting a major resistance movement.

The most serious threats facing these groups today are dams, mining, and agribusiness, all of which would displace them from their lands. Since 1973 the government's National Power Corporation (NPC) has been attempting to implement its planned construction of 21 hydroelectric projects which would flood tribal lands in Mindanao and northern Luzon. These projects directly support the efforts of multinational companies, such as DelMonte, who are turning tribal lands into giant pineapple plantations. The tribal peoples quite correctly see their land and cultures as inseparable, and understandably they do not want them sacrificed for the benefit of a wealthy few. The official government program for tribal peoples is to crowd them into carefully controlled "Service Centers" in order to free tribal lands for development. Since 1968 this resettlement process has been methodically carried out by PANAMIN (Presidential Assistant on National Minorities), the special government agency established for that purpose. By 1979 an estimated 2.6 million tribal people were being "assisted" by PANAMIN (Rocamora, 1979:2).

So far the tribal peoples have utilized a variety of approaches to prevent the loss of their lands. At first they sent delegations with petitions directly to Philippine President Marcos. When these appeals were rejected they held organizational meetings, issued formal declarations, and turned to more active resistance. Their basic demands were quite simple and are eloquently expressed in the formal declaration prepared by the Mangyan people of Mindoro at a meeting of tribal representatives in 1976:

1. We want land for our tribe, enough for all of us, a piece of land that is titled and secure, that others cannot steal . . . We will not retreat anymore.
2. We want our own way of life. We are willing to live side-by-side with others but we want to live our own culture and traditions (cited Rocamora, 1979:9-10).

The 500,000 Igorots (Kalinga and Bontoc) in northern Luzon were traditional enemies, but in 1975 they signed a formal peace treaty and combined to fight together against the government's plan to build four major dams on the Chico River in their territory (Rocamora, 1979; Winnacker, 1979; Razon, 1976). They agreed to reject all overtures from PANAMIN and the NPC, and refused all cooperation with the construction effort. At first the united Igorots managed to stall construction by dismantling survey camps, but the workers kept returning. Finally, when antigovernment guerrillas belonging to the New People's Army (NPA) came to the support of the Igorots and began to encourage them to violent action, the Philippine army was called in. The entire zone was militarized and Philippine army units moved to block further protests. Many tribal leaders were arrested and entire villages were forcibly relocated, but resistance to the dams continued. The Igorots appealed to President Marcos and even attempted to prevent funding of the projects by presenting their case to an International Monetary Fund-World Bank conference in Manila, but all of their efforts only succeeded in gaining time. Unfortunately, given the Marcos government's determination to promote large-scale developments that are detrimental to tribal groups and opposed by them, the tribal peoples may increasingly join antigovernment guerrillas and turn to violent resistance as their only alternative.

THE INTERNATIONAL ARENA

So far we have examined representative regional and national level indigenous political movements in several countries. In this section we move to the international level, where indigenous peoples have become

CHAPTER
NINE

increasingly active in their struggle for self-determination. International indigenous political organizations, combining related indigenous peoples separated only by national boundaries, have existed for some time. For example, the Nordic Sami Council, uniting the Sami of Norway, Sweden, and Finland, was founded in 1953. However, coordinated, large-scale political action by diverse indigenous peoples from many different countries is a very recent phenomenon. Since the widespread establishment of regional native organizations, which began in earnest only in the early 1970s, it has been an obvious step for indigenous leaders to convene international conferences of representatives of these national organizations and finally to establish permanent international organizations.

Perhaps the first major, multiethnic international conference organized and run by indigenous peoples was the First Circumpolar Arctic People's Conference held in Copenhagen, Denmark in November of 1973. This conference brought together Indian, Inuit (Eskimo), and Sami (Lapp) representatives from some 16 indigenous organizations in Alaska, Canada, Greenland, Norway, Finland, and Sweden. In their official resolutions they agreed to cooperate in the preservation of their cultures and claimed a common identity in their special relationship to the land which cross-cut their cultural differences. As they declared:

> *We are autochthonous peoples, that is we are an integral part of the very lands and waters we have traditionally used and occupied. Our identity and culture is firmly rooted in these lands and waters. It is this relationship which constitutes the very unique features of our cultural identity in contrast to the cultures of other peoples within each of the countries from which we come* (Boye, 1974:69).

The delegates called upon national governments to recognize and respect their unique claims of collective ownership of their traditional lands and waters, and stressed:

> *. . . there must not be any displacement or interference with our rights by government and/or industry, nor can there be disturbance of our lands* (Boye, 1974:70).

A few months later in 1974 another international, multiethnic conference, the American Indian Parliament of the Southern Cone, was convened by indigenous peoples in Paraguay for the purpose of defining common problems and proposing solutions. Representatives from 15 Indian groups from Argentina, Bolivia, Brazil, Venezuela, and Paraguay attended the week-long conference. The official conclusions of the parliament emphasized the common Indian identity rooted in a cultural heritage that was thousands of years old and which has existed quite independently of any affiliations with present nation states. Specific statements were issued on a variety of topics including land, labor, education, language, health, and political organization. The basis of their position in regard to land closely resembled the view presented earlier by the arctic peoples and was expressed in their uncompromising statement of principle:

> *. . . the land is of the Indian. The Indian is the earth itself.*
> *The Indian is the owner of the land, with property titles or without*
> *them* (cited Chase-Sardi and Colombres, 1975:240).

More specifically, they stated that Indian land should be recognized as communally held and Indian communities should be legally recognized, self-governing, corporate entities. They felt that the natural resources of their lands should only be exploited by themselves for their own benefit. They wanted an educational system that promoted their own cultural values and languages. In regard to their own political mobilization, they stressed the need for greater unity and the rapid formation of more regional federations, but they warned against possible manipulation of their new organizations by alien political interests or by false native leaders who were promoted by government authorities. They felt that any outside aid that they accepted should be without ideological preconditions. They also emphasized that divisions promoted by religious sects must not hinder their political unity, and they warned specifically against the dangers of any trend toward the emergence of internal stratification within Indian communities.

Even before the First Circumpolar Arctic People's Conference, preliminary plans were being worked out by the National Indian Brotherhood of Canada for the establishment of a permanent international organization of indigenous peoples having official status as a Non-Governmental Organization (NGO) of the United Nations. The advantage of such an organization was that it would be in a position to present the case of indigenous people before the world community much more effectively than any existing national indigenous organizations. This new oganization, the World Council of Indigenous Peoples (WCIP), was formally inaugurated in 1975 at its first general assembly hosted by the Sheshaht (Nootka) Indians on their tribal lands on Vancouver Island, British Columbia (Sanders, 1977). Fifty-two delegates representing indigenous organizations from 19 countries attended. In addition to the numerous Indians from North and South America, there were also indigenous peoples from Australia, New Zealand, Greenland, and Scandinavia. A formal charter was adopted by the assembly which opened its membership to organizations of indigenous people who were working, " . . . to further their economic self-sufficiency and to obtain self-determination." The principle objectives of the WCIP included the following points:

1. to ensure political, economic and social justice to indigenous peoples
2. to establish and strengthen the concepts of indigenous and cultural rights

Policy for the World Council is formulated by the general assemblies and is carried out by the executive council which is composed of single representatives from major world regions such as Canada, Central America, South America, Europe and Greenland, and the South Pacific. The World Council has obtained financial support from a wide variety of sources including international humanitarian organizations, religious bodies, and national governments. Since gaining NGO status it has also sought funding directly from the United Nations.

The World Council held its second general assembly in Swedish Samiland in 1977. This assembly issued a final report containing what is certainly the most comprehensive and sophisticated statement of rights and principles yet published by any organization of indigenous peoples (see Appendix D). The report (WCIP, 1977), which appeared in the Sami language, Swedish, and English, includes a major declaration listing fundamental principles, resolutions, and 14 basic rights. The fundamental principle stressed at the outset was the just claim of indigenous peoples to their lands. This was followed by the "irrevocable and inborn" right to self-determination. The other rights for the most part amplified these issues of land and self-determination.

The World Council is gradually expanding the scope of its organization to include more and more indigenous groups in various parts of the world. For example, in 1980 the Ainu of Japan joined the council, and CISA, the Indian Council of South America, was officially organized as the regional organization for South America with 18 representatives from nine countries. A third general assembly is to be held in Australia in 1981.

The activities of indigenous political organizations have clearly generated a response at the United Nations. It is to be expected that official international conventions will increasingly reflect the positions now being expressed by indigenous peoples themselves. In 1977 more than 50 leaders of indigenous organizations were given a unique opportunity to present their position when they were invited to attend the International Conference on Discrimination Against Indigenous

Populations in the Americas, organized in Geneva by the special United Nations NGO Committee on Human Rights. The conference was attended by delegates from 46 national and international organizations and by observers from 27 different national governments in addition to the special indigenous peoples delegations. At its conclusion, the conference adopted a number of resolutions strongly supporting indigenous peoples. The international response to the legitimate demands of indigenous peoples was even stronger in the declaration and programme of action presented by the 123 nations attending the United Nations World Conference to Combat Racism and Racial Discrimination held in Geneva in 1978 and approved by the United Nations General Assembly. The declaration specifically stated in article 21:

> *The Conference endorses the right of indigenous peoples to maintain their traditional structure of economy and culture, including their own language, and also recognizes the special relationship of indigenous peoples to their land and stresses that their land, land rights and natural resources should not be taken away from them . . .*

The full text of the proposed programme of action in favor of indigenous peoples is presented in Appendix C.

TEN
SUPPORT IN
THE STRUGGLE

The emphasis for all concerned in this struggle should be upon aiding the indigenous people to struggle on their own behalf.

(Turner, 1978:19)

There are now a bewildering array of nonindigenous organizations proclaiming support for indigenous peoples. Many of these organizations appeared with the rise of indigenous political organizations since 1970, but some have existed for many years. All of these groups are united in the expressed desire to assist indigenous peoples. However, they approach this objective in significantly different ways and as a result, not all groups have been equally welcomed by the indigenous peoples themselves. However well meaning they may be, some organizations are clearly out of touch with the current aims of indigenous groups. Other organizations which may seem to support the aspirations of indigenous peoples actually have special interests of their own that may weaken their effectiveness. The organizations that are the most well received by native peoples themselves are those that strengthen the native capacity for

191

self-defense through the direct provision of financial and technical assistance, unencumbered by ideological preconditions. Other groups that have been received positively are those that work to publicize the viewpoint of indigenous peoples and attempt to rally popular support for them while pressuring governments and multinational corporations to moderate their policies.

In order to clarify their different approaches, the organizations treated in this chapter will be grouped into three broad categories: Conservative-Humanitarian; Liberal-Political; and Primitivist-Environmentalist. These three general categories represent consistent constellations of differing premises, objectives, and strategies that are formally expressed by the organizations or can be inferred from their overall programs (see Table 3). The characteristics defining these dominant orientations are not always mutually exclusive nor incompatible. For example, organizations representing different orientations might jointly pursue a specific strategy, but they would do so because of different premises and perhaps for different objectives. There might be agreement on objectives, such as "self-determination," but organizations operating from different premises would probably pursue

Table 3

Primary Orientations of Organizations Supporting Indigenous Peoples

	Primitivist-Environmentalist	Liberal-Political	Conservative-Humanitarian
BASIC PREMISES	Tribal cultures are a superior adaptation. We must stop economic developments that threaten them.	Indigenous peoples are economically exploited and politically oppressed. We must help them defend their rights.	Progress is inevitable. We must help them make the best of it.
OBJECTIVES	Permit the persistence of traditional tribal cultures as a viable alternative.	Liberation, self-determination, decolonization of indigenous peoples.	Eventual integration into the national system with the preservation of ethnic identity.
STRATEGY	Promote cultural/environmental sanctuaries. Advocate conservation. Oppose specific development projects.	Promote political mobilization and consciousness-raising. Advocate human rights. Oppose oppressive policies.	Promote humanitarian assistance programs. Advocate use of native language and development of ethnic pride.

distinct strategies. It is even possible that different groups might agree on basic premises on certain issues, while employing different objectives or strategies. The picture is further complicated by the fact that a particular organization may shift its orientation through time. In the following discussion, other important distinctions that crosscut the three orientations will be dealt with, such as whether or not organizations represent formal political or religious interests.

THE CONSERVATIVE-
HUMANITARIAN APPROACH

> *Resource development of course cannot be halted, but the shock it deals to weaker societies can be moderated so that they are not shattered by it. These societies need and can be given time to adapt to modern pressures with major elements of their cultures intact*
> (Cultural Survival brochure, 1975).

The Aborigines Protection Society (APS), founded in England in 1839, was perhaps the first nonreligious, humanitarian organization to come to the defense of native peoples. This organization undoubtedly helped to moderate some of the worst abuses of the colonial period and still pursues its original aim of "protection and advancement of aboriginal and primitive peoples," although now it has merged with the Anti-Slavery Society. The concern of such Conservative-Humanitarian organizations is the same as the traditional missionary objective of "cushioning the shock" and smoothing the inevitable integration of tribal societies into the states that are beginning to dominate them. Today there are many other organizations concerned with indigenous peoples that continue in this tradition. Some of these groups, such as FUNAI and PANAMIN, are government bodies. Some, such as the Summer Institute of Linguistics (SIL), are religious organizations, and others such as Cultural Survival may be supported by anthropologists.

All of these groups share the conservative belief that "progress" cannot be stopped and the humanitarian concern for the native peoples that are being hurt by progress. This acceptance of the inevitability of progress directly conflicts with the basic premises of the Primitivist-Environmentalists, who argue that progress threatening the well being of indigenous peoples can and must be stopped. The Conservative-Humanitarian is unlikely to advocate fighting against a major development project threatening indigenous people. Rather, he or she would recommend measures that would allow the affected peoples to accommodate the "inevitable" changes as painlessly as possible. In this respect, the dominant orientation of Conservative-Humanitarian organizations emphasizes political "realism" and the strategies and objectives that it pursues are often quite compatible with established government policies and agencies. The conservative acceptance of integration as an important objective also conflicts directly with the Primitivist-Environmentalist insistence that traditional peoples should be allowed the option of nonintegration, and it may conflict with the Liberal-Political objective of self-determination. While Conservative-Humanitarian organizations may advocate self-determination, they are more likely to support specific culture-change projects designed to facilitate integration with the preservation of ethnic identity, whether or not such projects originate with the indigenous peoples themselves.

The Conservative-Humanitarian approach and some of the issues involved will be examined in more detail in the following sections which consider three concrete examples: the Summer Institute of Linguistics; the Sacha Runa Foundation; and Cultural Survival.

The SIL/WBT

The Summer Institute of Linguistics (SIL) is a conservative protestant missionary organization and is perhaps the single largest organization directly concerned with the welfare of tribal peoples throughout the world. It has carried out its particular Conservative-Humanitarian style of translation work, education, development, and evangelism in hundreds of tribal groups in more than 20 countries. In so doing it has been criticized by native political organizations and non-native individuals and organizations which are oriented more toward the Liberal-Political approach.

Technically the SIL is composed of two corporate entities: the Wycliffe Bible Translators (WBT) which presents its religious missionary role to the home churches in the United States and Europe which provide most of the organization's financial support; and the SIL proper, which operates in the field, emphasizing its scientific role in the preparation of grammars, vocabularies, and bilingual teaching materials. The SIL is also involved in promoting humanitarian projects that facilitate integration of indigenous peoples into the national society. This latter role is carried out with approval and support of the governments in the host countries, which might not be so readily available to a purely religious organization such as WBT.

The primary orientation of the SIL is entirely Conservative-Humanitarian in premises, objectives, and strategy as outlined in Table 3. It rejects the Primitivist-Environmentalist stance for several reasons, but most importantly because of the SIL's own interest in religious proselytism. The SIL does not want to see the persistence of undisturbed tribal cultures because these contain self-destructive, negative traits such as religious fears, which should be replaced by positive elements based on fundamentalist Christianity. This viewpoint was expressed recently by several SIL supporters as follows:

> . . . it would be erroneous not to recognize the necessity that the indigenous groups feel of having spiritual help to face the difficult life of the 20th century. The teachings of the gospel can replace the base of fear, common in their religions, with the security of the love of God . . . (Wise, Loos, and Davis, 1977:521).

Furthermore, they argue that only unrealistic romantics would object to outsiders introducing culture change, particularly in the area of religion, because there are no "pure natives" or "happy savages." The SIL supporters justify their own humanitarian intervention by stressing that change is normal, often desired by the natives, and inevitable anyway (Wise, Loos, and Davis, 1977:500). They do, of course, recognize that much culture change is detrimental, and they feel that they can play an important role in alleviating these "cultural shocks." However, it is significant that their primary efforts are clearly *not* directed at reducing the external pressures for change. In many cases, SIL teams have been the first to initiate contacts with isolated tribal groups, and they have on occasion directly supported development of tribal areas by outside corporate interests (Hart, 1973; Gesellschaft für bedrohte Völker 1979; Hvalkof and Aaby, 1980).

The SIL often recognizes that tribal peoples are economically exploited, and in this respect it agrees with the basic premises of Liberal-Political organizations. However, the SIL strategy seeks to correct this situation through the introduction of Christianity, literacy programs, and community development with the ultimate objective of integration, rather than through political mobilization directed toward self-determination. The SIL stresses that the natives need individual "self-realization" and a new ethnical base to "revitalize" their cultures (Wise, Loos, and Davis, 1977:521).

While the SIL officially advocates respect for other cultures and rejects any use of force to promote change (Wise, Loos, and Davis, 1977:509), in reality the material advantages of SIL missionaries make their program extremely persuasive and its assaults on traditional religions may seriously undermine tribal cultures. A very substantial infrastructure normally accompanies SIL missionaries in the field. They typically operate out of a comfortable base, resembling a transplanted

American community, and make extensive use of aircraft and short-wave radios, all of which contrasts dramatically with the relative material simplicity of the tribal peoples. Their methods most often involve establishing a continuing relationship with a few select individuals within a given tribal community. These individuals receive special training and material advantages, are often converted to Christianity, and may eventually become teachers in the bilingual schools. The SIL also cooperates closely with official government agencies and may directly support the integration policies that some indigenous political organizations may reject.

In the SIL's own view of its work, it is intervening to improve conditions in cooperation with the native peoples, but a quite different interpretation of their role has been advanced by native political leaders. For example, in 1975 the leadership of the Arhuaco Indians of the Sierra Nevada in Colombia presented a formal petition to the Colombian president requesting the immediate removal of the three SIL teams working in their territory, accusing them of contributing to disunity and cultural disintegration. The Arhuaco clearly perceived the SIL presence as coercive and felt that any attack on their traditional religion threatened their entire culture. They explained that the SIL teams were:

> . . . *imposing on us the gospel as the only way to live, thereby ending our own religion, that urges us to work in accord with our own customs, traditions, and culture* (Unidad Indgena, 1975 vol. 1, no. 4:8, my translation).

Resolutions condemning the SIL and calling for its total expulsion from all indigenous areas were approved by both the second general assembly of the WCIP in 1977 and by the first Congress of South American Indian Movements in 1980 at Cuzco. The SIL was denounced by the Cuzco congress as an "institution of imperialist penetration" and for bringing "division and ethnocide" and fostering economic dependence. These intensely negative feelings toward the SIL are not just a response against religious proselytism, but the native leaders tutored by the SIL are seen as serious threats to the emerging self-determination, cultural revitalization movement. As the head of a Mexican Indian organization explained at the Cuzco conference:

> *The elements most faithful to the mission: the most catequized and mentally colonized are promoted to leadership and supported as such in order to fight the real traditional and modern chiefs, who are those that reject domination* (Carduño, 1980:116, my translation).

On the other hand, there is no doubt that the SIL has effectively prevented the total extinction of many threatened tribal groups and has also contributed to the preservation of language and cultural identity. Through its bilingual education programs it has also contributed, indirectly and unintentionally, to the creation of the new indigenous political leadership and the self-determination movement.

The Sacha Runa Foundation

The Sacha Runa Foundation is a unique example of a reciprocal arrangement between Ecuadorian forest Indians and American anthropologists in which the Indians receive medical assistance and in turn collaborate in the research interests of the anthropologists (Whitten and Whitten, 1977). This arrangement, which was developed largely in response to initiatives by the Canelos Quichua Indians, depends on funds generated by the foundation from donations and sale of artifacts in the United States which have been manufactured by the Indians. Medical services, which compliment traditional medical practices and counteract the effects of introduced diseases, are provided by a mission hospital in Ecuador selected by the Indians. The foundation, which is incorporated in the state of Illinois as a non profit corporation, settles the account each month through an intermediary church organization in the United States. In this example, the anthropologists are satisfying an obvious self-interest, but their research activities will also help preserve and strengthen the cultural heritage of the native group. The medical program itself has been designed by the natives to meet their own needs.

Cultural Survival

Cultural Survival was established in 1972 by a group of Harvard anthropologists to support special assistance programs for threatened tribal societies. The organization is squarely in the Conservative-Humanitarian tradition with its promotion of programs directed primarily at helping tribal peoples to retain their identities while accommodating the "inevitable" changes that are forced upon them by the dominant society. In contrast to the SIL and the Sacha Runa Foundation, Cultural Survival has no obvious religious or research self-interest in its work and can be considered a strictly humanitarian organization. In some respects its dominant orientation is very close to the Liberal-Political position because Cultural Survival's objectives include self-determination as well as recognizing the political and economic problems, and advocating human rights. However, Cultural Survival places greater emphasis on integration and "accommodation" rather than political liberation and its primary strategy is to support development and "adjustment" rather than political mobilization. The contrasts between Cultural Survival and the Primitivist-Environmentalist orientation are unmistakable. In terms of objectives, Cultural Survival rejects the possibility of permanent refuges for tribal cultures, because outsiders will simply not leave small isolated tribes alone. As Maybury-Lewis, anthropologist and president of Cultural Survival, explained:

> One might wonder if it would not have been better to leave them alone, but this is idle speculation. The push to explore and exploit the remotest corners of the earth cannot be stopped easily, if at all . . . (Maybury-Lewis, 1976a:15).

This position is presented even more strongly in the Culture Survival brochure cited above to the effect that: "Resource development of course cannot be halted . . ."

The Cultural Survival approach is also philosophically opposed to any "false sentimentality" (Pia Maybury-Lewis, 1979:25) and "static preservation" (Cultural Survival brochure) as might be implied by primitivist tribal sanctuaries. In this context, it is significant that when world-famous American anthropologist Margaret Mead agreed to serve on the Cultural Survival advisory board, it was stressed that the organization would work for positive changes and accepted her view that, "many small societies want changes in their ways of life" (cited Pia Maybury-Lewis, 1979:25). This viewpoint is the same kind of "realism" invoked by the SIL to support its program, but given these basic assumptions, the Cultural Survival objectives of helping small societies to become "successful ethnic minorities" (Maybury-Lewis, 1976b) and to "come into the wider society with something of their own culture and their own self respect intact" (Maybury-Lewis, 1976a:15), follow logically.

As of 1980, Cultural Survival was actively supporting fourteen small-scale projects in Central and South America, all of which were aimed at improving the ability of local Indian groups to successfully adapt to change. These projects included: a rubber coop for the Kaxinawa Indians in Brazil; legal aid for Colombian Indians, land demarcation in Ecuador; educational radio broadcasts by Nicaraguan Indians; bilingual education in Peru; and promotion of a native subsistence plant as a cash crop for the Cubeo in Colombia (Cultural Survival Newsletter, 1980, vol. 4(2):1-3, vol. 4(3):7). These projects differ from the kind of development examined in Chapter 7 in that the Cultural Survival projects aim to assist peoples who have already been seriously disrupted by outside influences, and in many cases have initiated the projects themselves to help restore some degree of self-reliance.

THE LIBERAL-POLITICAL APPROACH

In many respects the charter for the Liberal-Political approach to the support of indigenous peoples is stated in the *Declaration of Barbados* (IWGIA Document No. 1, Dostal, 1972:376-381). This document (see Appendix B) was drawn up by anthropologists attending the Symposium on Interethnic Conflict in South America, which was held in Barbados in 1971 under the sponsorship of the World Council of Churches through its Programme to Combat Racism. The most striking aspect of the declaration is its argument that the Indians are in effect internally colonized peoples who are economically exploited and politically oppressed by the class systems of the dominant national societies. The solution called for was:

> . . . *a radical break with the existing social situation; namely, the termination of colonial relationships, internal and external . . . the creation of a truly multi-ethnic state in which each ethnic group possesses the right to self-determination and the free selection of available social and cultural alternatives.* (IWGIA Document No. 1:3-4)

While the declaration did not outline precisely how these objectives were to be realized, it strongly condemned the state, religious missions, and anthropologists for their failure to meet their moral responsibilities to native peoples, and maintained that the Indians must "organize and lead their own liberation movement." However, it was suggested that anthropologists could play an important role in this "struggle for liberation" by helping to reveal the colonial situation of the Indians and by providing them with useful information. A complete suspension of all missionary activity was called for, because of its inherently colonial and ethnocentric character. The emphasis in the persuasively worded Barbados declaration was on political struggle, not passive accommodation, and this constituted a clear challenge to established Conservative-Humanitarian approaches to the defense of native peoples.

Since the creation of IWGIA (International Work Group for Indigenous Affairs) in 1968, a number of new organizations, representing the kind of Liberal-Political perspective broadly advocated by the Declaration of Barbados, have appeared in many parts of the world.

Many of these organizations, and particularly those with a religious affiliation, seem to have been organized as a response to the Declaration of Barbados, and all share the viewpoint expressed in the Barbados declaration that indigenous peoples are oppressed. These organizations are also in agreement on advocating self-determination as an objective and political action as a strategy. Liberal-Political organizations very often take a critical stand against established government policies, and they may oppose development of tribal areas by outside corporate interests. In this respect, they may share certain strategies, but not necessarily the objectives or underlying premises of Primitivist-Environmentalists.

Within their overall similarities there are many important differences between various Liberal-Political organizations. For example, some groups such as IWGIA and Survival International are nonpolitical and nonreligious, while other groups such as Project North in Canada and CIMI in Brazil represent religious interests. Many organizations are politically aligned and are therefore likely to oppose the maintenance of isolated, undisturbed tribal peoples. Isolation would deny such peoples the chance to participate politically in their own defense and in the building of multiethnic socialist states. Some might even consider cultural sanctuaries to be simply another form of political oppression.

In order to facilitate a more comprehensive treatment of Liberal-Political organizations, they will be grouped as follows into two broad subcategories, representing an obvious division of labor: (1) *international organizations* concerned with indigenous peoples worldwide (2) *regional task forces* working primarily in specific countries.

The International Organizations

> *We exist to help tribal peoples protect their rights; the simplest, unarguable rights of all people. . . . And, moreover, to support their right to determine, themselves, their own future and that of their children—tribal self-determination* (Corry, 1979:11, for Survival International).

The primary objective of the international Liberal-Political organizations is to help indigenous peoples gain self-determination and international recognition of their basic human rights. For example, IWGIA describes its purpose as "establishing the indigenous peoples' right to self-determination" and helping "to secure the future of indigenous people in concurrence with their own efforts and desires"

(IWGIA leaflet 1980). With this emphasis on human rights and self-determination, the question of isolation versus some form of integration as a preferred policy is left to indigenous peoples to decide for themselves. In many respects these organizations could be considered to be human rights organizations that specialized exclusively in indigenous peoples. Their methods of operation closely resemble other, more generalized human rights organizations such as Amnesty International. Their overall strategy is threefold:

1. to focus international attention on the contemporary situation of indigenous peoples
2. to pressure governments to respect the internationally recognized rights of indigenous peoples
3. to provide financial assistance to indigenous peoples in support of their self-determination struggle

In pursuit of their objectives, these organizations maintain constant communication with each other, with more specialized regional organizations, and with indigenous organizations. Together they now form a wide network composed of indigenous leaders, anthropologists, and other fieldworkers, who are all in close touch with events that influence tribal peoples throughout the world. It is now possible to respond almost immediately to any particular crisis situation, and a very powerful coalition of informed opinion can be mobilized to influence government authorities to act responsibly in the expressed interests of indigenous peoples.

For example, in 1978 the international organizations learned that the Brazilian government was quietly preparing to "emancipate" Amazon Indians and thereby terminate their legally protected status. An international protest movement was immediately mounted and the government was forced to withdraw the decree. Since then the Anthropology Resource Center (ARC) in Boston, IWGIA in Denmark, and Survival International in London have coordinated an international campaign, together with other international organizations and 27 pro-Indian organizations in Brazil, in support of a proposal to create a 6.4-million-hectare reserve for the Yanomamo Indians to counteract a government plan to isolate them in 21 small reserves.

Most international organizations have focused heavily on the issue of protecting tribal land rights. For example, Survival International lists land rights as its first essential priority. Another organization, CIMRA (Colonialism and Indigenous Minorities Research and Action), also London based, has campaigned heavily in favor of aboriginal land rights in Australia. As part of its campaign, CIMRA offers the following very concrete action proposals to concerned individuals who agree that something should be done to help Aborigines, but ask, "Yes, but what can I do?":

1. "Support . . . Aborigine land rights movements."
2. "Protest . . . to foreign corporations mining Aborigine land.
3. "Lobby . . . the Australian Government." (CIMRA, 1979:27)

These recommendations are followed by names and addresses of aboriginal organizations, mining companies, and government offices that can be contacted.

International Development Action (IDA), founded in Australia in 1970 as a research organization, focuses on tribal land rights as a development issue. IDA calls itself a "development education group" and is funded by Australian religious charities, development aid, student and educational organizations. One of its early projects was an extended study of the role of multinational mining corporations in the expropriation of aboriginal lands on the Cape York Penninsula of Queensland, Australia. This research was carried out in close cooperation with the Aborigines, and the results were published in a series of monographs (Roberts, 1975; Roberts, Parsons, and Russell, 1975; Roberts and McLean 1976; Roberts, 1978). More recently IDA investigated the Purari hydro-electric scheme that would uproot thousands of Papua New Guinea tribal peoples so that massive amounts of electricity could be generated to enable Japanese companies to produce aluminum from the bauxite taken from tribal lands in the nearby Cape York Penninsula of Australia. IDA's New Guinea work was a joint effort between IDA and the Purari Action Group, a native New Guinea organization opposing the development project.

In their efforts to focus world attention on the problems of indigenous peoples, the international organizations arrange press conferences, sponsor lectures, and carry out ambitious publication programs. IWGIA, for example, has published over 40 separate documents reporting on conditions in Central and South America, Canada, Australia, India, and the Philippines. In addition, it publishes a newsletter in English and Spanish. These materials are distributed to some two thousand social scientists throughout the world, to indigenous organizations, and governments, special United Nations organizations, and to other interested international organizations. Organizations such as IWGIA operate on very small budgets with limited staffs. They support themselves through grants from philanthropic organizations and governments (IWGIA is heavily supported by Scandinavian governments), and from private donations and subscriptions.

Increasingly, these unique organizations have become important sources of funds to meet requests from indigenous political organizations

or to carry out specific projects in support of self-determination for
indigenous peoples. While the total amount of this aid is still very
modest, it represents a significant shift from traditional international aid
which often supports massive, inappropriate programs that may
adversely affect indigenous peoples. Ideally, the kinds of projects being
sponsored by these new organizations are small in scale and are usually
initiated and directed by the native peoples themselves. For example,
IWGIA has channeled funds to support conferences organized by
indigenous peoples and to help free imprisoned indigenous political
leaders. Together with Survival International, IWGIA has helped to
finance the operation of Indian organizations in Colombia and Ecuador.
Most of the funds ultimately originate from large foundations, charities,
and church aid organizations.

Regional Task Forces

The regional Liberal-Political task forces are relatively small, specialized,
sometimes temporary organizations concerned with indigenous peoples
in specific regions. These organizations are more likely to be involved
directly in field projects and more often represent special religious or
political interests than the international organizations. Depending on the
situation of local indigenous groups, the regional organizations may
work primarily to promote campaigns against specific government
policies and economic interests threatening native peoples; they may
assist native communities to acquire land titles and to secure financial
support; or they may carry out consciousness-raising projects to
strengthen native self defense movements. For example, Brazilian
anthropologists formed the Comissão Pró-Indio in 1978 to fight the
government's "emancipation" decree, but it quickly broadened its scope
to include the following objectives:

1. to support the Indian peoples in the efforts to reclaim and
   guarantee the inviolability of their lands, their permanent
   possession, the exclusive use of the natural wealth and of all the
   resources existing within them
2. to recognize, respect, and support their cultural autonomy and
   the right to self-determination, and the free organization of the
   Indian peoples (Nimuendaju, 1979, vol. 1, no. 1, my translation)

The Aboriginal Treaty Committee, a special Australian task force,
launched a national campaign in 1979 to persuade the Commonwealth
Government to acknowledge the priority of the aboriginal land claim and
to negotiate a treaty with aboriginal representatives. The Committee is
run by non-aboriginals who have been actively involved in aboriginal

affairs and is sponsored by 87 prominent Australians from professions representing a cross-section of the national society.

In South America there are many politically aligned regional support groups that are anxious to incorporate the native groups into the struggle to restructure their national governments along socialist lines. Seen from this perspective, indigenous peoples are simply part of the exploited peasantry and working classes, who happen to also be distinguished by language and customs. Furthermore, in many obvious cases, the powerful economic interests that are forcing native peoples off their lands often are supported by the political establishments that the socialists would like to replace. The political interests of these leftist support groups are sometimes very openly expressed. For example, a Colombian organization which publishes the newsletter, "Yavi: Support to the Indigenous Struggles," considers the Indian movement to be part of Colombia's revolutionary struggle against capitalist oppression. Their position is represented as follows:

> To modify the correlation of forces actually favorable to the classes in power, is a task of all the people. The unification of all the popular sectors, and among them the Indians, is a necessity. The role that the Indians play in this process depends on the unity and clarity that they have to obtain their specific claims in concert with the class struggle (Yavi, 1979, no. 4, p. 5, my translation).

In Peru, a support organization called COPAL proclaims "solidarity with the native groups," and works for political mobilization and defense of Indian lands in the Amazon region. Prior to the presidential elections of 1980, COPAL circulated a booklet among the forest Indians entitled "Know the Political Parties," in which they explained that the parties on the right represented the exploiters who wanted to take away Indian lands, while the leftist parties represented the natives, their rights to land, and their own cultures and organizations.

Since indigenous peoples do in fact share many common enemies, an alliance between them might seem very advantageous for both groups. Such an alliance might appear even more obvious because traditional native communities are highly "socialistic" with their communal land base and cooperative forms of production and distribution. However, a community-based tribal society is not the same as a socialist state, and one need not oppose state socialism to recognize that indigenous peoples do not automatically fare any better under socialism than under other forms of state organization. It is true that conditions for the Mapuche Indians in Chile improved under the socialist Allende government and they were dealt with harshly by the rightist military government that deposed Allande. But at the same time the Akawaio Indians of Guyana will be forced off their lands by a giant hydroelectric project under the sponsorship of a socialist government (Bennet, Colson, and Wavell, 1978). A socialist Indian policy recently proposed for Panama (Falla, 1979c:36-42) contains several principles that might worry Indian leaders. The proposed policy would acknowledge the justice of Indian land claims, but it would grant the state the right to expropriate Indian lands for development purposes for the "true good of the Panamanian community, to which the Indian also belongs" (Falla, 1979c:41). The new policy also envisioned a development program involving the concentration of the Indian population, highway construction, and the introduction of "improved" technology.

In some cases Indians have specifically rejected alliances with the political left because they feel that it represents a foreign ideology, which is as foreign to their cultural reality as Christianity. This viewpoint was well expressed by Ramiro Reynaga, a Bolivian Quechua and general coordinator of the Indian Council of South America, in the following terms:

> *The Andean political parties, all of them, of left and right,*
> *believe themselves destined to direct our movement . . . they want to*
> *detour it toward their immediate partisant advantage . . . Foreign*
> *theories will not unite the Indians . . . We will unite ourselves . . .*
> *around our ignored ancestral rights, around our own liberation*
> *objectives* (Reynaga, 1980:65-73, my translation).

This rejection of the leftist political orientation was also expressed by Russell Means, Lakota Indian and cofounder of the American Indian Movement, in a speech in 1980 to the Black Hills International Survival Gathering, as follows:

> *Revolutionary Marxism is committed to even further*
> *perpetuation and perfection of the very industrial process which is*
> *destroying us all* (Means, 1980:28).

There may be considerable justification for these native fears of politically aligned support groups. It is quite likely that national political parties will see no long-term interest in encouraging genuine self-determination for local indigenous populations. Some indication of this is the clear tendency of such organizations to work for the entitlement of relatively small individual community land holdings for indigenous peoples, rather than for more extensive regional holdings that would provide a realistic basis for cultural self-determination.

CHAPTER
TEN

In the following sections three regional task forces—Project North, CIMI, and the Marandu Project—are examined. These organizations represent respectively: a religious group that has allowed native groups to set the objectives; a religious group that retains its self interest; and a nonpolitical, nonreligious consciousness-raising group.

Project North

Project North was founded in Canada in 1975 as a coalition of several major denominations, and is an outstanding example of an effective interdenominational support group. The organization's principal objective is to strengthen native efforts to gain recognition of their land rights before the massive energy development projects planned for the north overwhelm them. The Project North group stresses that it is the moral obligation of southern Canadians to see that northern development will only be carried out if there is justice for the native population. The project sees its own role primarily as that of a task force to create a communication channel and serve as an intermediary between the native people of the north and the members of the churches they represent in the south, who make up nearly three fourths of the Canadian population. To this end, the Project North team maintains close contacts with the native organizations in the north and with a number of groups based in the south that oppose irresponsible northern development. The project publishes a newsletter and the staff confers directly with many official government bodies on these issues. Among the churches, they coordinate innumerable workshops, conferences, seminars, and special national campaigns, providing opportunities for native leaders to present their case as widely as possible and to rally popular support. One of their primary policy goals, to see a moratorium declared on major development projects until native claims could be fairly satisfied, was at least partially supported by the 1977 Berger Commission Report discussed earlier.

Perhaps the most significant aspect of Project North is that it represents a complete reversal of the missionary role. The "missionaries" are not trying to impose changes on the native peoples, but instead the natives are defining their own goals in terms of self-determination. Also, the church groups are attempting to bring about change within their own societies to help the native peoples realize their goals and in the process create a more just society for everyone. The connection between economic structures and consumption patterns in the dominant society and resource extraction and injustice in the north is clearly understood by the Project North team, as demonstrated by the following observation reprinted in a Project North pamphlet:

> *In the final analysis, what is required is nothing less than*
> *fundamental social change. Until we as a society begin to change our*
> *own life styles based on wealth and comfort, until we begin to change*
> *the profit-oriented priorities of our industrial system, we will continue*
> *placing exorbitant demands on the limited supplies of energy in the*
> *North and end up exploiting the people of the North in order to get*
> *those resources* (Roman Catholic Bishop's Labour Day Message,
> 1975).

CIMI

In Brazil, the *Conselho Indigenista Misionario* (CIMI, a predominantly Catholic group formed to promote Indian self-determination and land rights) has been an outspoken critic of FUNAI (the official Indian service) for its failure to adequately defend Indian interests. CIMI has fostered the political mobilization of Brazilian Indians by convening assemblies of Indian leaders from throughout the country. However, their defense program for the Indian, as outlined in a recent strategy statement (Suess, 1980), specifically rejects the possibility of a purely Indian self-defense movement, which they dismiss as a return to the past. In this respect CIMI seems to depart from the admonition of the Declaration of Barbados, "That Indians organize and lead their own liberation is essential, or it ceases to be liberating" (IWGIA Document No. 1, p. 7).

CIMI considers the Indian to be part of a struggle for global liberation in which their best hope is to join a triple alliance organized by the missionaries. This alliance would consist of Indians united with other Indians on the basis of their ethnic identity; Indians united with other oppressed peoples; and finally the Indians would unite with the church. It is not clear what kind of Indian culture would emerge from such an alliance, but the missionary-dominated ideological component and the self-interest are obvious. There is also a striking difference here between CIMI's view of itself as a leader in the Indian struggle and Project North's efforts to rally support for the expressed demands of native peoples from within the dominant society. It is certain that under CIMI's guidance Brazilian Indians have made very positive moves in recent years toward self-determination, but the missionaries remain a major factor in this movement. It is significant that a fully independent Indian movement does not yet exist in Brazil.

The Marandu Project

The Marandu Project was a unique program initiated in 1972 by Paraguayan anthropologists and local Indian leaders to encourage self-determination for the oppressed Indian groups in the Paraguayan Chaco along the lines suggested by the Declaration of Barbados. One of the primary organizers of the project was, in fact, a signer of the Barbados declaration. The consciousness-raising objectives of the project are clear in the following statement of philosophy:

> . . . the only way in which the Indian population will be able to achieve the long-term developments which will enable them to survive is by giving the Indians complete control of their destiny, as only they fully understand what their problems are and what they hope to achieve for the future (Renshaw, 1976:15).

The Marandu Project was designed for action on three levels: (1) with local Indian groups; (2) with the national Paraguayan society; and (3) with international support groups.

With the Indians, the primary focus of the project was a series of informational courses. This important function is implied in the name of the project itself, because in the Guarani language *marandu* means "giving information." The courses employed audio-visual techniques to convey factual information about the national society that the Indians needed in order to organize a more effective self defense, such as how to obtain identity cards, land titles, the formation of cooperatives, legal rights, etc. The project also included the establishment of an Indian Council, organized entirely by the Indians. The Council had complete control over the project itself and was envisioned to be the nucleus for a pan-Indian organization. The anthropologists associated with the project did not participate in the council's decision making and did not attend any council meetings in order to avoid any possibility of outside interference.

At the national level, the team used the mass media to combat anti-Indian attitudes and arranged mediation discussions between Indian leaders and local representatives of the national society. At the international level, contacts were maintained with support groups such as IWGIA and Survival International, which were able to obtain funds for the project.

It appears that the Marandu Project was well on the way to achieving its basic objectives when it was abruptly terminated by the Paraguayan government. In December 1975, four members of the staff were arrested. The Indian council was placed under the control of a newly created government Indigenist Institute where its role could be strictly limited. Paradoxically, in the end the project was accused of being both CIA and communist inspired, and it was obvious that the ruling powers in the country felt that letting Indians actually control their futures was somehow subversive (Renshaw, 1976; Temple, 1977; Chase-Sardi and Colombres, 1975).

THE PRIMITIVIST-
ENVIRONMENTALIST APPROACH

The disappearance of these ways of life is not inevitable,
but can become so in the absence of deliberate policies intended to
maintain them. (Dasmann, 1973:29)

The Primitivist-Environmentalist orientation combines the conservation concerns of environmentalists with what could be called a primitivist anthropological perspective. It advocates the establishment of large, permanently protected zones where natural ecosystems and the traditional peoples adapted to them would not be disturbed or exploited by outsiders. Such a course of action was recommended by a group of ecologists at the 1972 United Nations Stockholm conference on the Human Environment (Goldsmith, 1972), and was endorsed by the 12th general assembly of the International Union for Conservation of Nature and Natural Resources, the IUCN, at Kinshasa, Zaire in 1975 (IUCN Bulletin, 6(11), special supplement). The IUCN even recognizes a land category that it refers to as *protected anthropological areas*, which would be specifically set up to allow a given people to "continue traditional ways of life" (Dasmann, 1973). However, there are no organizations dedicated exclusively to the establishment of cultural sanctuaries; in general this approach has found little favor with organizations directly concerned with indigenous peoples. Only one such organization, Tribal Life Fund, founded in Brussels in 1978, lists "diplomatic approaches toward the creation of internationally protected zones" as one of its objectives (Tribal, March 1979).

Support for tribal peoples by environmentalists is a relatively new and significant development. In the past, traditional subsistence use within nature preserves and parks was often banned as "unnatural" and traditional occupants were forcibly removed. This happened, for example, to the IK in Uganda (see page 109). However, environmentalists have increasingly recognized that traditional cultures can exist in relative balance with natural ecosystems and environmental organizations have aligned themselves with indigenous peoples in opposition to the outside exploitation of tribal lands. For example, in 1978 environmentalists joined the Sami effort to block the Alta hydroelectric project in northern Norway which would flood one of the largest undeveloped river valleys in Scandinavia and disrupt Sami reindeer herding. Environmentalists also criticized the Jonglei Canal project which would adversely affect the Nilotic pastoralists in the southern Sudan, and they have supported the resistance of native peoples to uranium mining on tribal lands in Australia, Canada, Greenland, and the United States.

The principal concern of the Primitivist-Environmentalist position is to defend a particular culture type or "way of life" that is considered to be a positive value in itself. This idealized culture type is characterized by egalitarian social systems and predominantly nonmarket, low energy, subsistence economies dependent on local ecosystems. As we have seen in Chapter 9, this culture type corresponds closely to the common self-identity presented by many spokesmen for the indigenous peoples movement, even though there is little agreement on acceptable labels. Cultures of this type may be designated *primitive* in the sense that they perpetuate key elements of the *earliest* or *primary* cultures that originated thousands of years prior to the emergence of stratified cultures. The term *primitive* or "ecosystem" culture (Dasmann, 1975) may also be used to emphasize the adaptive environmental success of these original cultures and their relative superiority to industrial civilization in this respect (Bodley, 1976:25-55). Given the positive features of such cultures, it is also assumed that they will continue to exist, as they have in the past, if given the chance. Their disappearance is only inevitable if the presently dominant industrial cultures choose to eliminate them.

The basic premise that primitive cultures are a superior adaptation that need not disappear, and the special emphasis on culture or culture type, are important Primitivist-Environmentalist viewpoints that are frequently attacked by partisans of both Liberal-Political and Conservative-Humanitarian orientations. Supporters of these latter approaches may consider the Primitivist-Environmentalist stress on culture to be dehumanizing objectification because such an emphasis tends to ignore the individuals within traditional cultures that might actually desire change, or because a static, idealized concept of culture provides an inadequate basis for progressive political struggle (Aaby, 1977; Turner, 1979). Some critics feel that culture is an irrelevant issue in this context because it is difficult to define "abstraction" (Hippler, 1979:348), or they object to the implicit "romanticism" in the primitivist view. These arguments disregard the fact that primitivists do recognize dynamic processes within primitive cultures. It is also perfectly possible to "objectify" culture by recognizing the importance of culture types, without simultaneously "dehumanizing" the people who are inseparable parts of cultural systems. However, an emphasis on people, as distinct from culture, leads naturally to objectives such as liberation, decolonization, and the preservation of ethnic identity. It also implies strategies involving political mobilization and humanitarian assistance programs. On the other hand, stressing the concept of primitive culture leads immediately to objectives and strategies that would preserve the material conditions that would ensure the persistence of primitive cultures for those desiring that alternative.

The Primitivist-Environmentalist viewpoint does in fact reject the frequent Liberal-Political argument that *all* traditional peoples must learn about the dominant society and mobilize themselves politically for "self-determination." Instead, it is argued that what is needed is restraint on the part of the international community and what could be called *zoning restrictions* to maintain the conditions permitting the continuation of traditional cultures. From the Primitivist-Environmentalist perspective, there must be deliberate decisions by national states to pursue such policies, but the primary political struggle to achieve them must be carried out by political organizations and individuals already integrated into national societies. The few surviving, fully traditional, self-sufficient cultures should not be compelled into politicalization and "consciousness-raising" in order to ensure their own survival because paradoxically the mobilization process itself can undermine self-reliance. Furthermore, the actual political power of these peoples, given their numerical weakness, is likely to be too small to outweigh the potential cultural costs that they might incur while seeking that power. Of course, the existing indigenous political organizations discussed in Chapter 9 are playing a dominant role in the overall struggle to insure the independent existence of radically diverse cultures. But it must be remembered that these organizations arise out of cultures that have already been seriously disrupted and are at a point where the advantages of political mobilization are obvious.

There are many other objections to a cultural sanctuary approach (see also Bodley, 1977). Some might argue that it is racist, or discriminatory, because it would give some peoples preferential access to resources because of their ancestry. This can perhaps best be answered by pointing out that it is *culture* or way of life that is the critical criteria here, not racial ancestry *per se*. The real issue is zoning by type of use, and peoples who could establish a certain type of prior use would be favored over others. This would indeed be discriminatory, as is any land use regulation, but it would not be *racial* discrimination.

Others might object that traditional peoples living within environmental sanctuaries would be denied actual ownership and would thus be placed in a new colonial situation. They would not be given clear property titles to the lands they occupied, but would only hold limited

FIGURE 21. *A traditionally oriented Campa family in the Gran Pajonal of the Peruvian Amazon. Tribal peoples should be given the option of pursuing their traditional cultures.* (K. M. Bodley)

use rights. This would be true, but use rights do constitute the essence of collective traditional ownership, and these would be assured.

In spite of the intense criticisms that are often raised against it, the Primitivist-Environmentalist philosophy has at least partially inspired a few recent attempts to establish combined culture-environment sanctuaries. Potentially, there are many possible applications of this general approach to cultural protection, and in order to illustrate this possible diversity, the following three specific examples will be briefly examined; the Xingu Park in Brazil, the Manu Park in Peru, and the Kobuk Valley National Monument in Alaska.

The Xingu Experiment

The Xingu National Park in Brazil was the first and most famous attempt to protect tribal cultures by deliberately restricting entry into their area and by prohibiting exploitation of tribal resources by outsiders. This case is often cited as an example of the futility of isolationist policies and it has even been condemned as a "human zoo" approach, but it can also be interpreted as a noble and very successful experiment. Whichever viewpoint one wishes to take, there can be no doubt that by 1970, after nearly ten years of park administration that effectively held back the frontier, some 1,500 Indians of 14 distinct tribes were thriving, while countless groups in other areas were threatened with extinction.

Because of the extreme natural isolation of their territory, the Xingu Indians were not in permanent contact with members of the national society until 1946 when an expedition led by the Villas Boas brothers established an outpost in the area as the first phase of the government's planned development program. The Villas Boas brothers had great respect for the Indians and admiration for their way of life. They also knew what the advancing frontier would do to the Indians and decided to remain in the Xingu and work to safeguard the traditional Indian way of life by maintaining the original isolation of their natural environment. The brothers were not opposed to communication as such between Indians and civilization, but they felt that Brazilian society was simply not ready to coexist on equal terms with the Indian. As they explain:

> In our modest opinion, the true defense of the Indian is to respect him and to guarantee his existence according to his own values. Until we, the "civilized" ones, create the proper conditions among ourselves for the future integration of the Indians, any attempt to integrate them is the same as introducing a plan for their destruction. We are not yet sufficiently prepared (Orlando and Claudio Villas Boas, 1973:vii).

The protection policy envisioned by the Villas Boas brothers took the form of the national park established in 1961 and administered directly by them until 1974. The Villas Boas brothers pursued a program of strict noninterference in the internal affairs of the Indians, even to the extent of not intervening in such matters as witch killings. However, they did make western medicine available to the Indians in order to prevent the disastrous mortality being caused by accidentally introduced epidemic diseases, and they distributed certain useful manufactured articles that were already highly prized by the Indians. At the same time they prohibited alcohol, casual tourism, missionary work, and formal schooling within the park, and they discouraged the use of cash and the introduction of most exotic consumer goods. Only two small posts were maintained in the park with a total staff in 1967 of only nine persons to supervise the medical program and regulate visitors; no other permanent residence by outsiders was permitted. Anthropological research was allowed however, and during a two and a half year period in the 1960's some 370 people visited the park, most staying only a few days (Agostinho da Silva, 1972; Junqueira, 1973).

Critics of the park point out that the distribution of metal tools by the post is potentially manipulative and has created economic dependency. However, relations with the outside world have not been exploitative and seem not to have altered the traditional socioeconomic system in any significant way. Charges that the park officials have prohibited Indians from leaving seem to have little foundation. As long as the quality of life inside the park remains high, the outside remains relatively unattractive. So far only social outcasts would even contemplate the "social suicide" that leaving would mean (Gregor, 1977:215). Those who have gone out have been apalled at what they see. For example, a Waura Indian, after spending a week in São Paulo for medical treatment, could not imagine why his anthropologist companion, who had just spent two years in the Xingu, would ever prefer São Paulo to the Xingu. The Waura asked in dismay: "How could you return to this world after seeing how we live?" (Brecher, 1973:xi).

Unfortunately, the success of the Xingu experiment ultimately depended on the willingness of the Brazilian government to restrain the pressures for its dissolution. For many years the Xingu park served the government as a brilliant showpiece to divert international attention from some of the more glaring deficiencies of Brazil's Indian policies. However, in 1971 the government made the political decision to permit a highway to be constructed across the northern third of the park and thereby opened the way for invasion. By 1980 ranchers were encroaching on the park in several areas, and the Xingu Indians were beginning to kill the intruders in order to defend their lands (ARC Bulletin No. 3, 1980:9–10). These recent events could certainly be used to argue that protective isolation cannot succeed, but perhaps the real significance of the Xingu experience is that it demonstrates that traditional tribal cultures can thrive as long as they are given the chance.

The Manu Park

The policies developed for the administration of the Manu Park in the tropical forests of southeastern Peru would potentially allow for different degrees of contact between tribal peoples and the national society within an overall context of environmental protection. In contrast to the Xingu Park, which was intended specifically for Indian protection, the Manu Park was officially established in 1973 as a nature preserve for scientific research and tourism. The fact that there were Indians living in the area had no bearing on the original decision to establish the park. The park itself comprises an area of over 15,000 square kilometers and is situated within a much larger region that has so far largely escaped development and has been only superficially explored. When the park was first designated as a "reserved" area in 1968, preliminary exploration revealed that several groups of uncontacted and defensively hostile Indians existed in the proposed park area. Some of these groups were so independent that they continued to use stone axes. At the other extreme there was a small village of Machiguenga Indians concentrated around a school founded by SIL missionaries in 1963 (d'Ans, 1972, 1980).

The original guidelines proposed for the park recommended a zoning policy that would permit undisturbed traditional occupation by the Indians as long as they did not use guns, engage in commerical exploitation of their resources, or otherwise threaten the environment. The regions occupied by the most isolated Indians were to be designated "anthropological areas" with the main entry points protected by guard posts, but they were to be otherwise left alone. The settled Machiguenga were to be alloted special hunting grounds from which visitors were to be excluded, and those that wished to participate in market hunting, logging, or cash cropping were to be provided with lands in a "buffer zone" adjacent to the park and protected by park personnel (d'Ans, 1980; Jungius, 1976). Except for the restriction on commercial activities, the Indians within the park were to be given complete freedom, and the mission-oriented village was allowed to remain. However, the SIL found these conditions unacceptable, and soon withdrew from the park, taking half of the Machiguenga villagers with them. Those that remained returned to their more traditional dispersed settlements (d'Ans, 1980).

The Manu Park in many ways might seem to be an ideal approach, but it depends on adequate funding to regulate entry and prevent abuses of park regulations. In 1972 there were only eight guards and an annual budget of a mere $34,000 (Harroy, 1972:77). Furthermore, there must be a willingness on the part of the park administration to maintain its enlightened policy toward the Indians, in the face of strong pressures to remove the Indians and promote extensive tourism. Unfortunately, by 1975 there were clear indications of official "indifference" toward the Indians, and it was unclear whether or not the original policies would really be seriously pursued.

The Kobuk National Monument

In 1980 President Carter signed into law the Alaska Conservation Act, placing over 422,000 square kilometers of land, an area larger than the state of California, into protected conservation areas. A unique feature of this act was that it permitted subsistence hunting and fishing to continue, and these traditional activities were given priority over sport and commercial uses. The Kobuk Valley National Monument, one of the nine new conservation areas, was specifically designed to "foster the continuation of the Alaska Eskimo culture by providing for traditional resource uses" (U.S. Interior Department, 1975:5). In the environmental impact statement prepared in support of the proposed Kobuk monument, it was argued that prohibiting subsistence use by the approximately 1,000 Eskimo people immediately dependent on the 7,500-square-kilometer area for caribou, fish, and other resources, would leave the Eskimo embittered, reduce their quality of life, and make them more dependent on welfare. It was also argued that eliminating subsistence use of the monument would upset the natural ecosystem, because the present culture represented 700 years of successful continuous participation in the environment, and it would only be replaced by some form of artificial management.

In contrast to both the Xingu and Manu parks, the Kobuk monument would permit the use of guns and motorized transport (snowmobiles) by the natives, as well as the limited sale of trapped furs. These policies recognize that the Kobuk Valley Eskimo have incorporated many exotic technological items into their culture since their first direct contact with western civilization in 1884. However, these new items, and even the partial dependence on the cash economy, appear not to have altered the traditional subsistence economy or the basic culture in any significant way (Anderson et al., 1977:652-653). Establishment of the monument would prevent mining, road building, sport hunting, and settlement in the area, and it would therefore provide the native population with the opportunity to continue their traditional subsistence way of life (U.S. Interior Department, 1975:136). In this case there is no question of people being kept in isolation to preserve their culture, possibly against their will. The Kobuk Valley Eskimo live primarily in villages outside of the monument, and are certainly not being forced to maintain their culture. The Interior Department explained its position as follows:

> *The NPS (National Park Service) will make the monument area available for subsistence pursuits, but it would not dictate to residents of the region what kind of lifestyle, cash or subsistence, they may pursue (U.S. Interior Department, 1975:379).*

APPENDIX A
ORGANIZATIONS AND PERIODICALS

In this Appendix I have compiled a selection of contemporary organizations concerned with the present situation of indigenous peoples and some of the important periodicals that they publish. Current addresses are listed for anyone who might wish to contact these organizations or subscribe to their periodicals.

PERIODICALS PUBLISHED BY INDIGENOUS PEOPLES

AKWESASNE NOTES

Mohawk Nation
via Rooseveltown, NY 13683

CHICHAM

Federación Shuar
Domingo Comín 17–38
Sucua, Ecuador

LAND RIGHTS NEWS (published by the Northern Land Council)

P.O. Box 3046
Darwin, NT 5794
Australia

MESSAGESTICK

North Queensland Land Council
P.P. Box 1429
Cairns, North Queensland 4870
Australia

NATIVE PRESS

P.O. Box 1919
Yellowknife, NWT
XOE 1 HO
CANADA

UNIDAD INDIGENA

Apartado Aereo 3239
Bogata, Colombia

SUPPORT ORGANIZATIONS

The Anti-Slavery Society/Aborigines Protection Society

60 Weymouth Street
London W1N 4DX
England

ARC, Anthropology Resource Center

59 Temple Place, Suite 444
Boston, Massachusetts 02111
Publishes *ARC Newsletter* as well as a series of specialized
monographs. Also publishes the *ARC Bulletin,* which is devoted
exclusively to the current situation of Brazilian Indians.

Canadian Association in Support of the Native Peoples

Publishes *CASNP Bulletin.*

CIMI, Conselho Indigenista Misionario

Avenida Joaquim Nabuco 1023
Caixa Postal 984–6900 Manaus
Amazonas, Brazil
Publishes *Porantim* newspaper and special bulletins concerned with
Brazilian Indians.

CIMRA, Colonialism and Indigenous Minorities Research/Action

92 Plimsoll Road
London N.4. England
Publishes *Natural People News.*

CIPA, Centro de Investigacion y Promocion Amazonica

Ricardo Palma 666–D
Lima 18, Peru
Special publications devoted to Peruvian Amazon Indians.

Comissaõ Pro-Indio

A/c de Setor de Antropologia
Departamento de Ciençias Sociais
Universidade de São Paulo (USP)
C.P. 8105, São Paulo
Brasil
Publishes news bulletin, *Nimuendaju*.

Boletin COPAL

Santa Isabel 180
Miraflores, Lima
Peru
Journal devoted to Peruvian Amazon Indians.

Cultural Survival

11 Divinity Avenue
Cambridge, Massachusetts 02138
Publishes *Cultural Survival Newsletter*.

Gesellschaft für bedohte Völker

P.O. Box 159
D–3400 Gottingen
W. Germany
German section of *Survival International*. Publishes German language newsmagazine, *POGROM*, as well as many special monographs.

IDA, International Development Action

73 Little George St.
Fitzroy 3065
Victoria, Australia
Specialized publications and a newsletter, concerned primarily with Australia and the Pacific.

IWGIA, International Work Group for Indigenous Affairs

Fiolstraede 10
DK–1171
Copenhagen, K—Denmark
Publishes *IWGIA Newsletter* (English and Spanish) and extensive document series and other specialized materials.

Project North

154 Glenrose Ave.
Toronto, Ontario
M4T 1K8, Canada
The Interchurch Project on Northern Development. Publishes *Project North Newsletter.* Concerned with development and native rights in Canada.

Survival International

36 Craven Street
London WC2N, 5NG
England
Publishes *Survival International Newsletter* as well as special document series.

Tribal Life Fund

Avenue du Fort Jaco 80
1180 Bruxelles, Belgium
Publishes journal *Tribal.*

WCIP, World Council of Indigenous Peoples

WCIP-Secretariat
Suite B-844
University of Lethbridge
Lethbridge, Alberta
Canada T1K 3M4

YAVI

Apartado Aereo 14789
Bogata, Colombia
Newsletter in Spanish, concerned with Indians in Colombia.

APPENDIX B
WORLD COUNCIL OF CHURCHES
Programme to Combat Racism
PCR 1/71 (E)
Declaration of Barbados*

FOR THE LIBERATION OF THE INDIANS

The anthropologists participating in the Symposium on Inter-Ethnic Conflict in South America, meeting in Barbados, January 25–30 1971, after analyzing the formal reports of the tribal populations' situation in several countries, drafted and agreed to make public the following statement. In this manner, we hope to define and clarify this critical problem of the American continent and to contribute to the Indian struggle for liberation.

The Indians of America remain dominated by a colonial situation which originated with the conquest and which persists today within many Latin American nations. The result of this colonial structure is that lands inhabited by Indians are judged to be free and unoccupied territory open to conquest and colonization. Colonial domination of the aboriginal groups, however, is only a reflection of the more generalized system of the Latin American states' external dependence upon the imperialist metropolitan powers. The internal order of our dependent countries leads them to act as colonizing powers in their relations with the indigenous peoples. This places the several nations in the dual role of the exploited and the exploiters, and this in turn projects not only a false image of

"The Barbados Symposium was sponsored jointly by the Programme to Combat Racism and the Churches Commission on International Affairs of the World Council of Churches, together with the Ethnology Department of the University of Berne (Switzerland). A report of the Symposium is in preparation. The views expressed are those of the members of the Symposium, and not necessarily those of the co-sponsors of the Symposium.

Indian society and its historical development, but also a distorted vision of what constitutes the present national society.

We have seen that this situation manifests itself in repeated acts of aggression directed against the aboriginal groups and cultures. There occur both active interventions to "protect" Indian society as well as massacres and forced migrations from the homelands. These acts and policies are not unknown to the armed forces and other governmental agencies in several countries. Even the official "Indian policies" of the Latin-American states are explicitly directed towards the destruction of aboriginal culture. These policies are employed to manipulate and control Indian populations in order to consolidate the status of existing social groups and classes, and only diminish the possibility that Indian society may free itself from colonial domination and settle its own future.

As a consequence, we feel the several States, the religious missions and social scientists, primarily anthropologists, must assume the unavoidable responsibilities for immediate action to halt this aggression and contribute significantly to the process of Indian liberation.

The Responsibility of the State

Irrelevant are those Indian policy proposals that do not seek a radical break with the existing social situation; namely, the termination of colonial relationships, internal and external; breaking down of the class system of human exploitation and ethnic domination; a displacement of economic and political power from a limited group or an oligarchic minority to the popular majority; the creation of a truly multi-ethnic state in which each ethnic group possesses the right to self-determination and the free selection of available social and cultural alternatives.

Our analysis of the Indian policy of the several Latin American nation states reveals a common failure of this policy by its omissions and by its actions. The several states avoid granting protection to the Indian groups' rights to land and to be left alone, and fail to apply the law strictly with regard to areas of national expansion. Similarly, the states sanction policies which have been and continue to be colonial and class oriented.

This failure implicates the State in direct responsibility for and connivance with the many crimes of genocide and ethnocide that we have been able to verify. These crimes tend to be repeated and responsibility must rest with the State which remains reluctant to take the following essential measures:

1. Guaranteeing to all the Indian populations by virtue of their ethnic distinction, the right to be and to remain themselves,

living according to their own customs and moral order, free to
develop their own culture;

2. Recognition that Indian groups possess rights prior to those of
   other national constituencies. The State must recognize and
   guarantee each Indian society's territory in land, legalizing it as
   perpetual, inalienable collective property, sufficiently extensive
   to provide for population growth;

3. Sanctioning of Indian groups' right to organize and to govern in
   accordance with their own traditions. Such a policy would not
   exclude members of Indian society from exercising full citizenship, but would in turn exempt them from compliance with those
   obligations that jeopardize their cultural integrity.

4. Extending to Indian society the same economic, social, educational and health assistance as the rest of the national population
   receives. Moreover, the State has an obligation to attend to those
   many deficiencies and needs that stem from Indians' submission
   of the colonial situation. Above all the State must impede their
   further exploitation by other sectors of the national society,
   including the official agents of their protection.

5. Establishing contacts with still isolated tribal groups is the States'
   responsibility, given the dangers—biological, social and ecological—that their first contact with agents of the national society
   represents.

6. Protection from the crimes and outrages, not always the direct
   responsibility of civil or military personnel, intrinsic to the
   expansion process of the national frontier.

7. Definition of the national public authority responsible for relations with Indian groups inhabiting its territory; this obligation cannot be transferred or delegated at any time or under any
   circumstances.

Responsibility of the Religious Missions

Evangelization, the work of the religious missions in Latin America also
reflects and complements the reigning colonial situation with the values
of which it is imbued. The missionary presence has always implied the
imposition of criteria and patterns of thought and behavior alien to the
colonized Indian societies. A religious pretext has too often justified the
economic and human exploitation of the aboriginal population.

The inherent ethnocentric aspect of the evangelization process is
also a component of the colonialist ideology and is based on the following
characteristics:

1. Its essentially discriminatory nature implicit in the hostile relationship to Indian culture conceived as pagan and heretical;
2. Its vicarial aspect, implying the reidentification of the Indian and his consequent submission in exchange for future supernatural compensations;
3. Its spurious quality given the common situation of missionaries seeking only some form of personal salvation, material or spiritual;
4. The fact that the missions have become a great land and labour enterprise, in conjunction with the dominant imperial interests.

As a result of this analysis we conclude that the suspension of all missionary activity is the most appropriate policy on behalf of both Indian society as well as the moral integrity of the churches involved. Until this objective can be realized the missions must support and contribute to Indian liberation in the following manner:

1. Overcome the intrinsic Herodianism of the evangelical process, itself a mechanism of colonialization, Europeanization and alienation of Indian society;
2. Assume a position of true respect for Indian culture, ending the long and shameful history of despotism and intolerance characteristic of missionary work, which rarely manifests sensitivity to aboriginal religious sentiments and values;
3. Halt both the theft of Indian property by religious missionaries who appropriate labor, lands and natural resources as their own, and the indifference in the face of Indian expropriation by third parties;
4. Extinguish the sumptuous and lavish spirit of the missions themselves, expressed in various forms but all too often based on exploitation of Indian labor.
5. Stop the competition among religious groups and confessions for Indian souls—a common occurrence leading to the buying and selling of believers and internal strife provoked by conflicting religious loyalties;
6. Suppress the secular practice of removing Indian children from their families for long periods in boarding schools where they are imbued with values not their own, converting them in this way into marginal individuals, incapable of living either in the larger national society or their native communities;
7. Break with the pseudo-moralist isolation which imposes a false puritanical ethic, incapacitating the Indian for coping with the national society—an ethic which the churches have been unable to impose on that same national society;

8. Abandon those blackmail procedures implicit in the offering of goods and services to Indian society in return for total submission;

9. Suspend immediately all practices of population displacement or concentration in order to evangelize and assimilate more effectively, a process that often provokes an increase in morbidity, mortality and family disorganization among Indian communities;

10. End the criminal practice of serving as intermediaries for the exploitation of Indian labor.

To the degree that the religious missions do not assume these minimal obligations they, too, must be held responsible by default for crimes of ethnocide and connivance with genocide.

Finally, we recognize that, recently, dissident elements within the churches are engaging in a conscious and radical self-evaluation of the evangelical process. The denunciation of the historical failure of the missionary task is now a common conclusion of such critical analyses.

The Responsibility of Anthropology

Anthropology took form within and became an instrument of colonial domination, openly or surreptitiously; it has often rationalized and justified in scientific language the domination of some people by others. The discipline has continued to supply information and methods of action useful for maintaining, reaffirming and disguising social relations of a colonial nature. Latin America has been and is no exception, and with growing frequency we note nefarious Indian action programmes and the dissemination of stereotypes and myths distorting and masking the Indian situation—all pretending to have their basis in alleged scientific anthropological research.

A false awareness of this situation has led many anthropologists to adopt equivocal positions. These might be classed in the following types:

1. A *scientism* which negates any relationship between academic research and the future of those peoples who form the object of such investigation, thus eschewing political responsibility which the relation contains and implies;

2. An *hyprocrisy* manifest in the rhetorical protestation based on first principles which skillfully avoids any commitment in a concrete situation;

3. An *opportunism* that although it may recognize the present painful situation of the Indian, at the same time rejects any possibility of

transforming action by proposing the need "to do something" within the established order. This latter position, of course, only reaffirms and continues the system.

The anthropology now required in Latin America is not that which relates to Indians as objects of study, but rather that which perceives the colonial situation and commits itself to the struggle for liberation. In this context we see anthropology providing on the one hand, the colonised peoples those data and interpretations both about themselves and their colonizers useful for their own fight for freedom, and on the other hand, a redefinition of the distorted image of Indian communities extant in the national society, thereby unmasking its colonial nature with its supportive ideology.

In order to realise the above objectives, anthropologists have an obligation to take advantage of all junctures within the present order to take action on behalf of the Indian communities. Anthropologists must denounce systematically by any and all means cases of genocide and those practices conducive to ethnocide. At the same time, it is imperative to generate new concepts and explanatory categories from the local and national social reality in order to overcome the subordinate situation of the anthropologist regarded as the mere "verifier" of alien theories.

The Indian as an Agent of his own Destiny

That Indians organize and lead their own liberation movement is essential, or it ceases to be liberating. When non-Indians pretend to represent Indians, even on occasion assuming the leadership of the latter's groups, a new colonial situation is established. This is yet another expropriation of the Indian populations' inalienable right to determine their future.

Within this perspective, it is important to emphasize in all its historical significance, the growing ethnic consciousness observable at present among Indian societies throughout the continent. More peoples are assuming direct control over their defense against the ethnocidal and genocidal policies of the national society. In this conflict, by no means novel, we can perceive the beginnings of a Pan-Latin-American movement and some cases too, of explicit solidarity with still other oppressed social groups.

We wish to reaffirm here the right of Indian populations to experiment with and adopt their own self-governing development and defense programmes. These policies should not be forced to correspond with national economic and socio-political exigencies of the moment. Rather, the transformation of national society is not possible if there remain groups, such as Indians, who do not feel free to command their own destiny. Then, too, the maintenance of Indian society's cultural and social integrity, regardless of its relative numerical insignificance, offers alternative approaches to the traditional well-trodden paths of the national society.

Barbados, 30 January 1971

Miguel Alberto Bartolome—Argentina   *Darcy Ribeiro—Brazil*

Guillermo Bonfil Batalla—Mexico   *Scott S. Robinson—USA*

Victor Daniel Bonilla—Colombia   *Stefano Varese—Peru*

Gonzalo Castillo Cardenas—Colombia   *Nelly Arvelo de Jiminez—Venezuela*

Miguel Chase Sardi—Paraguay   *Esteban Emilio Mosonyi—Venezuela*

Georg Grünberg—Switzerland

APPENDIX C

UNITED NATIONS DECLARATION AND PROGRAMME OF ACTION TO COMBAT RACISM AND RACIAL DISCRIMINATION, GENEVA, 1978

Declaration, Article 21:

> 21.   *The Conference endorses the right of indigenous peoples to maintain their traditional structure of economy and culture, including their own language, and also recognizes the special relationship of indigenous peoples to their land and stresses that their land, land rights and natural resources should not be taken away from them;*

PROGRAMME OF ACTION

Measures at the National Level (Articles 8–11)

8. The Conference urges States to recognize the following rights of indigenous peoples:

 (a) To call themselves by their proper name and to express freely their ethnic, cultural and other characteristics;

 (b) To have an official status and to form their own representative organization;

 (c) To carry on within their areas of settlement their traditional structure of economy and way of life; this should in no way affect their right to participate freely on an equal basis in the economic, social and political development of the country;

 (d) To maintain and use their own language, wherever possible, for administration and education;

 (e) To receive education and information in their own language, with due regard to their needs as expressed by themselves, and to disseminate information regarding their needs and problems.

9. Funds should be made available by the authorities for investments, the uses of which are to be determined with the participation of the indigenous peoples themselves, in the economic life of the areas concerned, as well as in all spheres of cultural activity.

10. The Conference urges States to allow indigenous peoples within their territories to develop cultural and social links with their own kith and kin everywhere with strict respect for the sovereignty, territorial integrity and political independence and non-interference in the internal affairs of those countries in which the indigenous peoples live.

11. The Conference further urges States to facilitate and support the establishment of representative international organizations for indigenous peoples, through which they can share experiences and promote common interests.

APPENDIX D
WORLD COUNCIL OF INDIGENOUS PEOPLES SECOND GENERAL ASSEMBLY KIRUNA, SWEDEN, AUGUST 24–27, 1977

DECLARATION ON HUMAN RIGHTS

The Indigenous Delegates present at the Second General Assembly of the World Council of Indigenous Peoples, assembling at Kiruna, Samiland, Sweden, have studied the Universal Declaration of the United Nations on Human Rights and other international agreements and, having analysed our present situation as aboriginals, we submit to the opinion of the world the following:

Declaration

We have surveyed those areas were (sic) invaded by the Europeans. To make their intrusion they used various means: direct or indirect violence, fraud and manipulation. These were the methods they used to occupy the land of the indigenous populations and acquire titles to such property which was rightfully owned by the aboriginals. These infamous conditions still prevail as of today, without any consideration to the fundamental declarations of the United Nations on Human Rights.

The most important ones are the Declaration of the General Assembly of 1948 and United Nations Convention on the Abolishment of all forms of Racial Discrimination.

Here is not the question of ordinary political persecution, but of the white man's use of medieval methods to encroach upon and exterminate the indigenous peoples and take over their lands. This is possible thanks

231

to the complicity between the land owners, the multinational companies, and the governments.

Through our own members and individuals as well as international organizations, the World Council of Indigenous Peoples has received documented reports, at the First as well as at the Second General Assembly, of daily violations against indigenous groups and individuals. These are violations aimed at the most elementary needs which are denied and the human rights such as we understand them and as they have been explained by the official agencies of the United Nations.

This applies in particular to the greater part of South America, where the conditions have been described as especially severe. Outright massacres have taken place, in the style of those enacted by the conquerors and usurpers, in the 15th and 16th centuries. People have been imprisoned without legal cause, they have been tortured and murdered. In this way almost all the articles in the Convention of 1948 have been violated.

Even participation in the World Council for Indigenous Peoples has constituted grounds for imprisonment, torture, loss of civil rights, and expulsion.

No less serious is the inclination of certain states to deny the indigenous population, in groups or as individuals, the right to land and water. These are the fundamental resources for human life and prerequisites to an indigenous development of their own institutions, culture and language. All this also constitutes principles which have been manifested in international conventions:

1. International Convention on Economic, Social and Cultural Rights
2. The International Labour Organization's Convention No. 107
3. International Convention on Civil and Political Rights

Fundamental Principle

The World Council of Indigenous Peoples upholds, as a fundamental principle, that the Indigenous Peoples are the rightful owners of the land, whether they hold formal title deeds, issued by the colonists and usurpers, or not. It is, anyway, up to the colonists, usurpers, and intruders to submit evidence to their title, and this should be required on the part of the aboriginals. This principle should be considered as a fundamental element of legal justice.

I. All those Conventions and Declarations on the Human Rights which have been approved in the United Nations or in other international bodies by the representatives of the National

Government, are not adhered to because the United Nations has no mandatory power nor are the member states particularly keen on realising them in practice. These conventions, furthermore, do not take account of the true situation and rights of the Indigenous Peoples.

II. We, therefore, wish to make clear those irrevocable and inborn rights which are due to us in our capacity as Aboriginals:

1. Right to self-determination;
2. Right to maintain our culture, language and traditions in freedom;
3. Right to have the World Council of Indigenous Peoples as a United Nations member, representing our people;
4. Right to recover the land which rightfully and according to millenary tradition belongs to us, but has been robbed from us by the foreign intruders;
5. Right to occupy land collectively with sole rights as something irrevocable and nontransferable;
6. Right to organize ourselves and administer our land and natural resources;
7. Right to demand from the governments of the countries sufficient land to improve the conditions of the Indigenous communities and promote their development under their own tutorship;
8. Right to make use of the natural resources exisent in the areas of the indigenous peoples, such as forests, rivers, ore deposits and the riches of the sea, and a right for the indigenous people to take part in the project and construction work and the use of it;
9. Right to demand the states that such laws are passed, that will be of benefit to the Indigenous People, particularly for the protection of their right to land ownership, recognizing representative aboriginal organizations and their full involvement in the process of making laws;
10. Right to secure requisite funds for the Indigenous Peoples from the individual countries to be used for agrarian and natural resources development;
11. Right to acquire a share in the funds accruing from the member states to the United Nations, either through a project or directly, and right to exchange technical and scientific information between the Indigenous Populations of different countries;
12. Right to subsidies from governmental or international economic institutions through the granting of long-term credit at low interest;

13. Right to respect our Indigenous culture in all its modes of expression, for the protection of which appropriate by-laws should be passed;
14. Right to an appropriate education in accordance with our culture and our traditions, without any foreign elements and within the framework of an educational system which recognizes the values of our culture and acknowledges an official status to our language at all educational levels.

The Second General Assembly of the World Council of Indigenous Peoples addresses itself to all the peoples of the world, to individuals and to nations, to the United Nations and all its agencies, and to other international organizations, with an urgent appeal that all the violent actions and measure against indigenous peoples, as related above, be immediately brought to an end.

The World Council of Indigenous Peoples requests all its members to exert strong pressure wherever possible on the agencies in their respective countries, to make those agencies co-operate with international organizations to ensure that the inhuman conditions of Aboriginals is abolished.

The World Council of Indigenous Peoples urges the United Nations to establish a special fund for the support of groups or individual Aboriginals, so that they many be able to bring their cases to national or international courts and that they may be able to develop their areas, economic and culture.

The World Council of Indigenous Peoples should also work for the establishment of an international university for Indigenous Peoples having its seat in, for instance, the capital of Collasuyo (Bolivia).

WCIP
August 24-27, 1977
Kiruna, Samiland, Sweden

BIBLIOGRAPHY

Aaby, Peter
1978 "What Are We Fighting For? 'Progress' or 'Cultural Autonomy'?" *Cultural Imperialism and Cultural Identity,* edited by Carola Sandbacka. Helsinki: Transactions of the Finnish Anthropological Society No. 2, pp. 61–76.

Ackermann, F. L.
1962 *Geologia e Fisiografia da Regiao Bragantina, Estado do Para.* Belem, Brazil.

Allan, William
1965 *The African Husbandman.* New York: Barnes & Noble.

Anderson, Douglas et. al.
1977 *Kuunanmiit Subsistence: Traditional Eskimo Life in the Latter Twentieth Century.* Washington, D.C.: National Park Service, U.S. Department of the Interior.

Andrist, Ralph K.
1969 *The Long Death: The Last Days of the Plains Indian.* New York: Collier Books.

Anonymous
1945 "Indians Shoot at Plane." *Life* 18 (March 19):70–72.

1963–64 "Statement on Ethics of the Society for Applied Anthropology." *Human Organization* 22:237.

1972 "Columbia Trial Reveals Life ('Everyone Kills Indians') on Plains." *Akwesasne Notes* 4(4):26.

d'Ans, André-Marcel
1972 "Les Tribus Indigenes du Parc National du Manu." *Proceedings of the 39th International Americanists Congress,* Lima: Vol. 4:95–100.

1980 "Begegnung in Peru." *Ist Gott Amerikaner?* edited by Søren Hvalkof and Peter Aaby, pp. 309–351. Göttingen, Germany: Lamuv Verlag.

Arcand, Bernard
1972 *The Urgent Situation of the Cuiva Indians of Colombia.* Copenhagen: IWGIA Document No. 7.

BIBLIOGRAPHY

Arensberg, Conrad M. and Arthur H. Niehoff
    1964 *Introducing Social Change: A Manual for Americans Overseas.* Chicago: Aldine.

Arnold, Robert
    1978 *Alaska Native Land Claims.* Anchorage, Alaska: The Alaska Native Foundation.

Asch, Michael
    1977 "The Dene Economy." *Dene Nation—The Colony Within,* edited by Mel Watkins. pp. 47–61. Toronto: University of Toronto Press.

Australia, Commonwealth Bureau of Census and Statistics
    1970 *Official Yearbook of the Commonwealth of Australia,* No. 56. Canberra.

Australia, DAA (Department of Aboriginal Affairs)
    1977 "Address by the Minister for Aboriginal Affairs the Honourable R. I. Viner at the Announcement of the Poll Results for the National Aboriginal Conference Elections, Perth, 28 Novemeber 1977." Pamphlet.

    1978 "Statement by the Honorable R. I. Viner, M. P., Minister for Aboriginal Affairs, on Aboriginal Policies & Achievements in Aboriginal Affairs, House of Representatives 24 November, 1978." Pamphlet.

Australia, Department of Territories, Territory of Papua.
    Report for 1964-1965.
    Report for 1967-1968.

Awad, Mohamed
    1962 "Nomadism in the Arab Lands of the Middle East." *The Problems of the Arid Zone,* pp. 325–339. Paris: UNESCO.

Barber, James
    1967 *Rhodesia: The Road to Rebellion.* London: Oxford University Press.

Barnaby, Georgy, George Kurszewski, and Gerry Cheezie
    1977 "The Political System and the Dene." *Dene Nation—The Colony Within,* edited by Mel Watkins. pp. 120–129. Toronto: University of Toronto Press.

Barnett, Homer G.
    1956 *Anthropology in Administration.* New York: Row, Peterson.

Barth, Fredrik
    1962 "Nomadism in the Mountain and Plateau Areas of South West Asia." *The Problems of the Arid Zone,* pp. 341–355. Paris: UNESCO.

Bartolomé, Miguel Alberto
    1972 "The Situation of the Indians in the Argentine: the Chaco Area and Misiones Province." *The Situation of the Indian in South America,* edited by W. Dostal, pp. 218–251. Geneva: World Council of Churches.

Bascom, William R.
    1965 "Ponape: A Pacific Economy in Transition." *Anthropological Records* 22.

Bauer, Peter T. and Basil S. Yamey
    1957 *The Economics of Under-Developed Countries.* Cambridge Economic Handbooks.

Bennett, Gordon
1978 "Aboriginal Rights in International Law." Occasional Paper No. 37, *Royal Anthropological Institute of Great Britain & Ireland.*

Bennett, Gordon, Audrey Colson, and Stuart Wavell
1978 "The Damned: the Plight of the Akawaio Indians of Guyana." *Survival International Document* No. 7.

Berkhofer, Robert F.
1965 *Salvation and the Savage: An Analysis of Protestant Missions and American Indian Response, 1787-1862.* University of Kentucky Press.

Beshir, Mohamed Omer
1968 *The Southern Sudan: Background to Conflict.* New York: Praeger.

Billington, Ray A.
1963 "The Frontier in American Thought and Character." *The New World Looks at its History,* edited by Archibald R. Lewis and Thomas F. McGann. Austin: University of Texas Press.

Birdsell, Joseph B.
1971 "Ecology, Spacing Mechanisms, and Adaptive Behavior in Aboriginal Land Tenure." *Land Tenure in the Pacific,* edited by Ron Crocombe, pp.334–361. Melbourne: Oxford University Press.

Bodley, John H.
1970 *Campa Socio-Economic Adaptation.* Ann Arbor: University Microfilms.

1976 *Anthropology and Contemporary Human Problems.* Menlo Park, Calif.: Cummings Publishing Company.

1977 "Alternatives to Ethnocide: Human Zoos, Living Museums, and Real People." *Western Expansion and Indigenous Peoples,* edited by Elias Sevilla-Casas, pp. 31–50. The Hague: Mouton Publishers.

Bodley, John H. and Foley C. Benson
1979 "Cultural Ecology of Amazonian Palms." *Reports of Investigations,* No. 56. Pullman: Laboratory of Anthropology, Washington State University.

Bonilla, Victor D.
1972 "The Destruction of the Colombian Indian Groups." *The Situation of the Indian in South America,* edited by W. Dostal, pp. 56–75. Geneva: World Council of Churches.

Bowman, James D.
1965 "They Like White Men—Broiled" (Associated Press). *Eugene Register-Guard* (Thursday, Oct. 7, page 2B).

Boye, Ellen
1974 "Samarbejde rundt om Nordpolen." *Grönland* pp. 65–70. Copenhagen.

Brecher, Kenneth S.
1973 "Forword." *Xingu: The Indians, Their Myths,* by Orlando Villas Boas and Claudio Villas Boas, pp. vii–xii. New York: Farrar, Straus & Giroux.

Bremaud, O. and J. Pagot
1962 "Grazing Lands, Nomadism and Transhumance in the Sahel." in *The Problems of the Arid Zone,* pp. 311–324. Paris: UNESCO.

BIBLIOGRAPHY

Brokensha, David
    1966 *Applied Anthropology in English-Speaking Africa.* Society for Applied
           Anthropology, Monograph No. 8.

Buell, Raymond L.
    1928 *The Native Problem in Africa.* 2 vols. New York: Macmillan.

Bugotu, F.
    1968 "The Culture Clash: A Melanesian's View." *New Guinea* 3(2):65–70.

Bunce, George E.
    1972 "Aggravation of Vitamin A Deficiency Following Distribution of
           Non-Fortified Skim Milk: An Example of Nutrient Interaction." In *The
           Careless Technology: Ecology and International Development,* edited by M.
           T. Farvar and John P. Milton, pp. 53–60. Garden City, New York:
           Natural History Press.

Burling, Robbins
    1963 *Rengsanggri: Family and Kinship in a Garo Village.* Philadelphia:
           University of Pennsylvania Press.

    1967 "Tribesmen and Lowlanders of Assam." *Southeast Asian Tribes,
           Minorities, and Nations,* edited by Peter Kunstadter, pp. 215–229.
           Princeton University Press.

Cana, Frank R.
    1946 "German South-West Africa," *Encyclopedia Britannica* Vol. 10, pp. 230–
           231.

Capot-Rey, R.
    1962 "The Present State of Nomadism in the Sahara." *The Problems of the
           Arid Zone,* pp. 301–310. Paris: UNESCO.

Carduño, Julio
    1980 "Carta Abierta a los Hermanos Indios de America." *Primer Congreso de
           Movimientos Indios de Sudamerica,* pp. 103–129. Paris: Ediciones Mitka.

Castillo-Cardenas, Gonzalo
    1972 "The Indian Struggle for Freedom in Colombia." *The Situation of the
           Indian in South America,* edited by W. Dostal, pp. 76–104. Geneva:
           World Council of Churches.

Chase-Sardi, Miguel
    1972 "The Present Situation of the Indians in Paraguay." *The Situation of the
           Indian in South America,* edited by W. Dostal, pp. 173–217. Geneva:
           World Council of Churches

Chase-Sardi, Miguel and Adolfo Colombres
    1975 *Por la Liberación del Indigena.* Buenos Aires: Ediciones del Sol.

Chatterjee, Suhas
    1967 "Language and Literacy in the North-Eastern Regions." *A Common
           Perspective for North-East India,* edited by Rathin Mittra and Barun Das
           Gupta, pp. 19–23. Calcutta: Pannalal Das Gupta.

Chirif, Alberto
    1975 "En torno a la Titulación de las Comunidades Nativas y a los Recursos
           Forestales y de Fauna Silvestre." *Marginacion y Futuro,* by Sistema

Nacional de Apoyo a la Movilizacion Social, Direccion General de Organizaciones Rurales, Serie: Communidades Nativas, pp. 66–76. Lima.

CIMRA (Colonialism & Indigenous Minorities Research and Action)
1979 "Yes, But What Can I Do?" *New Internationalist* No. 77 (July):27.

Clyde, Paul H.
1935 *Japan's Pacific Mandate*. New York: Macmillan .

Cole, Monica M.
1966 *South Africa*. London: Methuen & Co. Ltd.

Collier, John
1947 *The Indians of the Americas*. New York: W. W. Norton & Co.

Conrad, Joseph
1971 *Heart of Darkness*. Edited by Robert Kimbrough. New York: W. W. Norton & Co.

Cook, Sherburne F.
1955 "The Epidemic of 1830–33 in California and Oregon." *University of California Publications in American Archaeology and Ethnology* 43:303-326.

Coopens, Walter
1972 *The Anatomy of a Land Invasion Scheme in Yekuana Territory, Venezuela*. IWGIA Document No. 9. Copenhagen.

Cooper, John M.
1946 "The Patagonian and Pampean Hunters." *Handbook of South American Indians*, edited by Julian H. Steward, pp. 127–168 Vol. I. Bulletin 143, Bureau of American Ethnology. Smithsonian Institution.

Cornevin, Robert
1969 "The Germans in Africa Before 1918." In *The History and Politics of Colonialism 1870-1914*, edited by L. H. Gann and Peter Duignan, vol. 1 of *Colonialism in Africa 1870-1960*. Cambridge University Press.

Corris, Peter
1968 *Aborigines and Europeans in Western Victoria*. Occasional Papers in Aboriginal Studies No. 12, Ethnohistory Series No. 1. Canberra: Australian Institute of Aboriginal Studies.

Corry, Stephen
1976 "Towards Indian Self-Determination in Colombia." *Survival International Document* No. 2.

Cowan, James
1922–23 *The New Zealand Wars*. Wellington: R. E. Owen, Government Printer.

Crawford, J. R.
1967 *Witchcraft and Sorcery in Rhodesia*. London: Oxford University Press (for International African Institute).

Crocombe, Ron
1968 "Bougainville!: Copper, R. R. A. and Secessionism." *New Guinea* 3(3):39–49.

Crocombe, Ron (editor)
   1971 *Land Tenure in the Pacific.* Melbourne: Oxford University Press.
Crocombe, Ron and Robin Hide
   1971 "New Guinea: Unity in Diversity." in *Land Tenure in the Pacific,* edited by R. Crocombe, pp. 292–333. Melbourne: Oxford University Press.
Cunnison, Ian George
   1966 *Bagara Arabs: Power and Lineage in a Sudanese Nomad Tribe.* Oxford: Clarendon Press.

   1967 *Nomads in the Nineteen-Sixties.* Hull: Hull University.

DANE (Departemento Administrativo Nacional de Estadística)
   1978 *Elementos para el Estudio de los Resguardos Indígenas del Cauca.* Bogata.
Dasmann, R.F.
   1973 "Sanctuaries for Life Styles?" IUCN Bulletin ns Vol. 4(8):29.

   1975 "Difficult Marginal Environments and the Traditional Societies Which Exploit Them." *News From Survival International* No. 11 (July):11–15.
Davis, A. E. and T. D. Bolin
   1972 "Lactose Intolerance in Southeast Asia." *The Careless Technology: Ecology and International Development,* edited by M. T. Farvar and John P. Milton, pp. 61–68. Garden City, New York: Natural History Press.

Davis, Shelton H.
   1977 *Victims of the Miracle: Development and the Indians of Brazil.* Cambridge: Cambridge University Press.

   1980 "Brazilian Indian Policy: The Present Situation." *ARC Bulletin* 3:2–3.
De Marco, Roland R.
   1943 *The Italianization of African Natives: Government Native Education in the Italian Colonies 1890-1937.* Teacher's College, Columbia University Contributions to Education, No. 880. New York.

Diamond, Stanley
   1960 "Introduction: The Uses of the Primitive." In *Primitive Views of the World,* edited by Stanley Diamond, pp. v–xxix. New York: Columbia University Press.

   1968 "The Search for the Primitive." In *The Concept of the Primitive,* edited by Ashley Montagu, pp. 96–147. New York: Free Press.

Diao, Richard K.
   1967 "The National Minorities of China and Their Relations with the Chinese Communist Regime." In *Southeast Asian Tribes, Minorities, and Nations,* edited by Peter Kunstadter, pp. 169–201. Princeton University Press.

Dilley, M. R.
   1966 *British Policy in Kenya Colony.* New York: Barnes & Noble.

Dobyns, Henry F.
   1966 "Estimating Aboriginal American Population: An Appraisal of Techniques With a New Hemispheric Estimate." *Current Anthropology* 7(4):395–449.

Docker, Edward W.
 1970 *The Blackbirders: the Recruiting of South Seas Labour for Queensland, 1863-1907*. Sydney: Angus and Robertson.

Dostal, W. (editor)
 1972 *The Situation of the Indian in South America*. Geneva: World Council of Churches.

Dyson-Hudson, Neville
 1962 "Factors Inhibiting Change in an African Pastoral Society." *Transactions of the New York Academy of Sciences* Series II, Vol. 24, pp. 771–801.

Dyson-Hudson, Rada and Neville Dyson-Hudson
 1969 "Subsistence Herding in Uganda." *Scientific American* 220(2):76–89.

Eiselen, W. M.
 1934 "Christianity and the Religious Life of the Bantu." In *Western Civilization and the Natives of South Africa*, edited by I. Schapera, pp. 65–82. London: George Routledge and Sons, Ltd.

Elkin, A. P.
 1951 "Reaction and Interaction: A Food Gathering People and European Settlement in Australia." *American Anthropologist* 53:164–186.

Elwin, Verrier
 1939 *The Baiga*. London: John Murray.

 1959 *A Philosophy for NEFA*. 2d ed. Shillong: J. N. Chowdhury.

 1969 *The Nagas in the Nineteenth Century*. Oxford University Press.

Fabre, D.G.
 1963 *Más Allá del Rio das Mortes*. Buenos Aires: Ediciones Selectas.

Falla, Ricardo
 1979a *Historia Kuna—Historia Rebelde*. Serie El Indio Panameño No. 4. Panamá: Ediciones "CCS" (Centro de Capacitacion Social).

 1979b *El Tesoro de San Blas*. Serie El Indio Panameño No. 5. Panama: Ediciones "CCS" (Centro de Capacitacion Social).

 1979c *El Indio y las Clases Sociales*. Serie El Indio Panameno No. 7. Panama: Ediciones "CCS" (Centro de Capacitacion Social).

Federacion de Centros Shuar
 1976 *Solucíon Original a un Problema Actual*. Sucua, Ecuador.

Fenbury, David
 1968 "Those Mokolkols!: New Britain's Bloody Axemen." *New Guinea* 3(2):33–50.

Fey, Harold E. and D'Arcy McNickle
 1970 *Indians and Other Americans: Two Ways of Life Meet*. New York: Harper and Row.

Forde, Daryll
 1953 "Applied Anthropology in Government: British Africa." In *Anthropology Today*, edited by A. L. Kroeber, pp. 841–865. Chicago: University of Chicago Press.

Formosa, Bureau of Aboriginal Affairs
   1911   *Report on the Control of the Aborigines of Formosa.* Taihoku.

Foster, George M.
   1969   *Applied Anthropology.* Boston: Little, Brown.

Fuentes, Hildebrando
   1908   *Loreto—Apuntes Geográficos, Históricos, Estadísticos, Politicos y Sociales.* Vol. II. Lima: Imprenta de la Revista.

Furneaux, Rupert
   1963   *The Zulu War: Isandhlwana and Rorke's Drift.* Philadelphia & New York: J. B. Lippincott Co.

Garra, Lobodon
   1969   *A Sangre y Lanza.* Buenos Aires: Edicíones Ana conda

Gesellschaft für bedrohte Völker
   1979   *Die frohe Botschaft unserer Zivilisations: Evangelikale Indianermission in Lateinamerika.* Gottingen & Wien.

Ghurye, G. S.
   1963   *The Scheduled Tribes.* 3d ed. Bombay: G. R. Bhatkal.

Goldschmidt, Walter R.
   1952   "The Interrelations Between Cultural Factors and the Acquisition of New Technical Skills." In *The Progress of Underdeveloped Areas,* edited by Bert F. Hoselitz, pp. 135–151. Chicago: University of Chicago Press.

Goldsmith, Edward, et al.
   1972   *Blueprint for Survival.* Boston: Houghton Mifflin Co.

Goodenough, Ward H.
   1963   *Cooperation in Change.* New York: John Wiley & Sons.

Goulet, Denis
   1971   *The Cruel Choice: A New Concept in the Theory of Development.* New York: Atheneum.

Graham, A. C.
   1971   "China, Europe and the Origins of the Modern Science." *Asia Major 16* (parts 1–2):178–196.

Great Britain, Parliamentary Papers
   1836   "Report From the Select Committee on Aborigines (British Settlements)." Imperial Blue Book no. VII, 538.

Gregor, Thomas
   1977   *Mehinaku: The Drama of Daily Life in a Brazilian Indian Village.* Chicago and London: The University of Chicago Press.

Grosart, Ian
   1972   "Direct Administration." In *Encyclopedia of Papua and New Guinea,* edited by Peter Ryan, vol. I, pp. 266–269. Melbourne University Press.

Gross, Daniel R. and Barbara A. Underwood
   1971   "Technological Change and Caloric Costs: Sisal Agriculture," *American Anthropologist* 73(3):725–740.

Gross, Daniel R., et al.
   1979   "Ecology and Acculturation Among Native Peoples of Central Brazil." *Science* Vol. 206(4422):1043–1050.

Hames, Raymond B.
1979 "A Comparison of the Efficiencies of the Shotgun and the Bow in Neotropical Forest Hunting." *Human Ecology* 7(3):219–252.

Hardenburg, Walter E.
1912 *The Putumayo, the Devil's Paradise: Travels in the Peruvian Amazon Region and an Account of the Atrocities Committed Upon the Indians Therein.* London.

Harding, Thomas G.
1960 "Adaptation and Stability." *Evolution and Culture,* edited by Marshall Sahlins and Elman Service, pp. 45–68. Ann Arbor: University of Michigan Press.

Harrop, Angus J.
1937 *England and the Maori Wars.* New York: Books for Libraries Press.

Harroy, Jean-Paul (editor)
1972 *United Nations List of National Parks & Equivalent Reserves,* second edition, Vol. 2. Brussels: IUCN.

Hart, Laurie
1973 "Story of the Wycliffe Translators: Pacifying the Last Frontiers." *NACLA's Latin America & Empire Report* Vol. 7(10):15–31.

Hastings, Peter
1968 "West Irian—1969," *New Guinea* 3(3):12–22.

Heilbroner, Robert L.
1963 *The Great Ascent: the Struggle for Economic Development in Our Time.* New York: Harper Torchbooks.

Henry, Jules
1941 *Jungle People.* New York: J. J. Augustin.

Hickey, Gerald C.
1967 "Some Aspects of Hill Tribe Life in Vietnam." *Southeast Asian Tribes, Minorities, and Nations,* edited by Peter Kunstadter, pp. 745–769. Princeton University Press.

Hippler, Arthur E.
1979 "Comment on 'Development in the Non-Western World'." *American Anthropologist* 81:348–349.

Hooton, Earnest A.
1945 "Introduction." *Nutrition and Physical Degeneration: A Comparison of Primitive and Modern Diets and their Effects* (Weston A. Price). Redlands, Calif.: The author.

Huff, Lee W.
1967 "The Thai Mobile Development Unit Program," *Southeast Asian Tribes, Minorities, and Nations,* edited by Peter Kunstadter, pp. 425–486. Princeton University Press.

Hughes, Charles C. and John M. Hunter
1972 "The Role of Technological Development in Promoting Disease in Africa." *The Careless Technology: Ecology and International Development,* edited by M. T. Farvar and John P. Milton, pp. 69–101. Garden City, New York: Natural History Press.

Hunter, Guy
1967 *The Best of Both Worlds: A Challenge on Development Policies in Africa.* Oxford University Press.

Hurault, J.
1972 "The 'Francization' of the Indians." *The Situation of the Indian in South America,* edited by W. Dostal, pp. 358–370. Geneva: World Council of Churches.

Hutt, W. H.
1934 "The Economic Position of the Bantu in South Africa." *Western Civilization and the Natives of South Africa,* edited by I. Schapera, pp. 195–237. London: George Routledge & Sons, Ltd.

Hvalkof, Søren and Peter Aaby (editors)
1980 *Ist Gott Amerikaner?* Göttingen, Germany: Lamuv Verlag.

Illich, Ivan
1970 *Deschooling Society.* World Perspectives Vol. 44. New York: Harper & Row.

International Labour Office
1953 *Indigenous Peoples: Living and Working Conditions of Aboriginal Populations in Independent Countries.* Studies and Reports, New Series No. 35. Geneva.

Iyer, L. A. Krishna and L. K. Bala Ratnam
1961 *Anthropology in India.* Bombay: Bharatiya Vidya Bhavan.

Jabavu, D. D. T.
1934 "Bantu Grievances." *Western Civilization and the Natives of South Africa,* edited by I. Schapera, pp. 285–299. London: George Routledge & Sons, Ltd.

Jimenez, Nelly Arevalo de
1972 "An Analysis of Official Venezuelan Policy in Regard to the Indians. *The Situation of the Indian in South America,* edited by W. Dostal, pp. 31-42. Geneva: World Council of Churches.

Jones, Garth N.
1965 "Strategies and Tactics of Planned Organizational Change: Case Examples in the Modernization Process of Traditional Societies." *Human Organization* 24(3):192–200.

Jones, J. D. Rheinallt
1934 "Economic Condition of the Urban Native." *Western Civilization and the Natives of South Africa,* edited by I. Schapera, pp. 159–192. London: George Routledge & Sons, Ltd.

Jungius, Hartmut
1976 "National Parks and Indigenous Peoples—A Peruvian Case Study." *Survival International Review* Vol. 1(14):6–14.

Junqueira, Carmen
1973 *The Brazilian Indigenous Problem and Policy: the Example of the Xingu National Park.* AMAZIND/IWGIA Document No. 13. Copenhagen/ Geneva.

Kaplan, David
> 1960 "The Law of Cultural Dominance." In *Evolution and Culture*, edited by Marshall D. Sahlins and Elman R. Service, pp. 69–92. Ann Arbor: University of Michigan Press.

Kar, Parimal Chandra
> 1967 "A Point of View on the Garos in Transition." In *A Common Perspective for North-East India*, edited by Rathin Mittra and Barun Das Gupta, pp. 91–102. Calcutta: Pannalal Das Gupta.

Keesing, Felix M.
> 1941 *The South Seas in the Modern World*. Institute of Pacific Relations International Research Series. New York: John Day.

Keesing, Felix M. and Marie Keesing
> 1934 *Taming Philippine Headhunters: A Study of Government and of Cultural Change in Northern Luzon*. London: George Allen & Unwin.

Kelm, Heinz
> 1972 "The Present Situation of the Indian Populations in Non-Andean Bolivia." *The Present Situation of the Indian in South America*, edited by W. Dostal, pp. 158–172. Geneva: World Council of Churches.

Klima, George J.
> 1970 *The Barabaig: East African Cattle Herders*. New York: Holt, Rinehart and Winston.

Kloos, Peter
> 1972 "Amerindians of Surinam," In *The Situation of the Indian in South America*, edited by W. Dostal, pp. 348–357. Geneva: World Council of Churches.

> 1977 "The Akuriyo of Surinam: A Case of Emergence From Isolation." *IWGIA* Document No. 27. Copenhagen.

Kolarz, Walter
> 1954 *The Peoples of the Soviet Far East*. New York: Frederick A. Praeger.

Kosokov, K.
> 1930 *Voprosu o Shamanstve v Severnoy Azii* [On the Question of Shamanism in Northern Asia]. Moscow.

Kruyt, A. C.
> 1929 "The Influence of Western Civilization on the Inhabitants of Poso (Central Celebes)." *The Effect of Western Influence on Native Civilizations in the Malay Archipelago*, edited by B. Schrieke, pp. 1–9. Batavia: Java Royal Batavia Society of Arts and Sciences.

Kunstadter, Peter (editor)
> 1967 *Southeast Asian Tribes, Minorities, and Nations*. Princeton University Press.

La Raw, Maran
> 1967 "Toward a Basis for Understanding the Minorities in Burma: the Kachin Example." *Southeast Asian Tribes, Minorities, and Nations*, edited by Peter Kunstadter, pp. 125–146. Princeton University Press.

Lehman, F. K.
1963   *The Structure of Chin Society: A Tribal People of Burma Adapted to a Non-Western Civilization.* Illinois Studies in Anthropology No. 3.

Levin, M. G. and L. P. Potapov
1964   *The Peoples of Siberia.* Chicago: University of Chicago Press.

Lindley, M. F.
1926   *The Acquisition and Government of Backward Territory in International Law.* London: Longmans, Green & Co.

Lipkind, William
1948   "The Carajá." In *Handbook of South American Indians,* edited by Julian Steward, pp. 179–191 Vol. III. Bulletin 143, Bureau of American Ethnology. Smithsonian Institution.

Lizot, Jacques
1976   "The Yanomami in the Face of Ethnocide." IWGIA Document No. 22. Copenhagen.

Loram, C. T.
1932   "Native Labor in Southern Africa," in *Pioneer Settlement.* American Geographical Society, Special Publication No. 14. pp. 169–177.

Louis, Roger and Jean Stengers
1968   *E. P. Morel's History of the Congo Reform Movement.* Oxford: Clarendon Press.

Lugard, Sir F. D.
1928   "The International Institute of African Languages and Cultures." *Africa* 1(1):1–12.

1965   *The Dual Mandate in British Tropical Africa.* London: Frank Cass.

Lurie, Nancy Oestreich
1957   "The Indian Claims Commission Act." *American Indians and American Life,* edited by George E. Simpson and J. Milton Yinger, pp. 56–70. The Annals of the American Academy of Political and Social Science (May) Vol. 311. Philadelphia.

Mair, Lucy Philip
1970   *Australia in New Guinea.* Melbourne: Melbourne University Press.

Malinowski, Bronislaw
1929   "Practical Anthropology." *Africa* 2(1):22–38.

Manners, Robert A.
1956   "Functionalism, Realpolitik, and Anthropology in Underdeveloped Areas." *America Indigena* 16(1):7–33.

1967   "The Kipsigis of Kenya: Culture Change in a 'Model' East African Tribe." *Contemporary Change in Traditional Societies,* edited by Julian Steward, Vol. 1, pp. 205–359. Urbana: University of Illinois Press.

Maunier, Rene
1949   *The Sociology of Colonies.* Vol. 2. London: Routledge and Kegan Paul.

Maybury-Lewis, David
1976a   "Submerging Peoples: an Anthropologist's View." *Survival International Review* Vol. 1(15):15–16.

1976b "Message From the President of Cultural Survival." *Cultural Survival Newsletter* Vol. 1(1):1.

Maybury-Lewis, Pia
1979 "Margaret Mead 1901–1978." *Cultural Survival Newsletter* Vol. 3(1):25.

McCullum, Hugh, Karmel McCullum, and John Olthuis
1977 *Moratorium: Justice, Energy, the North, and the Native People.* Toronto, Canada: Anglican Book Centre.

McNeil, Mary
1972 "Lateritic Soils In Distinct Tropical Environments: Southern Sudan and Brazil." in *The Careless Technology: Ecology and International Development* (edited by M. T. Farvar and John P. Milton), pp. 591–608. Garden City, New York: Natural History Press.

Mead, Margaret
1961 *New Lives for Old.* New York: New American Library.

Means, Russell
1980 "Fighting Words on the Future of the Earth." *Mother Jones* Vol. 5(10):22–38.

Meggers, Betty J.
1971 *Amazonia: Man and Culture in a Counterfeit Paradise.* Chicago: Aldine.

Merivale, Herman
1861 *Lectures on Colonization and Colonies.* London: Green, Longman & Roberts.

Mittra, Rathin and Barun Das Gupta
1967 *A Common Perspective for North-East India.* Calcutta: Pannalal Das Gupta.

Moasosang, P.
1967 "The Naga Search for Self-Identity." *A Common Perspective for North-East India,* edited by Rathin Mittra and Barun Das Gupta, pp. 51–57. Calcutta: Pannalal Das Gupta.

Mönckeberg, F.
1968 "Mental Retardation from Malnutrition." *Journal of the American Medical Association* 206:30–31.

Montagu, Ashley
1972 "Sociogenic Brain Damage." *American Anthropologist* 74 (5):1045–1061.

Moreira Neto, Carlos de Araujo
1972 "Some Data Concerning the Recent History of the Kaingang Indians." In *The Situation of the Indian in South America,* edited by W. Dostal, pp. 284–333. Geneva: World Council of Churches.

Morel, E. D.
1906 *Red rubber.* New York: The Nassau Print.
1969 *The Black Man's Burden.* Northbrook, Illinois: Metro Books.

Mosonyi, Esteban E.
1972 "The Situation of the Indian in Venezuela: Perspectives and Solutions." In *The Situation of the Indian in South America,* edited by W. Dostal, pp. 43–55. Geneva: World Council of Churches.

Mountjoy, A. B.
1967 *Industrialization and Underdeveloped Countries.* Chicago: Aldine.

BIBLIOGRAPHY

Münzel, Mark
    1973   *The Aché Indians: Genocide in Paraguay.* IWGIA Document No. 11. Copenhagen.

Murdock, George P.
    1959   *Africa: Its Peoples and Their Culture History.* New York: McGraw-Hill.

Murphy, Robert and Julian Steward
    1956   "Trappers and Trappers: Parallel Processes in Acculturation." *Economic Development and Culture Change* 4:335–355.

Nag, Amit Kumar
    1967   "The Society in Transition in the Mizo District." In *A Common Perspective for North-East India,* edited by Rathin Mittra and Barun Das Gupta, pp. 80–90. Calcutta: Pannalal Das Gupta.

Nahanni, Phoebe
    1977   "The Mapping Project." *Dene Nation—Colony Within,* edited by Mel Watkins. pp. 21–27. Toronto: University of Toronto Press.

Netting, Robert M.
    1977   *Cultural Ecology.* Menlo Park, Calif.: Benjamin/Cummings.

New Zealand, Department of Statistics
    1960   *The New Zealand Official Year-Book* Wellington.

Nimuendaju, Curt
    1946   *The Eastern Timbira.* University of California Publications in American Archaelogy and Ethnology, Vol. 41. University of California Press.

Nishi, Midori
    1968   "An Evaluation of Japanese Agricultural and Fishery Developments in Micronesia During the Japanese Mandate 1914–1941." *Micronesia* 4(1)1–18.

Oliver, Douglas L. (editor)
    1951   *Planning Micronesia's Future: A Summary of the United States Commercial Company's Economic Survey of Micronesia.* Harvard University Press.

Palacios i Mendiburu, S.
    1892   "Conferencia Sobre la Colonizacion de Loreto." *Boletin de la Sociedad Geografica de Lima* 2:267–312.

Palmer, George
    1871   *Kidnapping in the South Seas.* Edinburgh.

Pittock, A. Barrie
    1972   *Aboriginal Land Rights.* IWGIA Document No. 3. Copenhagen.

    1975   *Beyond White Australia: A Short History of Race Relations in Australia.* Race Relations Committee of the Religious Society of Friends (Quakers) in Australia.

Pitt-Rivers, George H.
    1927   *The Clash of Culture and the Contact of Races.* London: George Routledge & Sons.

Portas, Julio Aníbal
    1967   *Malón Contra Malón: la Solucion Final del Problema del Indio en la Argentina.* Buenos Aires: Ediciones de la Flor.

Portugal, Pedro
1980 "Entrevista con Pedro Portugal." In *Primer Congreso de Movimientos Indios de Sudamerica,* pp. 169–180. Paris: Ediciones Mitka.

Presland, Anna
1979 "An Account of the Contemporary Fight for Survival of the Amerindian Peoples of Brazil." *Survival International Review* Vol. 4, No. 1(25):14–40.

Powell, J. W.
1881 *First Annual Report of the Bureau of Ethnology to the Secretary of the Smithsonian Institution 1879-80.* Washington, D. C.: Government Printing Office.

Price, A. G.
1950 *White Settlers and Native Peoples.* London: Cambridge University Press.

Price, Weston Andrew
1945 *Nutrition and Physical Degeneration: A Comparison of Primitive and Modern Diets and Their Effects.* Redlands, Calif.: The Author.

Prior, Ian A. M.
1971 "The Price of Civilization." *Nutrition Today* 6(4):2–11.

Razon, Felix
1976 "Native Peoples Struggle Against U. S. Imperialism in the Philippines." Copenhagen: *IWGIA* Document No. 25:32–41.

Redfield, Robert
1953 *The Primitive World and its Transformations.* Ithaca, N. Y.: Cornell University Press.

1962 *A Village that Chose Progress: Chan Kom Revisited.* Chicago: University of Chicago Press, Phoenix Books.

Redfield, Robert, Ralph Linton, and M. J. Herskovits
1936 "Memorandum on the Study of Acculturation." *American Anthropologist* 38:149–152.

Reed, Stephen W.
1943 *The Making of Modern New Guinea.* Philadelphia: the American Philosophical Society.

Reining, Conrad C.
1966 *The Zande Scheme: An Anthropological Case Study of Economic Development in Africa.* Evanston, Illinois: Northwestern University Press.

Renshaw, John
1976 "Paraguay—The Marandu Project." *Survival International Review* Vol. 1(14):14–20.

Reynaga, Ramiro
1980 "Independencia Politica: Clave para la Victoria India." In *Primer Congreso de Movimientos Indios de Sudamerica,* pp. 49–86. Paris: Ediciones Mitka.

Ribeiro, Darcy
1957 *Culturas e Linguas Indigenas do Brasil.* Separata de Educacão e Cieñcias Socais No. 6. Rio de Janeiro: Centro Brasileiro de Pesquisas Educacionais.

Rivers, W. H. R.
1922 *Essays on the Depopulation of Melanesia.* Cambridge University Press.
Roberts, J. P. (editor)
1975 *Mapoon—Book One: The Mapoon Story by the Mapoon People.* Victoria, Australia: IDA (International Development Action).
Roberts, Janine
1978 *From Massacres to Mining: the Colonization of Aboriginal Australia.* London: War on Want.
Roberts, J., M. Parson, and B. Russell
1975 *Mapoon—Book Two: The Mapoon Story According to the Invadors.* Victoria, Australia: IDA (International Development Action).
Roberts, J. and D. McLean
1976. *Mapoon—Book Three: The Cape York Aluminum Companies and the Native Peoples.* Victoria, Australia: IDA (International Development Action).
Roberts, Stephen Henry
1969 *Population Problems of the Pacific.* New York: AMS Press.
Rocamora, Joel
1979 "Agribusiness, Dams and Counter-Insurgency." *Southeast Asia Chronicle* No. 67:2–10.
1979 "The Political Uses of PANAMIN." *Southeast Asia Chronicle.* 67:11–21.
Rotberg, Robert and Ali Mazrui (editors)
1970 *Protest and Power in Black Africa.* New York: Oxford University Press.
Rowley, Charles D.
1966 *The New Guinea Villager: The Impact of Colonial Rule on Primitive Society and Economy.* New York: Frederick A. Praeger.
1967 "The Villager and the Nomad: Aboriginals and New Guineans." *New Guinea* 2(1):70–81.
1970 *The Destruction of Aboriginal Society.* Aboriginal Policy and Practice, Vol. 1. Canberra: Australian National University Press.
1971 *The Remote Aborigines.* Aboriginal Policy and Practice, Vol. 3. Canberra: Snow, Alpheus Henry
Rushforth, Scott
1977 "Country Food." *Dene Nation—Colony Within,* edited by Mel Watkins. pp.47–61. Toronto: University of Toronto Press.
Russell, Peter H.
1977 "The Dene Nation and Confederation." *Dene Nation—Colony Within,* edited by Mel Watkins. pp. 163–173. Toronto: University of Toronto Press.
Ryan, John
1969 *The Hot Land: Focus on New Guinea.* New York: Macmillan.
Said, Beshir Mohammed
1965 *The Sudan, Crossroads of Africa.* Chester Springs, Pa.: Dufour Editions.
Sanders, Douglas E.
1977 "The Formation of the World Council of Indigenous Peoples." Copenhagen: *IWGIA* Document No. 29.

Saussol, Alain
  1971 "New Caledonia: Colonization and Reaction." In *Land Tenure in the Pacific,* edited by Ron Crocombe, pp. 227–245. Melbourne: Oxford University Press.

Scarr, Deryck
  1968 "Introduction." In *A Cruise in a Queensland Labour Vessel to the South Seas* (W. E. Giles). Canberra: Australian National University Press.

Schapera, I.
  1934 *Western Civilization and the Natives of South Africa.* London: George Routledge & Sons.

Schneider, David
  1955 "Abortion and Depopulation on a Pacific Island: Yap." In *Health, Culture, and Community, edited by B. D. Paul, pp. 211-235. New York:* Russel Sage.

Schoen, Ivan L.
  1969 "Contact With the Stone Age," *Natural History* 78(1).

Sinclair, Keith
  1961 *The Origins of the Maori Wars.* 2d ed. Wellington: New Zealand University Press.

Smith, Wilberforce
  1894 "The Teeth of Ten Sioux Indians," *Journal of the Royal Anthropological Institute* 24:109–116.

Snow, Alpheus Henry
  1921 *The Question of Aborigines: In the Law and Practice of Nations.* New York:G. P. Putnam's Sons.

Soja, Edward W.
  1968 *The Geography of Modernization in Kenya.* Syracuse Geographical Series, no. 2.

Spooner, Brian
  1973 *The Cultural Ecology of Pastoral Nomads.* Reading, Massachusetts: Addison-Wesley Modules in Anthropology.

Starr, Cecie (editor)
  1971 *Anthropology Today.*Del Mar, Calif.: Communications Research Machines, Inc.

Steward, Julian H.
  1948 "The Witotoan Tribes." In *Handbook of South American Indians,* edited by Julian H. Steward, pp. 749–762, Vol. III. Bulletin 143, Bureau of American Ethnology, Smithsonian Institution.

Steward, Julian H. (editor)
  1967 *Contemporary Change in Traditional Societies.* Urbana: University of Illinois Press.

Sturtevant, William C.
  1967 "Urgent Anthropology: Smithsonian–Wenner–Gren Conference." *Current Anthropology* 8(4):355-361.

1970 "Resolution on Forced Acculturation." *Current Anthropology* Vol. 11(2):160.

Suess, Paulo
1980 "Tríplice Alianca na Luta Indígena." *Porantim* Vol. 3(17):8–9.

Suret-Canale, Jean
1971 *French Colonialism in Tropical Africa 1900-1945.* New York: Pica Press.

Temple, Dominique
1977 "Paraguay: The Two Directions of Indigenism." *Survival International Review* Vol. 2, No. 4(20):12–15.

Thiek, Hrilrokhum
1967 "An Outlook for a Better Understanding of the Tribal People." In *A Common Perspective for North-East India,* edited by Rathin Mittra and Barun Das Gupta, pp. 103–109. Calcutta: Pannalal Das Gupta.

Townsend, G.
1933 "The Administration of the Mandated Territory of New Guinea." *Geographical Journal* 82:424–434.

TTR *see under* United States

Turnbull, Colin M.
1963 "The Lesson of the Pygmies." *Scientific American.* 208(1).

1972 *The Mountain people.* New York: Simon & Schuster.

Turner Terence S.
1978 "The Txukahamae Kayapo Are Alive and Well in the Upper Xingu." *Survival International Review* Vol. 3 No. 2(22):18–21.

1979 "Anthropology and the Politics of Indigenous Peoples' Struggles." *Cambridge Anthropology* Vol. 5(1):1–43.

United States, Department of the Interior, Alaska Planning Group
1975 *Kobuk Valley National Monument.* Final Environmental Statement. Washington, D. C.: U. S. Government Printing Office.

United States, Department of the Interior, Office of Territories
1953 *Report on the Administration of the Trust Territory of the Pacific Islands* (by the United States to the United Nations) for the Period July 1, 1951 to June 30, 1952.

1954 *Annual Report, High Commissioner of the Trust Territory of the Pacific Islands to the Secretary of the Interior.* (for 1953).

United States, Department of State
1955 *Seventh Annual Report to the United Nations on the Administration of the Trust Territory of the Pacific Islands* (July 1, 1953 to June 30, 1954).

1959 *Eleventh Annual Report to the United Nations on the Administration of the Trust Territory of the Pacific Islands* (July 1, 1957 to June 30, 1958).

1964 *Sixteenth Annual Report to the United Nations on the Administration of the Trust Territory of the Pacific Islands* (July 1, 1962 to June 30, 1963).

1973 *Twenty-Fifth Annual Report to the United Nations on the Administration of the Trust Territory of the Pacific Islands* (July 1, 1971 to June 30, 1972).

Valcarcel, Carlos A.
1915 *El Proceso del Putumayo y sus Secretos Inauditos.* Lima.

Villas Boas, Orlando and Claudio
1973   *Xingu: The Indians, Their Myths.* New York: Farrar, Straus & Giroux.

Wagley, C.
1951   "Cultural Influences on Population." *Revista do Museu Paulista* 5:95–104.

Watkins, Mel (editor)
1977   *Dene Nation—The Colony Within.* Toronto: University of Toronto Press.

WCIP (World Council of Indigenous Peoples)
1977   World Council of Indigenous Peoples Second General Assembly, Kiruna, Sweden, August 24–27, 1977 (report).

Webb, W. E.
1966   "Land Capacity Classification and Land Use in the Chittagong Hill Tracts of East Pakistan." *Proceedings of the Sixth World Forestry Congress* 3:3229–3232.

Webb, Walter Prescott
1952   *The Great Frontier.* Boston: Houghton Mifflin Co.

Wellington, John H.
1967   *South West Africa and Its Human Issues.* Oxford: Clarendon Press/Oxford University Press.

Whitten, Norman E.
1976   "Ecuadorian Ethnocide and Indigenous Ethnogenesis: Amazonian Resurgence Amidst Andean Colonialism." Copenhagen: *IWGIA* Document No. 23.

Whitten, Norman E. and Dorothea S.
1977   "Report of a Process Linking Basic Science Research With an Action Oriented Program for Research Subjects." *Human Organization* 36(1):101–105.

Winnacker, Martha
1979   "The Battle to Stop the Chico Dams." *Southeast Asia Chronicle* No. 67:22–29.

Wise, Mary Ruth, Eugene E. Loos, and Patricia Davis
1977   "Filosofía y Métodos del Instituto Linguistico de Verano." Proceedings of the 42nd International Americanists Congress, Paris. Vol. 2:499–525.

Woodruff, William
1966   *Impact of Western Man.* London: Macmillan.

Zallez, Jaime and Alfonso Gortaire
1978   *Organizarse o Sucumbir: La Federacíon Shuar.* Mundo Shuar Serie "B," No. 14. Sucua, Ecuador: Centro de Documentatcion e Investigacíon Cultural Shuar.

INDEX